ACCA

Strategic Professional

Advanced Financial Management (AFM)

Workbook

For exams in September 2022, December 2022, March 2023 and June 2023

BPP
LEARNING
MEDIA

Fourth edition 2022

ISBN: 9781 5097 4606 4

Previous ISBN: 9781 5097 3752 9

ISBN (for internal use only): 9781 5097 4750 4

e-ISBN: 9781 5097 4706 1

British Library Cataloguing-in-Publication Data

A catalogue record for this book is available from the British Library

Published by

BPP Learning Media Ltd

BPP House, Aldine Place

142–144 Uxbridge Road

London W12 8AA

www.bpp.com/learningmedia

Printed in the United Kingdom

Your learning materials, published by BPP Learning Media Ltd, are printed on paper obtained from traceable sustainable sources.

Contains public sector information licensed under the Open Government Licence v3.0

We are grateful to the Association of Chartered Certified Accountants for permission to reproduce past examination questions and extracts from the syllabus. The suggested solutions in the further question practice bank have been prepared by BPP Learning Media Ltd, except where otherwise stated.

Contents

Helping you to pass

BPP Learning Media – ACCA Approved Content Provider

As an ACCA Approved Content Provider, BPP Learning Media gives you the opportunity to use study materials reviewed by the ACCA examining team. By incorporating the examining team's comments and suggestions regarding the depth and breadth of syllabus coverage, the BPP Learning Media Workbook provides excellent, ACCA-approved support for your studies.

These materials are reviewed by the ACCA examining team. The objective of the review is to ensure that the material properly covers the syllabus and study guide outcomes, used by the examining team in setting the exams, in the appropriate breadth and depth. The review does not ensure that every eventuality, combination or application of examinable topics is addressed by the ACCA Approved Content. Nor does the review comprise a detailed technical check of the content as the Approved Content Provider has its own quality assurance processes in place in this respect.

BPP Learning Media do everything possible to ensure the material is accurate and up to date when sending to print. In the event that any errors are found after the print date, they are uploaded to the following website: www.bpp.com/learningmedia/Errata.

The PER alert

Before you can qualify as an ACCA member, you not only have to pass all your exams but also fulfil a three-year practical experience requirement (PER). To help you to recognise areas of the syllabus that you might be able to apply in the workplace to achieve different performance objectives, we have introduced the 'PER alert' feature (see the next section). You will find this feature throughout the Workbook to remind you that what you are learning to pass your ACCA exams is equally useful to the fulfilment of the PER requirement. Your achievement of the PER should be recorded in your online My Experience record.

Chapter features

Studying can be a daunting prospect, particularly when you have lots of other commitments. This Workbook is full of useful features, explained in the key below, designed to help you to get the most out of your studies and maximise your chances of exam success.

Key term

Central concepts are highlighted and clearly defined in the Key terms feature. Key terms are also listed in bold in the Index, for quick and easy reference.

Formula to learn

This boxed feature will highlight important formula which you need to learn for your exam.

PER alert

This feature identifies when something you are reading will also be useful for your PER requirement (see 'The PER alert' section above for more details).

Real world examples

These will give real examples to help demonstrate the concepts you are reading about.

Illustration

Illustrations walk through how to apply key knowledge and techniques step by step.

Activity

Activities give you essential practice of techniques covered in the chapter.

Essential reading

Links to the Essential reading are given throughout the chapter. The Essential reading is included in the free eBook, accessed via the Exam Success Site (see inside cover for details on how to access this).

Figure 1.1: Key to icons

At the end of each chapter you will find a Knowledge diagnostic, which is a summary of the main learning points from the chapter to allow you to check you have understood the key concepts. You will also find a Further study guidance which contains suggestions for ways in which you can continue your learning and enhance your understanding. This can include: recommendations for question practice from the Further question practice and solutions (available in the digital edition of the Workbook), to test your understanding of the topics in the Chapter; suggestions for further reading which can be done, such as technical articles, and ideas for your own research.

Introduction to the Essential reading

The electronic version of the Workbook contains additional content, selected to enhance your studies. Consisting of revision materials and further explanations of complex areas including illustrations and activities, as well as practice questions and solutions and background reading, it is designed to aid your understanding of key topics which are covered in the main printed chapters of the Workbook.

A summary of the content of the Essential reading is given below.

	Chapter	Summary of Essential reading content
1	Financial strategy: formulation	• Further discussion of dividend policy including brought forward knowledge from the FM exam • Examples of ethical issues in different business functions • Discussion of integrated reporting and triple bottom line
2	Financial strategy: evaluation	• Recap of the dividend growth model and its use in calculating the cost of equity: brought forward knowledge from the FM exam • Further discussion of the CAPM model • Recap of other techniques for calculating the cost of debt: brought forward knowledge from the FM exam • Recap of basic ratio analysis, brought forward knowledge from the FM exam • Examples of different types of risk and risk mapping
3	Discounted cash flow techniques	• Discussion of post-audits • Recap of the basics of discounting: brought forward knowledge from the FM exam • Further discussion of IRR re-investment assumption • Recap of other techniques for analysing risk and uncertainty: brought forward knowledge from the FM exam • Recap of capital rationing: brought forward knowledge from the FM exam
4	Application of option pricing theory	• Discussion of the factors determining option value for call and put options
5	International investment and financing decisions	• Further discussion of economic risk, exchange controls, purchasing power parity theory and interest rate parity theory • Alternative approaches to international investment appraisal, and alternative strategies for international expansion • Discussion of eurobonds (or international bonds)
6	Cost of capital and changing risk	• Recap of theories of capital structure: brought forward knowledge from the FM exam • Further discussion of APV looking at the treatment of subsidised loans • Extra example illustrating how to deal with projects that change business risk
7	Financing and credit risk	• Background information on how credit ratings are calculated • Further example to practise calculating the duration of a bond • Recap of sources of finance: brought forward knowledge from the FM exam

Chapter		Summary of Essential reading content
		• Further discussion of the pros and cons of Islamic finance
8	Valuation for acquisition and mergers	• Extra notes on asset and market-based models • Discussion of the use of the Black–Scholes model in valuing start-ups
9	Acquisitions: strategic issues and regulation	• Discussion of different types of mergers and acquisitions • Further detail regulatory issues and defensive tactics
10	Financing acquisitions and mergers	• Discussion of different types of paper issues • Evaluation of the effect of an offer on the acquiring company's financial statements
11	The role of the treasury function	• Discussion of the organisation of the treasury function
12	Managing currency risk	• Recap of internal hedging techniques, forward contracts and money market hedging: brought forward knowledge from the FM exam • Further discussion different approaches to dealing with currency futures
13	Managing interest rate risk	• Recap of basic hedging techniques: brought forward knowledge from the FM exam
14	Financial reconstruction	• Discussion of leveraged buy-outs
15	Business reorganisation	• Further discussion of demergers
16	Planning and trading issues for multinationals	• General issues in international trade • International institutions • Outline of developments in financial markets

Introduction to Advanced Financial Management (AFM)

Overall aim of the syllabus

This exam requires students to apply relevant knowledge and skills and exercise professional judgement as expected of a senior financial adviser in taking or recommending decisions concerning the financial management of the organisation.

Brought forward knowledge

The Advanced Financial Management syllabus includes a number of topics which were covered in Financial Management but develops them further and requires candidates to be able to apply them to more complex scenarios in the exam.

The syllabus

The broad syllabus headings are:

A	Role of the senior financial adviser in the multinational organisation
B	Advanced investment appraisal
C	Acquisition and mergers
D	Corporate re-organisation and reconstruction
E	Treasury and advanced risk management techniques
F	Professional skills
G	Employability and technology skills

Main capabilities

On successful completion of this exam, candidates should be able to:

- Explain and evaluate the role and responsibility of the senior financial executive or adviser in meeting conflicting needs of stakeholders and recognise the role of international financial institutions in the financial management of multinationals

- Evaluate potential investment decisions and assessing their financial and strategic consequences, both domestically and internationally

- Assess and plan acquisitions and mergers as an alternative growth strategy

- Evaluate and advise on alternative corporate re-organisation strategies

- Apply and evaluate alternative advanced treasury and risk management techniques

- Apply a range of professional skills in addressing requirements within the AFM exam, and in preparation for, or to support, current work experience

- Apply employability and technology skills

Links to other exams

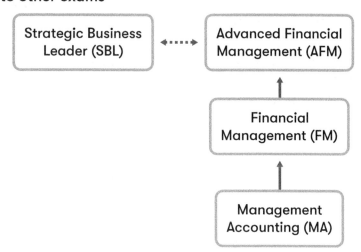

This diagram shows where direct (solid line arrows) and indirect (dashed line arrows) links exist between this exam and others that may precede or follow it.

Achieving ACCA's Study Guide Outcomes

This BPP Workbook covers all the AFM syllabus learning outcomes. The tables below show in which chapter(s) each area of the syllabus is covered.

A	Role of senior financial adviser in the multinational organisation	
A1	The role and responsibility of senior financial executive/adviser	Chapter 1
A2	Financial strategy formulation	Chapter 2
A3	Ethical and governance issues	Chapter 1
A4	Management of international trade and finance	Chapter 16
A5	Strategic business and financial planning for multinational organisations	Chapter 16
A6	Dividend policy in multinationals and transfer pricing	Chapter 16

B	Advanced investment appraisal	
B1	Discounted cash flow techniques	Chapter 3
B2	Application of option pricing theory in investment decisions	Chapter 4
B3	Impact of financing on investment decisions and adjusted present values	Chapter 6 & 7
B4	Valuation and the use of free cash flows	Chapter 8
B5	International investment and financing decisions	Chapter 5

C	Acquisitions and mergers	
C1	Acquisitions and mergers versus other growth strategies	Chapter 9
C2	Valuation for acquisitions and mergers	Chapter 8
C3	Regulatory framework and processes	Chapter 9

C4	Financing acquisitions and mergers	Chapter 10
D	**Corporate reconstruction and reorganisation**	
D1	Financial reconstruction	Chapter 14
D2	Business re-organisation	Chapter 15
E	**Treasury and advanced risk management techniques**	
E1	The role of the treasury function in multinationals	Chapter 11
E2	The use of financial derivatives to hedge against forex risk	Chapter 12
E3	The use of financial derivatives to hedge against interest rate risk	Chapter 13
F	**Professional skills**	
F1	Communication	**Exam skill; covered in Skills Checkpoint 3**
F2	Analysis and evaluation	**Exam skill: covered in Skills Checkpoint 2**
F3	Scepticism	**Exam skill: covered in Skills Checkpoint 1**
F4	Commercial acumen	**Exam skill: covered in Skills Checkpoint 4**
G	**Employability and technology skills**	
G1	Use computer technology to efficiently access and manipulate relevant information.	**Exam skill: covered in Skills Checkpoint 5**
G2	Work on relevant response options, using available functions and technology, as would be required in the workplace.	**Exam skill: covered in Skills Checkpoint 5**
G3	Navigate windows and computer screens to create and amend responses to exam requirements, using appropriate tools.	**Exam skill: covered in Skills Checkpoint 5**
G4	Present data and information effectively, using the appropriate tools.	**Exam skill: covered in Skills Checkpoint 5**

Syllabus section F is new from the September 2022 exam onwards. The four professional skills are introduced later in this section. **None of these skills are technically difficult;** they have been designed to reward candidates who are attempting to address the problems and issues being faced by a company in a scenario question in a thoughtful way. This is, of course, what you should naturally be aiming to do anyway.

Syllabus section G is present in the syllabus for all ACCA professional exams; it reflects the skills needed in a computer-based exam and has no specific detailed syllabus content. This area is covered in the exam success skills section later in this introduction.

The complete syllabus and study guide can be found by visiting the exam resource finder on the ACCA website: https://www.accaglobal.com/gb/en/student/exam-support-resources/professional-exams-study-resources/p4.html

The exam

Computer-based exams

Strategic Professional exams are all computer-based exams (CBE).

Approach to examining the syllabus

The Advanced Financial Management syllabus is assessed by a 3 hour 15 minute exam. The pass mark is **50%**. All questions in the exam are **compulsory**.

It examines **practical financial management issues** facing a company. You will be examined on your knowledge of the breadth of the AFM syllabus, and on your ability to **apply your knowledge** in a practical way.

The exam will have a significant numerical element, worth up to 50% of the marks, but you will also need to demonstrate your understanding of the **meaning and limitations** of your numerical analysis.

However, the AFM exam is not all about calculations and there will also be a strong emphasis on management issues which will require you to exercise **professional, commercial** and **ethical judgement**.

You will be required to adopt **the role of a senior financial adviser** in answering questions and, as such, will need to make points that are **relevant to the specific scenario** that your company is facing (not to make general 'textbook' style observations).

Format of the exam		Marks
Section A		
Question 1	Compulsory scenario-based question (10 of the marks are available for demonstrating professional skills)	50
Section B		
Questions 2, 3	2 × 25 mark scenario-based questions (5 of the marks in each question, so 10 marks in total, are available for demonstrating professional skills)	50
		100

All topics and syllabus sections will be examinable in either Section A or Section B of the exam, every exam will have questions which have a focus on syllabus Section B (advanced investment appraisal, covered in Chapters 3–7) and syllabus Section E (treasury and advanced risk management, covered in Chapters 11–13).

Analysis of past exams

The table below provides details of when each element of the syllabus has been examined in the ten most recent sittings and the section in which each element was examined.

Note that in exams before September 2018 there were three questions in Section B (of which two had to be answered).

* Covered in Workbook chapter

*		Sept/Dec 2021	Mar/June 2021	Sept/Dec 2020	Mar/June 2020	Sept/Dec 2019	Mar/June 2019	Dec 2018	Sep 2018	Mar/June 2018	Sept/Dec 2017
	ROLE OF SENIOR FINANCIAL ADVISER										
1	Financial strategy formulation		B	A		B	A			B	A
2	Financial strategy evaluation			A		B					B
16	Planning and trading issues for multinationals	A		B							
	ADVANCED INVESTMENT APPRAISAL										
3	Discounted cash flow techniques		B		B	A	A				B
4	Application of option pricing theory to investment decisions			B			A				B
5	International investment			B		A			A		
6	Cost of capital and changing risk	A					B	B		B	
7	Financial and credit risk			A							A
	ACQUISITIONS AND MERGERS										
8	Valuation techniques	B	A		A	B		A	B	A	B
9	Strategic and regulatory issues		A	A	A	B			B	A	
10	Financing acquisitions		A		A	B		A	B		
	CORPORATE RECONSTRUCTION AND REORGANISATION										
14	Financial reconstruction	B									A
15	Business reorganisation	B	A				B	A			B

		Sept/Dec 2021	Mar/June 2021	Sept/Dec 2020	Mar/June 2020	Sept/Dec 2019	Mar/June 2019	Dec 2018	Sep 2018	Mar/June 2018	Sept/Dec 2017
	TREASURY AND ADVANCED RISK MANAGEMENT TECHNIQUES										
11	Role of the treasury function	B	B		B		B		A		B
12	Managing foreign currency risk		B		B	A		B	A		
13	Managing interest rate risk	B		B			B				B

IMPORTANT!

The table above gives a broad idea of how frequently major topics in the syllabus are examined. It should **not** be used to question spot and predict for example that Topic X will not be examined because it came up two sittings ago. The examining team's reports indicate that the examining team is well aware some students try to question spot. The examining team avoid predictable patterns and may, for example, examine the same topic two sittings in a row.

Essential skills areas to be successful in Advanced Financial Management (AFM)

We think there are three areas you should develop in order to achieve exam success in AFM:

(a) **Knowledge application**; technical knowledge accounts for a high percentage of the marks in the AFM exam and it is essential to have a good knowledge of all syllabus areas.

(b) **AFM Professional skills**; these are worth 20% of the marks in the AFM exam (from September 2022 onwards) and are explained in detail in this section.

(c) **Exam success skills**; these are general skills required in the application of good exam technique and apply to any exam.

These are shown in the diagram below.

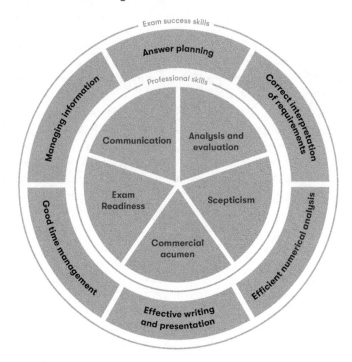

AFM professional skills

From the September 2022 exam onwards, 20 marks will be available for demonstrating the professional skills that would be expected from a proficient senior financial professional. Professional skills marks should not be thought of as being separate from the technical content of an answer; they are earned by providing comprehensive and relevant responses to the technical requirements.

There are four professional skills, which are introduced gradually in this workbook in a series of **skills checkpoints.**

The four professional skills are:

(a) **Scepticism – covered in skills checkpoint 1**

(b) **Analysis and Evaluation – covered in skills checkpoint 2**

(c) **Communication – covered in skills checkpoint 3**

(d) **Commercial Acumen – covered in skills checkpoint 4**

All of the professional skills will be examined in Section A of the exam, which is a single 50-mark case study. 10 of the 50 marks will be allocated to demonstrating professional skills.

Section B will consist of two compulsory scenario-based 25-mark questions. Each section B question will allocate 5 marks to professional skills, so 10 marks in total will be available for professional skills marks in Section B. Each question will contain **a minimum of two professional skills from Analysis and Evaluation, Scepticism and Commercial Acumen.**

There is also a 5th skills checkpoint, at the end of the workbook, that gives general advice on being exam ready and focuses on how to make best use of the computer-based exam software.

Exam success skills

Passing the AFM exam also requires the development of excellent exam technique through question practice.

We consider the following six skills to be vital for exam success.

Exam success skill 1

Managing information

Questions in the exam will present you with a lot of information. The skill is how you handle this information to make the best use of your time. The key is determining how you will approach the exam and then actively reading the questions.

Advice on developing this skill

To avoid being overwhelmed by the quantity of information provided, you must take an **active approach** to reading each question.

Active reading means focussing on the question's requirements first, highlighting key verbs such as 'evaluate', 'analyse', 'explain', 'discuss', to ensure you answer the question properly. Then, when you have an understanding of what the question will require you to do, read the rest of the question, highlighting important and relevant information, and making notes of any relevant technical information you think you will need.

Computer-based exam

In a computer-based exam (CBE) the **highlighter tool** provided in the toolbar at the top of the screen offers a range of colours:

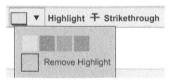

This allows you to choose **different colours to answer different aspects to a question**. For example, if a question asked you to discuss the pros and cons of an issue then you could choose a different colour for highlighting pros and cons within the relevant section of a question.

The **strikethrough function** allows you to delete areas of a question that you have dealt with - this can be useful in managing information if you are dealing with numerical questions because it can allow you to ensure that all numerical areas have been accounted for in your answer.

The CBE also allows you to **resize windows** by clicking on the bottom right-hand corner of the window as highlighted in the following section:

This functionality allows you to **display a number of windows at the same time**, so this could allow you review:

- the question requirements and the exhibit relating to that requirement, at the same time, or
- the window containing your answer (whether a word processing or spreadsheet document) and the exhibit relating to that requirement, at the same time.

Exam success skill 2

Correct interpretation of the requirements

The active verb used often dictates the approach that written answers should take (eg 'explain', 'discuss', 'evaluate'). It is important you identify and use the verb to define your approach. The **correct interpretation of the requirements** skill means correctly producing only what is being asked for by a requirement. Anything not required will not earn marks.

Advice on developing this skill

This skill can be developed by analysing question requirements and applying this process:

Step 1 Read the requirement

Firstly, read the requirement a couple of times slowly and carefully and **highlight the active verbs**. Use the active verbs to define what you plan to do. Make sure you identify any sub-requirements within a requirement – this is **often signalled by the use of the word 'and'** within a requirement.

Important active verbs for AFM include the following:

Advise

This requires you to provide someone with useful information, or to **tell them what you think they should do** based on a consideration of the issues presented in a scenario.

Analyse

This requires you to **break an issue into separate parts** and discuss, examine, or interpret each part. This may require you to **give reasons for** the current situation or what has happened.

Apply

This requires you to put a concept into action by applying it **to the scenario** in a relevant way.

Assess

This requires you to judge the importance or estimate the nature, quality or significance of an issue.

Discuss

This will require you to consider and debate/argue about the pros and cons of an issue.

Estimate

Calculate an **approximate value**, based on reasonable assumptions, and explaining those assumptions where appropriate.

Evaluate

This will require you to present **a 'balanced' discussion** of an issue looking at both the positive and negative issues. Where numbers feature in a question, an evaluation will require you to use the numbers provided to create a value from which a **judgement** can be made.

Explain

This involves making an idea clear and could require you to, for example, show logically how a concept is developed or to **give the reason** for an event.

Recommend

If you are asked to 'recommend' then you are expected to use details presented in the scenario to create **a logical and justified** course of action.

Step 2 Read the rest of the question

By reading the requirement first, you will have an idea of what you are looking out for as you read through the case overview and exhibits. This is a great time saver and means you don't end up having to read the whole question in full twice. You should do this in an active way – see Exam success skill 1: Managing Information.

Step 3 **Read the requirement again**

Read the requirement again to remind yourself of the exact wording before starting your written answer. This will capture any misinterpretation of the requirements or any missed requirements entirely. This should become a habit in your approach and, with repeated practice, you will find the focus, relevance and depth of your answer plan will improve.

Exam success skill 3

Answer planning: Priorities, structure and logic

This skill requires the planning of the key aspects of an answer which accurately and completely responds to the requirement.

Advice on developing this skill

Everyone will have a preferred style for an answer plan. For example, it may be a mind map, or bullet-pointed lists. Choose the approach that you feel most comfortable with, or, if you are not sure, try out different approaches for different questions until you have found your preferred style.

In a **computer-based exam** you can use the copy and paste functions to **copy the question requirements to the beginning of your answer**. This will allow you to ensure that your answer plan addresses all parts of the question requirements.

You can also **copy the question requirements to the main body your answer**. This will allow you to create sub-headings for your answer, again ensuring that your answer addresses all parts of the question requirements.

Copying and pasting simply involves highlighting the relevant information and either right clicking to access the copy and paste functions, or alternatively using Ctrl C to copy and Ctrl V to paste.

Exam success skill 4

Efficient numerical analysis

This skill aims to maximise the marks awarded by making clear to the marker the process of arriving at your answer. This is achieved by laying out an answer such that, even if you make a few errors, you can still score subsequent marks for follow-on calculations. It is vital that you do not lose marks purely because the marker cannot follow what you have done.

It is important to use the spreadsheet provided to produce a clear and efficient numerical analysis.

It is **not a sensible idea** to perform calculations on a calculator and then manually transfer them to the spreadsheet because this will not **show the marker where numbers have come from**.

It is important to remember that, in an exam situation, it is difficult to get every number 100% correct. It is important that you do not spend too long on any single calculation. If you are struggling with a solution then make a sensible assumption, state it and move on.

Using a spreadsheet allows you to **show the marker how numerical values have been calculated**, because the basis for a calculation is displayed if the marker clicks onto a cell.

Clear labelling should also help to show the marker what the numbers are intended to mean.

For example, in the following spreadsheet the marker can see that the highlighted calculation in cell F16 is calculated as 25% of the change in revenue given in cell C7 because this is what is recorded in the spreadsheet cell (as shown in the first row). The marker can also see from the **heading** in cell C4 that the value in cell C7 is a measure of the increase in sales revenue.

	A	B	C	D	E	F	G	H	I	J
2		part a	Workings							
3										
4			increase in revenue			$m		Notes		
5			20X6 revenue			133900		2% margin		
6			20X5 revenue			130000		3% growth		
7			change			3900				
8										
9			Divided capacity			$m				
10										
11				Pre-tax operating profit		2678				
12				interest		**-820**				
13						1858				
14				tax 30%		-557.4				
15										
16				spending on new capacity		-975				
17										
18				**dividend capacity**		**325.6**				

Workings

If the workings are visible in the cell and reflect straightforward calculations, then there is **less need to show detailed workings**. For example, in cell F16 in the previous spreadsheet extract workings are helpful, but in cell F14 there is no real need for workings as the marker will be able to follow the logic by looking at the basis for the calculation in F14, which will be something like =-F13*0.3).

However, a **workings section** (as shown in the previous spreadsheet) will sometimes be a useful feature of a spreadsheet answer if more detailed calculations are involved. A workings section reduces the likelihood of errors being made (if calculations are complex).

Keep your workings as clear and simple as possible and ensure they are cross-referenced to the main part of your answer. Where it helps, provide brief narrative explanations to help the marker understand the steps in the calculation. This means that if a mistake is made you should not lose any subsequent marks for follow-on calculations.

Spreadsheet short-cuts

You can also use useful spreadsheet short-cuts to improve the efficiency of numerical analysis. For AFM, useful short-cuts include the ability to calculate totals and averages, to insert different currency symbols, and also to calculate NPV, IRR and MIRR.

Further details are given in the following table.

Function	Guidance and examples
Sum	=SUM(A1:A10) adds all the numbers in spreadsheet cells A1 to A10.
Average	=AVERAGE(A1:A10) averages the numbers in spreadsheet cells A1 to A10.
NPV	Net present value is based on future cash flows, assuming that the first cash flow is in one year's time. For example, if the future cash flows from a project arise over five years and need to be discounted at 10% then the formula could be as follows: =NPV(0.1, B10:F10) This would give the present value of cash flows from time period 1-5; the cash outflow in time 0 would then need to be deducted to calculate the net present value.
IRR	Internal rate of return is based on future cash flows (looking at cash outflows and inflows) in each year of a project, from time 0 onwards. For example, to identify the internal rate of return of a project arising over five years (involving

Function	Guidance and examples
	time periods 0-5) the formula could be as follows: =IRR(A10:F10)
MIRR	Modified internal rate of return is based on future cash flows (looking at cash outflows and inflows) in each year of a project, from time 0 onwards. The formula is =MIRR (values, finance rate, reinvestment rate). The finance rate and reinvestment rate will normally be the same. For example, to identify the MIRR of the future cash flows from a project arising over five years (involving time periods 0-5) where the cost of capital to be applied to cash outflows (the finance rate) and cash inflows (reinvestment rate) is 10%, then the formula could be as follows: =MIRR(A10:F10, 0.1, 0.1)

Where numerical calculations require commentary then this can be provided in a word processing document with a **reference to calculations provided within the spreadsheet**.

Exam success skill 5

Effective writing and presentation

Written answers should be presented so that the marker can clearly see the points you are making, presented in the format specified in the question. The skill is to provide efficient written answers with sufficient breadth of points that answer the question, in the right depth, in the time available.

Advice on developing this skill

Step 1 **Use headings**

Using the headings and sub-headings from your answer plan will give your answer structure, order and logic. This will ensure your answer links back to the requirement and is clearly signposted, making it easier for the marker to understand the different points you are making. Underlining your headings will also help the marker.

Step 2 **Write your answer in short, but full, sentences**

Use short, clear sentences with the aim that every sentence should say something different and generate marks. Write in full sentences, ensuring your style is professional.

Exam success skill 6

Good time management

This skill means planning your time across all the requirements so that all tasks have been attempted at the end of the 3 hours 15 minutes available and actively checking on time during your exam. This is so that you can flex your approach and prioritise requirements which, in your judgement, will generate the maximum marks in the available time remaining.

Planning time

In AFM it is crucial to spend time on planning before starting to write your answer. This allows time for a candidate to immerse themselves in the question scenarios. Approximately 20% of your time should be allocated to planning to ensure that you are able to assimilate the key features of the scenario before starting to write.

For a 50-mark question, planning time should be 50 marks × 1.95 × 0.2 = **20 minutes**.

For a 25-mark question, planning time would be 25 marks × 1.95 × 0.2 = **10 minutes** per question.

Writing time

For time management purposes, candidates should allocate time based on the **technical marks available.** Professional skills marks should not be thought of as separate requirements as they are earned by providing **comprehensive and relevant responses to the technical requirements.**

Writing time can be calculated by **multiplying the technical mark allocation for each requirement by 1.95 minutes** (as the 20% of time spent planning is exactly offset by the extra 20% of marks available for professional skills marks).

So, time planning for a 25-mark question with, for example, a 12 mark part a and a 10 mark part b (and 5 professional skills marks) should be as follows:

Total time: 25 marks x 1.95 minutes per mark = <u>49 minutes</u>

Planning time: 49 minutes x 0.2 = 10 minutes

Writing time: part a = 12 x 1.95 minutes per mark = 23 minutes

Writing time: part b = 8 x 1.95 minutes per mark = 16 minutes

At the beginning of a question, work out the amount of time you should be spending on each requirement and note the finishing time next to each requirement on your exam.

Keep an eye on the clock

Aim to attempt all requirements, but be ready to be ruthless and move on if your answer is not going as planned. The challenge for many is sticking to planned timings. Be aware this is difficult to achieve in the early stages of your studies and be ready to let this skill develop over time.

Avoid discussing issues at great length, remember that the Strategic Professional Options examinations are normally marked on the basis of **one mark per point, possibly with an extra mark for more fully developing the same point.**

If you find yourself running short on time and know that a full answer is not possible in the time you have, consider recreating your plan in overview form and then add key terms and details as time allows. Remember, some marks may be available, for example, simply stating a conclusion which you don't have time to justify in full.

Question practice

Question practice is a core part of learning new topic areas. When you practise questions, you should focus on improving the Exam success skills – personal to your needs – by obtaining feedback or through a process of self-assessment.

This is a computer-based exam and practising as many exam-style questions as possible in the ACCA CBE practice platform will a key part of your exam preparation. You should attempt questions under timed conditions and ensure you produce full answers to the discussion parts as well as doing the calculations. Also ensure that you attempt all mock exams under exam conditions.

ACCA have launched a free on-demand resource designed to mirror the live exam experience helping you to become more familiar with the exam format. You can access the platform via the Study Support Resources section of the ACCA website, navigating to the CBE question practice section and logging in with your myACCA credentials.

Financial strategy: formulation

Learning objectives

On completion of this chapter, you should be able to:

	Syllabus reference no.
Develop **strategies** for the achievement of the organisational goals in line with its agreed policy framework	A1(a)
Recommend **strategies** for the management of the financial resources of the organisation such that they are utilised in an efficient, effective and transparent way	A1(b)
Advise the board of directors or management of the organisation in **setting the financial goals of the business** and in its policy development with particular reference to: • Investment selection and capital resource allocation • Minimising the cost of capital • Distribution and retention policy • Communicating financial policy and corporate goals to internal and external stakeholders • Financial planning and control • The management of risk	A1(c)
Recommend the optimum capital mix and structure within a specific business context and capital asset structure (also covered in Chapter 6)	A2(b)
Recommend appropriate distribution and retention policy	A2(c)
Assess **the ethical dimension within business issues** and decisions and advise on best practice in the financial management of the organisation.	A3(a)
Demonstrate an understanding of the interconnectedness of the ethics of good business practice between all functional areas of the organisation	A3(b)
Recommend, within specified problem domains, appropriate strategies for the resolution of stakeholder conflict and advise on alternative approaches that may be adopted	A3(c)
Recommend an ethical framework for the development of an organisation's financial policies and a system for the assessment of its ethical impact upon the financial management of the organisation	A3(d)

	Syllabus reference no.
Explore the areas within the ethical framework of the organisation which may be undermined by agency effects and/or stakeholder conflicts and establish strategies for dealing with them	A3(e)
Establish an ethical financial policy for the financial management of the organisation which is grounded in good governance, the highest standards of probity and is fully aligned with the ethical principles of the Association	A3(f)
Assess the impact on sustainability and environmental issues arising from alternative organisational business and financial decisions	A3(g)
Assess and advise on the impact of investment and financing strategies and decisions on the organisation's stakeholders, from a governance perspective	A3(h)

Exam context

This chapter we discuss **the role and responsibility of the senior financial adviser** in the context of setting **financial strategy**. This chapter and the next underpin the rest of the syllabus and introduce some of the key concepts of financial management, some of which will be familiar to you from the Financial Management exam.

Most of the areas that are introduced here are **developed in later chapters**. However, **dividend policy** is mainly covered in this chapter and should be studied with particular care.

Remember that **non-financial issues** are also important, and ethical and environmental issues are considered here reflecting the responsibility of senior financial managers for meeting the competing needs of a variety of **different stakeholders**.

Exam questions generally test elements of this chapter as **part of** a broader scenario-based question, in either in Section A or B of the exam.

You should already be familiar with the techniques covered here from your earlier studies (of the Financial Management syllabus). However, it is important to revise them here and to make sure that you can **apply them**, as necessary, to the scenario-based questions that you will face in the AFM exam.

Chapter overview

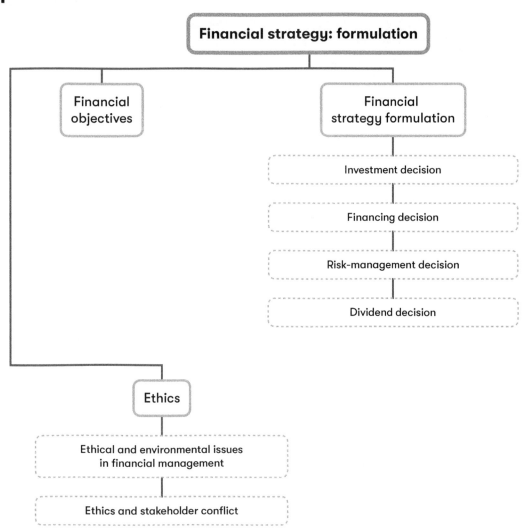

1 Financial objectives

Profit maximisation is often assumed, incorrectly, to be the primary objective of a business.

Reasons why profit is not a sufficient objective
• Investors care about the **future**
• Investors care about the **dividend**
• Investors care about **financing plans**
• Investors care about **risk management**

For a profit-making company, a better financial objective is the **maximisation of shareholder wealth**; this can be measured as **total shareholder return** (dividend yield + capital gain).

Formula to learn

Total shareholder return	=	dividend yield	+	capital gain (or loss)
		Dividend per share/share price		capital gain (or loss)/share price

Many companies have non-financial objectives that will also be important in assisting a company to achieve its **strategic goals**. For example, a manufacturing company that is aiming to differentiate itself on the basis of quality will require targets for defect rates. This does not negate the importance of financial objectives but emphasises the need for companies to have other targets than the maximisation of shareholders' wealth.

2 Financial strategy formulation

A **financial strategy** should organise an organisation's resources to maximise returns to shareholders by focussing on future cash flows, financing and risk.

2.1 Investment decision

Investment decisions (in projects or by making acquisitions) are often seen as **the key mechanism for creating shareholder wealth**, but they will need to be carefully analysed to ensure that they are likely to be beneficial to the investor.

The techniques for analysing investment decisions are covered in depth in Chapters 3–10.

2.2 Financing decision

2.2.1 Use of debt finance

One of the main aspects of **financing decisions** is how much debt a firm is planning to use and whether using debt finance can help to reduce a business's weighted average cost of capital.

The level of gearing that is appropriate for a business depends on a number of **practical issues**:

Practical issues	Explanation
Life cycle	A new, growing business will find it **difficult to forecast cash flows** with any certainty, so high levels of gearing are unwise.
Operating gearing	If fixed costs are a high proportion of total costs then **cash flows will be volatile**; so high gearing is not sensible.
Stability of revenue	If operating in a highly dynamic business environment then **cash flows will be volatile**; so high gearing is not sensible.
Security	If unable to offer security, debt will be difficult and expensive to obtain.

2.2.2 Financial planning and control

In order to survive, any business must have an adequate net inflow of cash. Businesses should try to plan for positive net cash flows but at the same time it is unwise to hold too much cash.

When a company is cash-rich the senior financial adviser will have to decide whether to do one (or more) of the following:

(a) **Plan to use the cash**, for example for a project investment or a takeover bid for another company

(b) **Pay out the cash** to shareholders as dividends, and let the shareholders decide how best to use the cash for themselves

(c) **Repurchase its own shares** (share buyback)

Where cash flow has become a problem, a company may choose to sell off some of its assets. However, it is important to recognise the difference between assets that a company can survive without and those that are essential for the company's continued operation.

Assets can be divided into three categories.

(a) Those that are needed to carry out the core activities of the business (eg plant and machinery)

(b) Those that are not essential for carrying out the main activities of the business and can be sold off at fairly short notice (eg short-term marketable investments)

(c) Those that are not essential for carrying out the main activities of the business and can be sold off to raise cash, but may take some time to sell (eg long-term investments, subsidiary companies)

The financing decision is discussed in Chapter 6 and techniques linked to the financing decision are covered in a number of later chapters.

2.3 Risk management decision

Risk management decisions, in the AFM exam, mainly involve management of exchange rate and interest rate risk and project management issues.

Again, the **volatility of an organisation's cash flows** are a powerful influence on its approach to risk management. The more volatile cash flows are, the more important risk management becomes. **Risk management is discussed in Chapter 2** and risk management **techniques** are **covered later** in Chapters 11–13.

2.4 Dividend decision

The **dividend decision** is related to how much a firm has decided to spend on **investments** and **also** to how much of the finance needed for investments is being raised externally (**financing decision**); this illustrates the **interrelationship** between these key **decisions**.

2.4.1 Influence of the investment decision

If a company is growing then much of the cash it has will be better used to invest in positive NPV projects, so it will not have the **liquidity** to pay dividends. **Shareholder expectations** will often be for low or even zero dividends in these circumstances.

2.4.2 Influence of the financing decision

However, if a company can borrow to finance its investments, it **can** still pay dividends. There are **legal constraints** over a company's ability to do this; it is only legal if a company has **accumulated** realised profits.

2.4.3 Influence of the lifecycle

Dividend policy often changes during the course of a business's **lifecycle**.

Time

Young company:	Mature company:
Zero or low dividend	**Higher dividend payouts**
High growth/investment needs	Lower growth/investment needs
Wants to minimise debt, as cash flows are unstable	Debt more suitable as cash flows stabilise

2.4.4 Dividend capacity

Investment and financing issues will impact on an organisation's **capacity** to pay a dividend.

KEY TERM

Dividend capacity: The cash generated in any given year that is **available** to pay to ordinary shareholders (it is also called free cash flow to equity).

You may be asked to calculate dividend capacity.

Dividend capacity
Profits after interest, tax and preference dividends
less
debt repayment, share repurchases, investment in assets
plus
depreciation, any capital raised from new share issues or debt

Activity 1: Dividend capacity

The following projected financial data relates to CX Co.

	$m
Operating profit	400
Depreciation	60
Finance charges paid	30
Preference dividends paid	15
Tax paid	75
Ordinary dividends paid	60

The book value of CX's non-current assets last year were $200 million. This is projected to rise by $40 million.

CX Co is planning to repay $100 million of debt during the next year.

Required

Estimate and comment on the dividend capacity of CX Co.

Solution

2.4.5 Practical dividend policies

Having considered these factors, companies will formulate and communicate their policy to ensure that shareholders have realistic **expectations** regarding the dividends they are likely to receive.

Policy	Explanation
Constant payout ratio	Logical but can create volatile dividend movements if profits are volatile
Stable growth	Set at a level that signals the growth prospects of the company, but may be difficult to maintain if circumstances change
Residual policy	Only pay a dividend after all positive NPV projects have been funded

2.4.6 Scrip dividends

A company will sometimes offer a **scrip dividend** (extra shares) instead of cash. Compared to a cash dividend, a scrip dividend boosts a company's cash flow and may benefit shareholders if the cash is re-invested in positive NPV projects that could not otherwise have been financed.

An **enhanced scrip dividend** involves giving the shareholder a choice over whether to take cash or shares but offering a generous amount of shares so that it is likely that shareholders will choose to take shares instead of cash.

2.4.7 Share buybacks

As an alternative to a cash dividend, a company can choose to return significant amounts of cash to shareholders by means of a **share buyback (or repurchase)**.

Advantages of share buybacks:

- **Avoids increasing expectations** of higher dividends in future (which may be a problem if dividends are increased).
- Provides disaffected shareholders with an **exit route**, in this sense it is a defence against a takeover.
- Taxed as a capital gain which may be advantageous if the **tax** on capital gains is below the rate used to tax dividend income.
- **If shares are under-valued**, the company may be able to buy shares at a low price which will benefit the remaining shareholders. Fewer shares will improve EPS and DPS ratios.

2.4.8 Special dividends

Another way of returning significant amounts of cash to shareholders is by a **special dividend;** a cash payment far in excess of the dividend payments that are normally made. This has a similar effect of returning significant amounts of cash to shareholders, but unlike a share buyback it impacts **all shareholders**.

A special dividend is more attractive than a share buy-back if shares are **over-valued**, and avoids shareholders potentially **diluting their control** by participating in a share buyback.

Essential reading

See Chapter 1 Section 1 of the Essential reading for more background information on dividend policy; this includes subject matter such as Modigliani and Miller's dividend irrelevance theory that should be familiar from your earlier studies.

The Essential reading is available as an Appendix of the digital edition of the Workbook.

3 Ethics

For financial strategy to be successful it needs to be communicated and supported by key **stakeholder groups**:

- **Internal** – managers, employees
- **Connected** – shareholders, banks, customers, suppliers
- **External** – government, pressure groups, local communities

Where a strategy creates a conflict between the interest of shareholders and those of other stakeholder groups then this can create ethical issues which need to be carefully managed.

3.1 Ethical and environmental issues in financial management

The key financial objective for a business is to create wealth for its shareholders. However, this can create adverse impacts on other stakeholders. You may be required to analyse this as a part of an exam question, which will require you to use your common sense to consider the impacts and how the stakeholders may react.

Activity 2: Ethical considerations in financial management

Complete the following table with ideas of potential issues in key areas of financial management.

Area of financial management	Ethical considerations
Investment	

Area of financial management	Ethical considerations
Financing	
Dividend policy	
Risk management	

3.2 Ethics and stakeholder conflict

Ethical issues often arise from a **conflict between the needs of different stakeholder groups**. Questions which include ethical considerations are likely to be of a practical nature and are likely to require you to give practical advice on a fair **resolution of stakeholder conflict**. Most commonly this will be a conflict between **shareholder needs** (ie financial gain) and the needs of another stakeholder, but other conflicts may also need to be managed.

3.2.1 Examples of stakeholder conflict

Directors and shareholders

Directors may be more risk averse than shareholders because a greater proportion of their income and wealth is tied up in the company that employs them, whereas many shareholders will hold a diversified portfolio of shares. Also, directors may focus their decision making on benefiting their own division instead of the company as a whole.

The relationship between management and shareholders is sometimes referred to as an **agency relationship**, in which managers act as agents for the shareholders.

The goal of **agency theory** is to find governance structures and control mechanisms (incentives) that minimise the problem caused by the separation of ownership and control.

Between different shareholder groups

Some shareholders might have a preference for short-term dividends, others for long-term capital gain (requiring more cash to be reinvested, and less to be paid as a dividend).

Between shareholders and debt holders

Debt holders may be more risk averse than shareholders, because it is only shareholders who will benefit if risky projects succeed.

Shareholders and staff/customers/suppliers

Pursuit of short-term profits may lead to difficult relationships with other stakeholders. For example, relationships with suppliers and customers may be disrupted by demands for changes to the terms of trade. Employees may be made redundant in a drive to reduce costs. These policies may aid short-term profits, but at the expense of damaging long-term relationships and consequently damaging shareholder value in the long term.

Shareholders and external stakeholders

The impact of a company's activities may impact adversely on its environment, eg noise, pollution.

3.2.2 Ethics and other functional areas of the organisation

Ethics should govern the conduct of corporate policy in all functional areas of a company, such as the company's **treatment of its workers, suppliers and customers**.

BPP
LEARNING
MEDIA

The ethical stance of a company is concerned with **the extent that an organisation will exceed its minimum obligations** to its stakeholders.

Essential reading

See Chapter 1 Sections 2 and 3 of the Essential reading for more background information on this area.

The Essential reading is available as an Appendix of the digital edition of the Workbook.

3.2.3 A framework for developing ethical policies

In principle, an effective framework will help to analyse some ethical issues in exam questions.

It will also be appropriate to apply your common sense to create practical solutions to the ethical problems that appear as part of an exam question.

1 Establish stakeholder concerns	2 Ensure that the company's fundamental ethical principles are understood by everyone	3 Introduce safeguards to reduce threats to an acceptable level
• Assess impact of activities (eg investments) on stakeholders, and ensure that solutions are researched to try to meet their needs where possible • Ethical concerns should then be reported to an ethics committee to ensure that the Board is aware and can take action	• Issue a code of conduct outlining key ethical values • Shows commitment from senior management • Provides guidance for staff	• Policies and procedure • Executive bonus schemes could be revamped to include ethical measures • Greater powers to the risk management function • Whistleblowers' hotline to ensure confidential responses to concerns

3.2.4 Governance

Safeguarding against the risk of unethical behaviour may also include the adoption of a **corporate governance** framework of decision making that restricts the power of executive directors and increases the role of independent non-executive directors in the monitoring of their duties.

In some countries this can include a **non-executive supervisory board** with representatives from the company's internal stakeholder groups including the finance providers, employees and the company's management. It ensures that the actions taken by the board are for the benefit of all the stakeholder groups and to the company as a whole.

Essential reading

See Chapter 1 Section 4 of the Essential reading for background information on integrated reporting. This area is no longer mentioned directly in the syllabus (as of September 2022) but some awareness of integrated reporting may help in a discussion of governance or of communication with stakeholders. The section on communicating with stakeholders is important.

The Essential reading is available as an Appendix of the digital edition of the Workbook.

Chapter summary

Financial strategy: formulation

Financial objectives

- Profit is **NOT** the key financial goal
  - It is **historic**
  - It is **not cash**
  - **It ignores** other factors, such as **risk**
- The key financial objective is **total shareholder return**, measured as dividend yield + capital gain

Financial strategy formulation

A financial strategy should organise an organisation's resources to maximise returns to shareholders by focusing on its:
- Investment decision
- Financing decision
- Risk management decision
- Dividend decision

The first and third of these decisions are covered more thoroughly in the next chapter.

Financing decision

- Debt is a cheap source of finance, and can be used to reduce the cost of capital; **the appropriate level of gearing depends on a number of practical factors**
- Practical issues:
  - **Life cycle** – a new, growing business will find it difficult to forecast cash flows so high levels of gearing are unwise
  - **Operational gearing** – if fixed costs are high then contribution (before fixed costs) will be high relative to profits (after fixed costs). High fixed costs mean cash flow is volatile, so high gearing is not sensible
  - **Stability of revenue** – if operating in a highly dynamic business environment then high gearing is not sensible
  - **Security** – if unable to offer security then debt will be difficult and expensive to obtain

Dividend decision

- Investment decision: Companies with many investment opportunities (young/high growth companies) may find it difficult to pay a dividend
- Financing decision: Companies that have volatile cash flows (and therefore prefer to minimise their use of debt finance) will often pay lower dividends.
- Dividend capacity (free cash flow to equity)
  - Cash available for paying a dividend
  - Calculated as:
    Profits after interest, tax and preference dividends **less** debt repayment, share repurchases, investment in assets **plus** depreciation, any capital raised from new share issues or debt
- Possible policies:
  - Constant payout
  - Stable growth
  - Residual
  - Scrip dividends
  - Special dividends
  - Share buybacks
- Dividend irrelevance theory (M&M)
  - In a tax-free world, shareholders are **indifferent** between dividends and capital gains, and the value of a company is determined solely by the 'earning power' of its assets and investments
  - Ignores impact of tax and practical difficulty and cost of raising finance

Ethics

Ethical and environmental issues in financial management

Unfair impact on stakeholders

Ethics and stakeholder conflict

- Companies need to understand the ethical issues it faces, resulting from stakeholder conflict
- It should state its ethical principles and introduce safeguards (eg to align interests of management to shareholders: agency theory).

Knowledge diagnostic

1. Total shareholder return

This is a measure of the change in shareholder wealth over a year. Calculated as dividend yield + capital gain/loss.

2. Financial strategy

Involves key decisions over investment, financing, dividends and risk management. Each decision affects the others.

3. Dividend capacity

Dividend capacity is the cash generated in any given year that is available to pay to ordinary shareholders (it is also called free cash flow to equity).

4. Scrip dividend

A dividend paid in shares.

Further study guidance

Question practice

Now try the following from the Further question practice bank (available in the digital edition of the workbook):

Q1 *Mezza*

Q2 *Agenda for change*

Both questions are past real exam questions and will give you a feel for the practical nature of the AFM exam, although at the time they were written (Agenda for Change is a 2007 question and Mezza is a 2011 question) exam questions were sometimes completely discussion-based and this is no longer the case (all exam questions now contain a calculation element).

Research exercise

Use an internet search engine to identify the ethical code of conduct for a company and have a look at the types of values and behaviours it contains. Choose any company you have an interest in, if you want a suggestion the BP code of conduct is an interesting document to analyse. This is available here:

https://www.bp.com/en/global/corporate/who-we-are/our-values-and-code-of-conduct.html

There is no solution to this exercise.

Activity answers

Activity 1: Dividend capacity

	$m
Profits after interest and tax (400 – 30 – 75)	295
Less preference dividends	(15)
Add back depreciation	60
Less capital expenditure (Closing non-current assets higher by 40 + depreciation 60 = capital expenditure of 100)	(100)
Less debt repaid	(100)
Dividend capacity	140

The ordinary dividend of $60 million is below this, which indicates that the dividend could potentially be increased.

Activity 2: Ethical considerations in financial management

Area of financial management	Ethical considerations
Investment	Examples include: • Fairness of wages and salaries, working conditions, training and career development • Potential impact on the environment • Bribery of government officials • Failing to invest because bonuses are based on short-term share performance (short-termism) • Over-priced takeovers indicate that managers are focused more on empire building than on shareholder value maximisation
Financing	Examples include: • A bank lending the company money may have an unethical profile • Tempting to suppress bad news at a time that finance is being raised
Dividend policy	An example could be: • May be at the expense of providing quality products or services or treating other stakeholders fairly
Risk management	An example could be: • Neglect of risk management in order to hit profit targets. Directors pursuing diversification strategies to protect their own positions, when it is not in the best interests of shareholders

2

Financial strategy: evaluation

Learning objectives

On completion of this chapter, you should be able to:

	Syllabus reference no.
Assess organisational performance using methods such as ratios and trends	A2(a)
Recommend the optimum capital mix and structure within a specific business context and capital asset structure (covered in Chapters 1 and 6)	A2(b)
Recommend appropriate distribution and retention policy (Chapter 1)	A2(c)
Explain the theoretical and practical rationale for the management of risk (also covered in Chapter 11)	A2(d)
Assess the organisation's exposure to business and financial risk including operational, reputational, political, economic, regulatory and fiscal risk	A2(e)
Develop a framework for risk management, comparing and contrasting risk mitigation, hedging and diversification strategies	A2(f)
Establish capital investment monitoring (see Chapter 3) and risk management systems	A2(g)
Advise on the impact of behavioural finance on financial strategies/securities prices and why they may not follow the conventional financial theories (also covered in Chapter 8)	A2(h)
Apply appropriate models, including term structure of interest rates, the yield curve and credit spreads, to value corporate debt	B4(a) in part
Calculate the cost of capital of an organisation, including the cost of equity and the cost of debt	B3(c) in part
Demonstrate detailed knowledge of business and financial risk and the capital asset pricing model	B3(d) in part

Exam context

This chapter starts by **examining** the **financing decision,** which is a key aspect of financial strategy. Cost of capital calculations are important in AFM and will be developed in later chapters. A sound knowledge of the capital asset pricing model is especially important for AFM. Basic cost of capital calculations are assumed knowledge from the Financial Management exam but are recapped in the Essential reading (available in Appendix 2 of the digital edition of the Workbook) as indicated in the relevant sections of this chapter.

We then move on to look at how the performance of a **financial strategy** can be **evaluated** using ratio analysis. This topic is frequently examined and must not be neglected.

This chapter also introduces the **important topic** of **risk management**. An understanding of risk is often important in evaluating a financial strategy. However, the main tools of risk management are covered in Chapters 11–13.

Finally, we introduce **behavioural finance** to explain why, when evaluating a financial strategy, we may find that it is not focused on shareholder value. This topic is considered further in Chapter 8.

Chapter overview

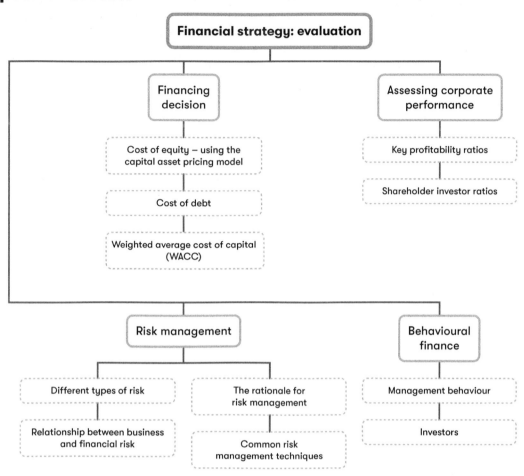

1 Financing decision

The primary objective of a profit-making company is normally assumed to be to **maximise shareholder wealth**. Investments will increase shareholder wealth if they **cover the cost of capital** and leave a surplus for the shareholders. The **lower the overall cost of capital** the **greater the wealth** that is created.

In order to be able to minimise the overall cost of finance, it is important initially to be able to **estimate the costs of each finance type**.

The **cost of the different forms of capital will reflect their risk**. Debt is lower risk than equity because debt ranks before equity in the event of a company becoming insolvent, and because interest has to paid. Therefore, debt will be cheaper than equity and the more security attached to the debt the cheaper it should be.

These cost of capital calculations can be performed as part of **an evaluation** of different proposed **financing strategies**, or as part of an evaluation of the **investment decision**.

1.1 Cost of equity – using the capital asset pricing model

Rational investors will create a diversified investment portfolio to reduce their exposure to risk.

Activity 1: Introductory activity

Complete the table below and comment on the return and risk of each investment opportunity.

		Annual returns on possible investments		
Oil price	Likelihood	Oil company	Airline company	50:50 portfolio
High	25%	25%	–5%	
Average	50%	10%	10%	
Low	25%	-5%	25%	
Expected return		10%	10%	

Solution

By continuing to diversify, shareholders can further reduce risk.

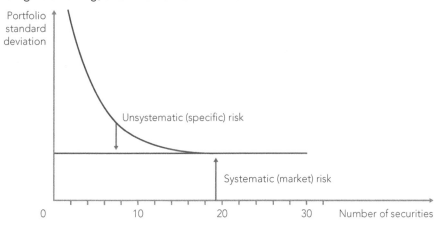

1.1.1 Unsystematic (or 'specific') risk

> **Unsystematic (or 'specific') risk:** The component of risk that is associated with investing in that particular company. This can be reduced by diversification.

Unsystematic (or 'specific') risk is gradually eliminated as the investor increases the diversity of their investment portfolio until it is negligible (the 'well-diversified portfolio').

Diversification is important because it enables investors to eliminate virtually all of the risks that are unique to particular industries or types of business. However, diversification does not offer any escape from general market factors (eg a recession) that can affect all companies.

1.1.2 Systematic (or 'market') risk

The risk that remains, for a diversified shareholder, is called systematic (or 'market') risk.

> **Systematic (or 'market') risk:** The portion of risk that will still remain even if a diversified portfolio has been created, because it is determined by general market factors.

Market risk is caused by factors which affect all industries and businesses to some extent or other, such as interest rates, tax legislation, exchange rates and economic boom or recession.

Commercial databases such as Reuters monitor the sensitivity of firms to general market factors by using historic data to calculate the **average change in the return on a share each time there is a change in the stock market as a whole**; this is called **a beta factor**.

1.1.3 Beta factors

> **Beta factors:** A measure of the sensitivity of a share to movements in the overall market. A beta factor measures market risk.

A **beta factor of 1 is average** because it means that the average change in the return on a share has been the same as the market, eg if the market fell by 1%, this share also fell by 1% on average.

Beta < 1.0	Beta = 1.0	Beta > 1.0
	Increasing risk →	
Share < Average risk	Share = Average risk	Share > Average risk
	Increasing return →	
Return < Average	Return = Average	Return > Average

Beta factors vary because **some shares are very sensitive to stock market downturns** due to:

- The nature of the products or services that are sold (luxuries will have a higher beta)
- The level of financial gearing (higher gearing creates higher financial risk)

1.1.4 Capital asset pricing model

The **Capital Asset Pricing Model (CAPM)** calculates the expected return (or cost) of equity (R_e or K_e) on the assumption that investors have a broad range of investments, and are only worried about market risk, as measured by the beta factor.

Formula provided

$$E(r_i) = R_f + \beta(E(R_m) - R_f)$$

Where $E(r_i)$ = the expected (target) return on security by the investor

R_m = expected return in the market

β = the beta of the investment

R_f = the risk-free rate of interest

$R_m - R_f$ = market premium

Activity 2: Technique demonstration

Mantra Co has an equity beta of 1.5. Assume there is a market premium for risk of 4%, and the risk-free rate is 2%.

Required

Estimate Mantra Co's cost of equity.

Solution

Limitations of the CAPM	Discussion
Estimating market return	This is estimated by considering movements in the stock market as a whole over time. This will overstate the returns achieved because it **will not pick up the firms that have failed** and have dropped out of the stock market.
Estimating the beta factor	Beta values are **historical** and will not give an accurate measure of risk if the firm has recently changed its gearing or its strategy.

Limitations of the CAPM	Discussion
Other risk factors	It has been argued the CAPM ignores the impact of: • The size of the company (the extra risk of failure for small companies); and • The ratio of book value of equity to market value of equity (shares with book values that are close to their market values are more likely to fail).

Essential reading

See Chapter 2 Section 1 of the Essential reading for more on the cost of equity from your earlier studies.

The Essential reading is available as an Appendix of the digital edition of the Workbook.

1.2 Cost of debt

There are many sources of debt finance including:

Bank loans

The cost of a loan will be given because a company will obtain tax relief on interest paid, the cost will be **multiplied by (1 – t)** to get the post-tax cost of debt.

Kay Co

Kay Co has a $1 million loan on which it pays 5% interest.

If the rate of tax on corporate profits is 20% then the interest payment of $50,000 will reduce taxable profit and Kay Co's tax bill will therefore fall by $50,000 × 0.20 = $10,000. The net cost of the loan is therefore $50,000 – tax saving of $10,000 = $40,000 or 4% (on a loan of $1 million).

A quick way of calculating this is 5% × (1 – 0.2) = 4%.

Bond/debenture/loan note

• A tradeable IOU (ie acknowledgement of the debt) with a nominal value $100 or $1000, normally maturing in 7-30 years and paying fixed interest; protected by covenants (eg restrictions on dividend policy; covenants are covered in detail in Section 3 of Chapter 14)

Example of a loan note:

> IOU $100
>
> Pay interest of 4%
>
> Repay $100 in 10 years' time

• Slower and more expensive to organise than a loan and less flexible than a bank loan in the event of default (a bank generally is more flexible in renegotiating a loan if a firm is unable to meet its loan repayments because it will want to maintain an ongoing commercial relationship with that firm)
• Normally redeemable at its nominal value ($100)
• Often cheaper interest costs compared to a loan (because it is a liquid investment, ie can be sold by the investor, so investors are happy to accept a lower rate of return in exchange for this convenience)

The cost of a **bond** can be estimated by considering:

(a) The **risk free rate** derived from the **yield curve** for a bond of that specified duration
(b) The **credit risk premium** derived from the bond's credit rating

1.2.1 Yield curve

The yield curve shows how the yield on government bonds vary according to the term of the borrowing. The curve shows the yield expected by the investor assuming that the bond pays all of the return as a single payment on maturity. Normally it is upward sloping.

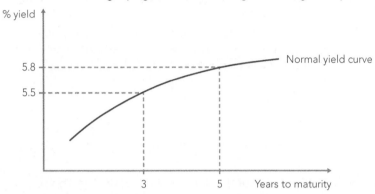

There are a number of factors influencing the yield curve, for example:

(a) **Expectations theory** – the curve reflects expectations that interest rates will rise in the future, so the government has to offer higher returns on long-term debt.

(b) **Liquidity preference theory** – the curve reflects the compensation that investors require higher annual returns for sacrificing liquidity on long-dated bonds.

1.2.2 Credit ratings

A bond's credit rating will also affect the return that is required by investors. An example of the ratings used by a major ratings agency are shown below:

Standard & Poor's	Definition
AAA, AA+, AAA–, AA, AA–, A+	Excellent quality, lowest default risk
A, A–, BBB+	Good quality, low default risk
BBB, BBB–, BB+	Medium rating
BB or below	Junk bonds (speculative, high default risk)

The extra return (or yield spread) required by investors on a bond will depend on its credit rating, and its maturity. This is often quoted as an adjustments to the risk free rate (as indicated by the yield curve) in basis points (1 point = 0.01%).

Maturity	3 years
Rating	
AAA	18
A	75

Activity 3: Technique demonstration

Mantra Co has issued AAA rate bonds with three years to maturity.

Tax is 30%.

Required

Complete the following table (using the yield curve in Section 1.2.1. and the yield spread in Section 1.2.2) to estimate Mantra's current cost of debt.

Solution

%

Credit spread on existing AAA rated bonds	[ ]
Yield curve benchmark	[ ]
Cost of debt (pre-tax)	[ ]
Cost of debt post-tax	[ ]

1.3 Weighted average cost of capital

To calculate a project NPV, or to assess a proposed financing plan, you may be required to calculate the weighted average cost of capital for the business (WACC). You will have covered this in your earlier studies of the Financial Management exam, and it is recapped here.

 Formula provided

$$WACC = \left(\frac{V_e}{V_e + V_d}\right)K_e + \left(\frac{V_d}{V_e + V_d}\right)K_d(1 - T)$$

V_e = total market value (ex-div) of issued shares

V_d = total market value (ex-interest) of debt

K_e = cost of equity in a geared company

K_d = cost of debt

The formula provided assumes that there are two sources of finance – debt and equity. You may have to adapt the formula if there are extra types of finance (for example, two different types of debt) by adding in additional terms for the cost and value of these extra types of finance.

1.3.1 Calculating market values of debt and equity

You may need to calculate these market values if they are not provided in a question.

Chapter 8 deals with the valuation of equity.

To value debt you need to calculate the present value of its future cash flows, discounted at the required return (pre-tax). This is illustrated below.

Activity 4: Technique demonstration

Mantra Co's bonds have a nominal value of £100 and a total nominal value of £0.49 billion. The bonds pay a coupon rate of 6.2% annually. Further information on credit spreads and yield curve spot rates are given below.

Maturity	1 year	2 years	3 years
AAA	8	12	18
Yield curve spot rate	4.5	5.0	5.5
Required return (pre-tax)	4.58%	5.12%	5.68%

Required

Complete the following calculations to estimate the total market value of Mantra Co's debt.

Solution

Time	1	2	3	Total
Per £100	6.2	6.2	106.2	
DF 4.58%	☐			
DF 5.12%		☐		
DF 5.68%			☐	
PV	☐	☐	☐	☐

1.3.2 Using the WACC formula

A brief reminder of how to use the basic WACC formula is provided in the next activity.

Activity 5: Calculating the WACC

Mantra has a total market value of £1 billion, split 50% debt and 50% equity.

Mantra has a cost of equity of 8% and a post-tax cost of debt of 3.98%. Tax is 30%.

Required

Calculate Mantra Co's WACC.

Solution

1.3.3 Assumptions made when using WACC for project evaluation

The WACC can only be used for project evaluation if:

(a) In the long term the company will maintain its existing capital structure (ie financial risk is unchanged)

(b) The project has the same risk as the company (ie business risk is unchanged)

If these factors are not in place (ie risk changes) then the company's existing cost of equity will change.

Where the risk of an extra project is different from normal, there is an argument for a cost of capital to be calculated for that particular project; this is a **project-specific cost of capital** and is covered in Chapter 7.

> **PER alert**
>
> One of the optional performance objectives in your PER is to advise on the appropriateness and cost of different sources of finance. Another is to identify and raise an appropriate source of finance for a specific business need. This chapter covers some of the common sources of finance and the linked area of dividend policy.

2 Assessing corporate performance

You may be expected to use **ratio analysis** to evaluate the success of a financial strategy.

Ratios are normally split into four categories: profitability, debt, liquidity, and shareholder investor ratios. In the context of assessing performance it is most likely that profitability and shareholder investor ratios will be most relevant. Debt and liquidity ratios are covered in later chapters.

You need to **learn these ratios**.

2.1 Key profitability ratios

Profitability ratios: ROCE, profit margin and asset turnover

> **Formula to learn**
>
> ROCE
> $$= \frac{\text{PBIT}}{\text{Capital employed}} = \frac{\text{PBIT}}{\text{Revenue}} \text{ (ie profit margin)} \times \frac{\text{Revenue}}{\text{Capital employed}} \text{ (ie asset turnover)}$$

ROCE should ideally be increasing. If it is static or reducing it is important to determine whether this is due to a reduced profit margin (which is likely to be bad news) or lower asset turnover (which may simply reflect the impact of a recent investment).

Capital employed = shareholders' funds + long-term debt finance

Alternatively, capital employed can be defined as total assets less current liabilities.

If ROCE is calculated **post tax** then it can be compared against the weighted average cost of capital (also post tax) to assess whether the return provided to investors is adequate.

2.2 Shareholder investor ratios

Total shareholder return (TSR) is often used to measure changes in shareholder wealth.

> **Formula to learn**
>
> $$TSR = \text{dividend yield\%} + \text{capital gain or loss\%}$$
>
> $$ie\ TSR = \frac{\text{dividend}}{\text{share price *}} + \frac{\text{capital gain or loss}}{\text{share price *}}$$
>
> *technically this should be the share price at start of year, although ACCA exam solutions often ignore this level of detail

Total shareholder return can be compared against the cost of equity (Ke) to assess whether the return being provided is adequate.

> **Formula to learn**
>
> $$\text{Return on equity} = \frac{\text{Earnings}}{\text{Shareholders' funds}}$$
>
> $$\text{Earnings per share} = \frac{\text{Profits distributable to ordinary shareholders}}{\text{Number of ordinary shares issued}}$$
>
> $$\text{Price - earnings ratio} = \frac{\text{Share price}}{\text{Earnings per share}}$$

Return on equity can also be compared against the cost of equity (K_e) to assess whether the return being provided is adequate.

The value of the P/E ratio reflects the market's appraisal of the share's future prospects – the more highly regarded a company, the higher its share price and its P/E ratio will be.

Activity 6: Ratio analysis

Splinter Co is considering selling its equity stake in Neptune Co.

Neptune Co. operates in a sector that is underperforming. Over the past two years, sales revenue has fallen by an average of 8% per year in the sector.

Given below are extracts from the recent financial statements and other financial information for Neptune Co and the sector.

Neptune Co year ending 31 May	20X6	20X7
	$m	$m
Equity		
Ordinary shares ($0.25)	150	150
Reserves	410	458
Total equity	560	608

Neptune Co year ending 31 May

	20X6 $m	20X7 $m
Non-current liabilities		
Bank loans	108	90
Bonds	210	200
Total non-current liabilities	318	290
Sales revenue	2,670	2,390
Profit for the year	288	144

Other financial information (based on annual figures to 31 May of each year)

	20X5	20X6	20X7
Neptune Co average share price ($)	5.00	4.80	4.00
Neptune Co dividend per share ($)	0.36	0.40	0.30
Sector average capital gain	+16.53%	−1.60%	+12.21%
Sector average P/E	12.29	13.54	13.57
Sector average dividend yield	+7.73%	+6.64%	+7.21%
Neptune Co's equity beta	1.4	1.5	1.6
Sector average equity beta	1.5	1.6	2.0

The risk-free rate and the market return are 4% and 10% respectively.

Required

1   Evaluate Neptune Co's total shareholder return.

2   Using your analysis from part (a), and other relevant ratios, analyse whether Splinter Co should dispose of its equity stake in Neptune Co.

Solution

Essential reading

See Chapter 2 Section 3 of the Essential reading for further discussion of basic ratio analysis.

The Essential reading is available as an Appendix of the digital edition of the Workbook.

3 Risk management

3.1 Different types of risk

3.1.1 Business risk

Business risk arises from the **type of business** an organisation is involved in and relates to uncertainty about the future and the organisation's **business prospects**.

- **Political risk** – the risk of government action which damages shareholder wealth (eg exchange control regulations could be applied that may affect the ability of the subsidiary to remit profits to the parent company).
- **Economic risk** – for example the risk of a downturn in the economy.
- **Fiscal risk** – including changes in tax policies which harm shareholder wealth.
- **Operational risk** – human error, breakdowns in internal procedures and systems.
- **Reputational risk** – damage to an organisation's reputation can result in lost revenues or significant reductions in shareholder value.

Business risk is **a mixture of systematic and unsystematic risk**. The systematic risk comes from such factors as revenue sensitivity to macro-economic factors and the mix of fixed and variable costs within the total cost structure. Unsystematic risk is determined by such company-specific factors as management mistakes, or labour relations issues, or production problems.

Activity 7: Business risk

DX Co is a retailer of sports equipment, with a reputation for selling low price reasonable quality products. The manufacture of its products is completely outsourced to companies operating in low-cost countries. Most of DX's staff are paid low wages and are on zero-hours contracts. Relations between staff and management are poor.

Required

Identify some examples of business risk for DX Co.

Solution

3.1.2 Non-business/financial risk

Non-business risk may arise from an adverse **event** (accident/natural disaster) or to risks arising from financial factors (**financial risk**).

KEY
TERM

> **Financial risk:** The volatility of earnings due to the financial policies of a business.

Long-term financial risks are mainly caused by the **structure of finance,** the **mix of equity and debt capital**, the risk of not being able to access funding, and whether the organisation has a sufficient long-term capital base for the amount of trading it is doing (overtrading).

Short-term financial risk also exists and needs to be managed.

Examples of short-term financial risk	Explanation
Exchange rate and interest rate risk	Risks arising from unpredictable cash flows due to interest rate or exchange rate movements (covered in later chapters)
Credit risk	Late or non-payment by a customer
Liquidity risk	Inability to obtain cash when needed

3.2 Relationship between business and financial risk

A business with high business risk may be **restricted in the amount of financial risk it can sustain** because, if financial risk is also high, this may push total risk above the level that is acceptable to shareholders.

It will be important for the **financial strategy** of an organisation facing **high business risk** to **minimise debt finance**, and to **hedge a greater proportion of its currency and interest rate exposure**, ie to **minimise financial risk**.

3.3 The rationale for risk management

3.3.1 Arguments against risk management

In order to generate returns for shareholders a company will need to accept a degree of risk. In addition, as we have seen, shareholders can diversify away some of the risk that they face themselves.

If risk management is unnecessary then the time and expense that it involves, it could be argued, reduces shareholder wealth.

3.3.2 Arguments in favour of risk management

The main arguments in favour of risk management (eg hedging) are based on the idea that in reality there is no guarantee that firms will be able to raise funds to finance attractive projects (ie capital markets are imperfect).

Hedging should reduce the volatility of a company's earnings, and this can have a number of beneficial effects:

(a) **Attracting investors**: because there is a **lower probability** of the firm encountering **financial distress**.

(b) **Encouraging managers to invest for the future**: especially for highly geared firms, there is often a **risk of underinvestment** because managers are concerned about the risk of not being able to meet interest payments. Risk management reduces the incentive to underinvest, since it reduces uncertainty and the risk of loss.

(c) **Attracting other stakeholders**: for example, suppliers and customers are more likely to look for long-term relationships with firms that have a **lower risk of financial distress**.

3.4 Common risk management techniques

KEY
TERM

Risk mitigation: The process of **transferring risks out of a business**. This can involve **hedging** (covered in Chapters 12–13) or insurance or even avoiding certain risks completely.

As already mentioned, a certain level of risk is inevitable and even desirable in business. The process of risk management needs to consider whether the company requires a risk mitigation strategy by considering the costs of such a strategy, the existing level of business and financial risk, and the risk preferences of the company.

KEY
TERM

Risk diversification: Reducing the impact of risk by investing in different business areas.

However, the benefits from diversification can normally be gained by shareholders building portfolios of different shares.

If this has already been done then diversification by a company may not benefit shareholders unless it involves moving into business areas that shareholders cannot access by themselves (eg new international markets where foreign share ownership is regulated), or if the diversification creates synergy with existing operations (synergy is discussed in Chapter 9).

Essential reading

See Chapter 2 Section 4 of the Essential reading for more detail about practical techniques for managing risk which you have seen in your earlier studies. It is **important to complete this reading (especially the section on risk mapping)** as this is an area of brought forward knowledge that you will be expected to be able to apply in your AFM exam.

The Essential reading is available as an Appendix of the digital edition of the Workbook.

4 Behavioural finance

Behavioural finance considers the impact of **psychological factors** on financial strategy. This challenges the idea that managers and investors behave in a rational manner based on sound economic criteria.

4.1 Management behaviour

Some of the main psychological factors affecting managerial decision-making are:

*   **Overconfidence** – tendency to overestimate their own abilities. This may help to explain why many acquisitions are overvalued (this aspect is covered further in Chapter 8). This could also help to explain why many boards believe that the stock market undervalues their shares.

    This can lead to managers taking actions that **may** not be in their shareholders' best interests, such as delisting from the stock market or defending against a takeover bid that they believe undervalues their company.

    Overconfidence can result from managers paying more attention to evidence confirming the logic of an investment than they will to evidence that questions this logic. This is **confirmation bias**.

*   **Entrapment** – managers are also reluctant to admit that they are wrong (they become trapped by their past decisions, sometimes referred to as cognitive dissonance). This helps to explain why managers persist with financial strategies that are unlikely to succeed.

    For example, in the face of economic logic managers will often delay decisions to terminate projects because the failure of the project will imply that they have failed as managers.

*   **Agency issues** – managers may follow their own self-interest, instead of focusing on shareholders.

Analysis of these types of behavioural factors can help to evaluate possible causes behind a failing financial strategy.

4.2 Investors

Some of the main behavioural factors are:

*   **Search for patterns** – investors look for **patterns** which can be used to justify investment decisions. This might involve analysing a company's past returns and using this to extrapolate future performance, or comparing peaks or troughs in the stock market to historical peaks and troughs. This can lead to **herding**. This is compounded by a reluctance of investors to admit that they are wrong (sometimes referred to as **cognitive dissonance**).

*   **Narrow framing** – many investors fail to see the bigger picture and focus too much on short-term fluctuations in share price movements; this can mean that if a single share in a large portfolio performs badly in a particular week then, according to theories such as CAPM, this

should not matter greatly to an investor who is investing in a large portfolio of shares over, say, a 20-year period. However, in reality, it does seem to matter – which indicates that investors show a greater aversion to risk than the CAPM suggests they should.

- **Availability bias** – people will often focus more on information that is **prominent (available)**. Prominent information is often the most **recent information**; this may help to explain why share prices move significantly shortly after financial results are published.
- **Conservatism** – investors may be resistant to changing their opinion so, for example, if a company's profits are better than expected the share price may not react significantly because investors underreact to this news.

If the stock markets are not behaving in a rational way, it may be difficult for managers to influence the share price of their company and the share price may not be a reliable estimate of the company's value.

Chapter summary

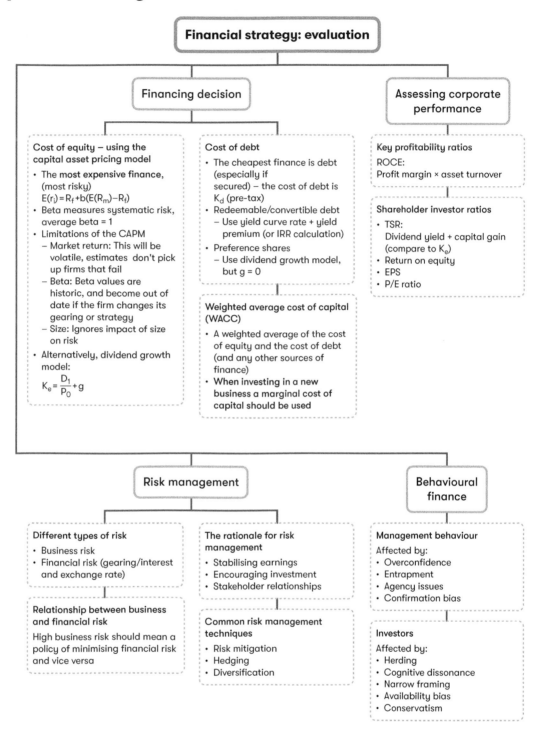

Financial strategy: evaluation

Financing decision

Cost of equity – using the capital asset pricing model
- The **most expensive finance,** (most risky)
  $E(r_i) = R_f + b(E(R_m) - R_f)$
- Beta measures systematic risk, average beta = 1
- Limitations of the CAPM
  - Market return: This will be volatile, estimates don't pick up firms that fail
  - Beta: Beta values are historic, and become out of date if the firm changes its gearing or strategy
  - Size: Ignores impact of size on risk
- Alternatively, dividend growth model:
  $K_e = \dfrac{D_1}{P_0} + g$

Cost of debt
- The cheapest finance is debt (especially if secured) – the cost of debt is K_d (pre-tax)
- Redeemable/convertible debt
  - Use yield curve rate + yield premium (or IRR calculation)
- Preference shares
  - Use dividend growth model, but g = 0

Weighted average cost of capital (WACC)
- A weighted average of the cost of equity and the cost of debt (and any other sources of finance)
- **When investing in a new business a marginal cost of capital should be used**

Assessing corporate performance

Key profitability ratios
ROCE:
Profit margin × asset turnover

Shareholder investor ratios
- TSR:
  Dividend yield + capital gain (compare to K_e)
- Return on equity
- EPS
- P/E ratio

Risk management

Different types of risk
- Business risk
- Financial risk (gearing/interest and exchange rate)

Relationship between business and financial risk
High business risk should mean a policy of minimising financial risk and vice versa

The rationale for risk management
- Stabilising earnings
- Encouraging investment
- Stakeholder relationships

Common risk management techniques
- Risk mitigation
- Hedging
- Diversification

Behavioural finance

Management behaviour
Affected by:
- Overconfidence
- Entrapment
- Agency issues
- Confirmation bias

Investors
Affected by:
- Herding
- Cognitive dissonance
- Narrow framing
- Availability bias
- Conservatism

Knowledge diagnostic

1. Unsystematic risk

This is the component of risk that is associated with investing in that particular company.

2. Systematic risk

The portion of risk that will still remain even if a diversified portfolio has been created, because it is determined by general market factors. Measured by a beta factor.

3. Credit risk premium

The expected return to bond holders can be calculated as the risk free rate (derived from the yield curve for a bond of that specified duration) + the credit risk premium (derived from the bond's credit rating).

4. Ratio analysis

This is an important mechanism for evaluating a financial strategy; make sure you learn the key ratios.

5. Risk management

Failure to manage risk can result in a business being unable to raise finance and having poor stakeholder relationships. Both business and financial risk should be considered in a financial strategy.

6. Behavioural finance

This gives insights into potential reasons for the failure of a financial strategy in terms of meeting shareholder expectations.

Further study guidance

Question practice

Now try the following from the Further question practice bank (available in the digital edition of the workbook):

Q3 *Airline Business*

Further reading

There is a Technical Article available on ACCA's website, called 'Patterns of behaviour'. This article examines behavioural finance and is written by a member of the AFM examining team.

Another useful Technical Article available on ACCA's website is called 'Risk Management'. This article examines the potential for risk management to 'add value' and is written by a member of the AFM examining team.

We recommend you read these articles as part of your preparation for the AFM exam.

Own research

Use an internet search engine to identify the beta factors for different companies. The Reuters website (reuters.com) is a good location from which to perform this search. Search for any company and you should find its beta factor in the section giving the key metrics of a company.

For example Ford's beta factor can be found here:

https://www.reuters.com/companies/F.N/key-metrics

There is no solution to this exercise.

Activity answers

Activity 1: Introductory activity

Each investment has an expected return of 10% but investing 100% in either company leaves risk, ie return might be as high as 25% or as low as −5%.

Investing in a 50:50 portfolio gives an expected return of 10% per year **under any scenario,** ie with no risk, and therefore the portfolio is preferable to only investing either in an airline company or an oil company.

Activity 2: Technique demonstration

Use the beta of the company: 1.5

$K_e = 2 + (4 × 1.5) = 8\%$

Activity 3: Technique demonstration

The cost of debt post-tax = 5.68 × (1 - 0.3) = 3.98

	%
Credit spread on existing AAA rated bonds	0.18%
Yield curve benchmark	5.50%
Cost of debt (pre-tax)	5.68%
Cost of debt post-tax	3.98%

Activity 4: Technique demonstration

Nominal value £0.49bn × 101.49/100 = market value £0.4973bn being approximately £0.50 billion.

Workings

1   DF 4.58% for 1 year = $(1 + 0.0458)^{-1}$
2   DF 5.12% for 2 years = $(1 + 0.0512)^{-2}$
3   DF 5.68% for 3 years = $(1 + 0.0568)^{-3}$

Time	1	2	3	Total
Per £100	6.2	6.2	106.2	
DF 4.58%	0.956			
DF 5.12%		0.905		
DF 5.68%			0.847	
PV	5.93	5.61	89.95	101.49

Activity 5: Calculating the WACC

After tax cost of debt is 3.98%

WACC = (8 × 50/100) + (3.98 × 50/100) = 5.99%

Activity 6: Ratio analysis

1   Both the company and the sector performed badly in 20X6. However, in 20X7, the sector appears to have recovered but Neptune Co's performance has worsened. Neptune Co's actual average returns are significantly below the required returns in both years.

Neptune Co

Return to shareholders (RTS)	20X6	20X7
Dividend yield*	8.0%	6.25
Share price gain	−4.0%	−16.67%
Total	4.0%	−10.42%
Required return (based on CAPM)	13.0%	13.60%

* Technically it is better to use the closing year share price from the previous year for this calculation (eg 0.4/5.0 = 8%) because this is the opening year share price and is consistent with the share price gain calculation but it is also acceptable to use the current year share price.

Sector (RTS)	20X5	20X6	20X7
Dividend yield	7.73%	6.64%	7.21%
Share price gain	16.53%	−1.60%	12.21%
Total	24.26%	5.04%	19.42%
Average: 16.2%			
Required return (based on CAPM)	13.0%*	13.6%	16.0%
Average: 14.2%			

*eg (4 + 1.5 × (10 − 4)) = 13.0%)

Note. The averages for Neptune Co and for the sector are the simple averages of the three years: 20X5 to 20X7.

2   **Ratio calculations**

Focus on investor and profitability ratios

Neptune Co	20X5	20X6	20X7
Profit margin (profit/sales)		10.8%	6.0%
Earnings per share	n/a	$0.48	$0.24
Price to earnings ratio	n/a	10.00	16.67
Gearing ratio (debt/(debt + equity))	n/a	36.2%	32.3%
Dividend yield	n/a	8.00%	6.25%
(Calculating on opening year share prices; alternatively closing year may be used)		(0.4/5.0)	(0.3/4.8)

Other calculations

Neptune Co, sales revenue annual growth rate average between 20X6 and 20X7 = (2,390/2,670) − 1 = −10.5%.

Discussion

In terms of Neptune Co's performance between 20X5 and 20X7, it is clear from the calculations above, that the company is experiencing considerable financial difficulties.

Sales have fallen more sharply than the sector average and profit margins have fallen (−44%) and so has the earnings per share (−50%).

The share price has decreased over this period as well and in the last year so has the dividend yield. This would indicate that the company is unable to maintain adequate returns for its investors (please also see below).

Although Neptune Co's price to earnings (P/E) ratio has increased significantly in 20X7, this is because of the large fall in the EPS, rather than an increase in the share price. However, this could be an indication that there is still confidence in the future prospects of Neptune Co.

Finally, whereas the sector's average share price seems to have recovered strongly in 20X7, following a small fall in 20X6, Neptune Co's share price has not followed suit. So, it would seem that Neptune Co is a poor performer within its sector.

This view is further strengthened by comparing the actual returns to the required returns based on the capital asset pricing model (CAPM). Taking the above into account, the initial recommendation is for Splinter Co to dispose of its investment in Neptune Co.

Activity 7: Business risk

Examples of **business risk here** could include:

- Threats of **technical change** leading to **product obsolescence**; although this would not appear to be high here as DX Co does not manufacture the products.

- **Social change** leading to a fall in the number of people participating in sports.

- **Operational risks**, including risks such as human error, breakdowns in internal procedures and systems or external events. Damage to an organisation's reputation (**reputational risk**) can arise from **operational failures**.

- Threats to the business or the industry from government action (change to laws regarding minimum wages, taxes or regulations for example surrounding working conditions), ie **political/fiscal/regulatory risk.**

3 Discounted cash flow techniques

Learning objectives

On completion of this chapter, you should be able to:

	Syllabus reference no.
Evaluate the potential value added to an organisation arising from a specified capital investment project or portfolio using the net present value model. Project modelling should include explicit treatment and discussion of: • Inflation and specific price variation • Taxation including tax allowable depreciation and tax exhaustion • Capital rationing. Multi-period capital rationing to be limited to discussion only • Probability analysis and sensitivity analysis when adjusting for risk and uncertainty in investment appraisal • Risk-adjusted discount rates (covered in Chapter 7) • Project duration as a measure of risk	B1 (a)
Outline the application of Monte Carlo simulation to investment appraisal. Candidates will not be expected to undertake simulations in an examination context but will be expected to demonstrate understanding of: • The significance of the simulation output and the assessment of the likelihood of project success • The measurement and interpretation of project value at risk	B1 (b)
Establish the potential economic return (using internal rate of return [IRR] and modified internal rate of return) and advise on a project's return margin. Discuss the relative merits of NPV and IRR.	B1 (c)

Exam context

This chapter moves into **Section B** of the syllabus, **'advanced investment appraisal',** which is covered in **Chapters 3–7.**

Every exam (from September 2018) **will have questions that have a focus on syllabus Sections B and E** (treasury and advanced risk management techniques).

This chapter briefly recaps on some of the **key fundamentals of investment appraisal,** which you should be familiar with from the Financial Management (FM) exam. **However, you will also be introduced to new techniques such as project duration, value at risk and modified IRR) and these will need to be studied carefully.**

Chapter overview

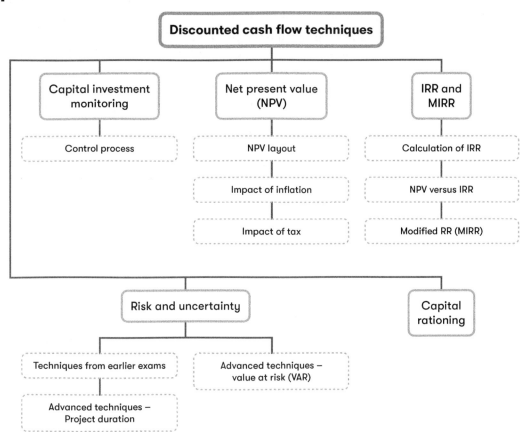

1 Capital investment monitoring

Capital investment projects are an important mechanism for creating wealth for shareholders, but they also expose a company to significant risk.

An important aspect of **risk management** (see Chapter 2) is the management of **project risk**; this will involve a set of capital investment controls to reduce the probability of a risk occurring, and is an example of **risk mitigation**.

Financial analysis is an important control, and the **analysis of risk and return** is covered in detail in **this chapter**, but this is only **one part of a broader capital investment monitoring process.**

1.1 Control process

> **1. Creating an environment encouraging innovation**
> This may involve using suggestion schemes, creating innovation targets, benchmarking.

↓

> **2. Preliminary screening**
> **– to remove ideas that do not fit with the company's strategy and resources**
> This may involve SWOT analysis and an approximate assessment of cash required and payback.

↓

> **3. Financial analysis**
> **– detailed investigation of risk and return**
> Involving the techniques covered later in this chapter (and the following two chapters).

↓

> **4. Authorisation**
> At central or divisional level, depending on the size of the project.

↓

> **5. Monitoring and review**
> This will cover both financial and risk factors. A post-audit is useful to learn from any mistakes.

Essential reading

See Chapter 3 Section 1 of the Essential reading for more background information on the role of post auditing; this should be familiar from your earlier studies.

The Essential reading is available as an Appendix of the digital edition of the Workbook.

2 Net present value (NPV)

Net present value should be familiar to you from previous studies:

> **Net present value (NPV) of a project:** The sum of the discounted cash flows less the initial investment.

Illustration 1: NPV

Project X requires an immediate investment of $150,000 and will generate net cash inflows of $60,000 for the next three years. The project's discount rate is 7%.

Required

If NPV is used to appraise the project, should Project X be undertaken?

Solution

Time	0	1	2	3
Cash flow $'000	(150)	60	60	60
Df 7%	1.000	0.935	0.873	0.816
Present value	**(150)**	**56.1**	**52.4**	**49.0**

Overall NPV ($'000s) = **+7.5**

As the NPV is positive, Project X should be undertaken, as it gives a return of above the cost of capital of 7% and will therefore increase shareholders' wealth.

Generally, only those projects with a **positive** NPV should be accepted, meaning that only those projects that will **increase** shareholders' wealth will be undertaken.

Alternatively, as AFM is **a computer-based exam**, it will be quicker to use the **=NPV spreadsheet function**. Here is an illustration using a spreadsheet extract:

	A	B	C	D
1	Time	1	2	3
2	Cash flow ($'000)	60	60	60
3	Present value of cash inflows from Time 1-3	157.5	Calculated using this formula: **=NPV(0.07,B2:D2)**	
4	Less outlay	(150)		
5	**Net present value**	**+7.5**		

Exam focus point

In a computer-based exam the =NPV function will allow you to complete your numerical analysis more quickly and accurately.

However, when using the =NPV function remember:

(a) To insert the cost of capital into the formula first [eg =NPV(**0.07**,B2:D2) in the previous illustration where the 0.07 is the 7% cost of capital]

(b) To only evaluate cash flows **after time 0** (the NPV formula assumes the first cash flow arises at time 1)

(c) Subtract the time 0 outlay to obtain the net present value

(d) Not to use annuities (there needs to be a separate column for time period if using the =NPV formula).

2.1 NPV layout

A neat layout will gain credibility in the exam and will help you make sense of the many different cash flows that you will have to deal with. It makes sense to start with the items that affect taxable profit and then to deal with capital items.

	A	B	C	D	E	F
1	*Time*	*0*	*1*	*2*	*3*	*4*
2	Sales receipts		X	X	X	X
3	Material cost		(X)	(X)	(X)	(X)
4	Labour cost		(X)	(X)	(X)	(X)
5	**Tax allowable depreciation**		(X)	(X)	(X)	(X)
6	Sales less costs		X	X	X	X
7	Taxation		(X)	(X)	(X)	(X)
8	Capital expenditure	(X)				
9	Scrap value					X
10	**Add back tax allowable depreciation**		X	X	X	X
11	Working capital impact	(X)	(X)	(X)	X	X
12	Net cash flows	(X)	X	X	X	X
13	Present value of cash flows from time 1 onwards	X				
14	Less time 0 outlay	(X)				
15	Project NPV	X				

The =NPV function for the net nominal cash flows would be used in cell B13 to calculate the present value of the cash flows from time 1 onwards. If the cost of capital was 7% for example, the formula in this cell would be **=NPV(0.07,C12:F12).** Then subtract the time 0 outlay to obtain the project NPV.

Calculation of the cost of capital is covered in Chapter 2 and 6.

Essential reading

See Chapter 3 Section 2 of the Essential reading for more background information on the basics of DCF; this should be familiar from your earlier studies.

The Essential reading is available as an Appendix of the digital edition of the Workbook.

2.2 Impact of inflation

In exam questions, it will normally be the case that cash flows are forecast to inflate at a variety of different rates. If so, inflation will have an impact on profit margins and therefore **inflation must be included in the cash flows.**

Investors will anticipate inflation, so the **cost of capital** will **normally include inflation**. So, there will be no need to adjust the cost of capital for inflation **unless** it is stated to be 'in real terms'. If this happens, which is rare in the AFM exam, the following formula (known as the Fisher formula) is provided and can be used to adjust a cost of capital for inflation.

Formula provided

[1 + real cost of capital] × [1 + general inflation rate] = [1 + inflated cost of capital]

or (1 + r) (1 + h) = (1 + i)

2.3 Impact of tax

Corporation tax can have **two impacts** on NPV calculations in the exam:

(a) **Tax will need to be paid on the cash profits from the project**

(b) **Tax will be saved if tax allowable depreciation can be claimed**

These impacts can be built into project appraisal as a **single cash flow** showing the tax paid **after tax allowable depreciation (TAD)** is taken into account as illustrated in Section 2.1. However, care must be taken to **add back TAD** because it is not in itself a cash flow.

In the final year a **balancing allowance or charge** will be claimed to reduce the written down value of asset to zero (after accounting for any scrap value).

The timing and rates of tax, and of tax allowable depreciation will be **given** in an exam question.

2.3.1 Tax exhaustion

There will be circumstances when TAD in a particular year will equal or exceed before-tax profits.

In most tax systems, **unused TAD can be carried forward** so that it is set off against the tax liability in any one year includes not only TAD for that year but also **any unused TAD from previous years**.

Activity 1: Avanti

Avanti Co is considering a major investment programme which will involve the creation of a chain of retail outlets. The following cash flows are expected.

Time	0	1	2	3	4
	$'000	$'000	$'000	$'000	$'000
Land and buildings	2,785				
Fittings and equipment	700				
Gross revenue		1,100	2,500	2,800	3,000
Direct costs		750	1,100	1,500	1,600
Marketing		170	250	200	200
Office overheads		125	125	125	125

- 60% of office overhead is an allocation of head office operating costs.
- The cost of land and buildings includes $80,000 which has been spent on surveyors' fees.
- Avanti Co expects to be able to sell the chain at the end of Year 4 for $4,000,000.

Avanti Co is paying corporate tax at 30% and is expected to do so for the foreseeable future. Tax is paid one year in arrears. Tax allowable depreciation is available on fittings and equipment at 25% on a reducing balance basis, any unused tax allowable depreciation can be carried forward. Estimated resale proceeds of $100,000 for the fittings and equipment have been included in the total figure of $4,000,000 given above.

Avanti Co expects the working capital requirements to be 14.42% of revenue during each of the four years of the investment programme.

Avanti's **real** cost of capital is 7.7% p.a.

Inflation at 4% p.a. has been **ignored** in the above information. This inflation will not apply to the resale value of the business which is given in **nominal** terms.

Required

Complete the solution to calculate the NPV for Avanti's proposed investment.

Solution

Time	0	1	2	3	4	5
Sales		1,100	2,500	2,800	3,000	
Direct costs		(750)	(1,100)	(1,500)	(1,600)	
Marketing		(170)	(250)	(200)	(200)	
Office overheads (40%)		(50)	(50)	(50)	(50)	
Net real operating flows		130 ×1.04	1,100 × 1.04²	1,050 × 1.04³	1,150 × 1.04⁴	
Inflated at 4% (rounded)		135	1,190	1,181	1,345	
Tax allowable depn (TAD) (W1)		☐	☐	☐		
Unused TAD from time 1			☐			
Taxable profit		0	1,019	1,082	1,150	
Taxation at 30% in arrears			☐	☐	☐	☐
Land/buildings (−80k sunk cost)	(2,705)					
Fixture and fittings	(700)					
Resale value					4,000	
Add back TAD (used)		☐	☐	☐	☐	
		☐	☐			
Working capital cash flows (W2)	☐	☐	☐	☐	☐	—
Net nominal cash flows	(3,570)	(90)	1,126	823	5,526	(345)
Discount rate (W3)	1.0	0.893	0.797	0.712	0.636	0.567
Present values	(3,570)	(80)	897	586	3,515	(196)
NPV						1,152

Alternatively use the =NPV function for the net nominal cash flows in time periods 1–5 and then subtract the time 0 outlay to obtain the project NPV.

Workings

1 **Tax allowable depreciation (TAD)**

Time	0	1	2	3	4	5
Written down value: start of year						
Scrap value						
TAD (25% reducing balance)						

2 **Working capital**

Time	0	1	2	3	4
Nominal sales					
Working capital					
Cash flow					

3 **Nominal discount rate**

Nominal discount rate [   ] × [   ] = [   ]

---

3 IRR and MIRR

Internal rate of return (IRR) should be familiar to you from previous studies.

> **Internal rate of return (IRR):** The discount rate at which the NPV is equal to zero. Alternatively, the IRR can be thought of as the return that is delivered by a project.

A project will be accepted if its IRR is higher than the required return as shown by the cost of capital.

3.1 Calculation of IRR

If calculating IRR manually, it can be estimated as follows:

Step 1 Calculate the NPV of the project at any (reasonable) rate (eg the cost of capital)

Step 2 Calculate the project NPV at any other (reasonable) rate.

Step 3 Calculate the internal rate of return using the formula.

> ### Formula to learn
>
> $$IRR = a + \frac{NPV_a}{NPV_a - NPV_b}(b - a)$$
>
> a = the lower of the two rates of return used
>
> b = the higher of the two rates used

If calculating IRR in a **computer-based exam** the =IRR function will allow you to complete your numerical analysis more quickly and accurately.

When using the =IRR function remember:

(a) To evaluate all (undiscounted) project cash flows **including time 0** (unlike =NPV which ignores the time 0 cash flow)

(b) Not to use annuities (there needs **to be a separate column for each time** period if using the =IRR formula).

Activity 2: IRR

Net present value working at 12% = +1,152

This analysis has been re-performed using a 20% required return as shown below:

Time	0	1	2	3	4	5
$'000	(3,570)	(90)	1,126	823	5,527	(345)
DF @20%	1.000	0.833	0.694	0.579	0.482	0.402
PV	(3,570)	(75)	781	477	2,664	(139)
NPV	+138					

Required

Using the above information, calculate the IRR of Avanti's proposed investment, either using the IRR formula or the =IRR spreadsheet function.

3.2 NPV versus IRR

IRR, as a percentage, is potentially an easier concept to explain to management.

However, **NPV is theoretically superior** because IRR it has a number of drawbacks when used to make decisions between competing projects (mutually exclusive projects).

- IRR ignores the size of a project, and may result in a small project with a better IRR being chosen over a bigger project even though the larger project is estimated to generate more wealth for shareholders (as measured by NPV).
- For projects with **non-normal cash flows**, eg flows where the present value each year changes from positive to negative or negative to positive more than once, **there may be more than one IRR.**
- IRR assumes **that the cash flows after the investment phase (here Time 0) are reinvested at the project's IRR; this may not be realistic.**

3.3 Modified IRR (MIRR)

IRR **assumes that the cash flows after the investment phase (here Time 0) are reinvested at the project's IRR.** A better assumption is that the funds **are reinvested at the investors' minimum required return (WACC),** here 12%. If we use this re-investment assumption we can calculate an alternative, modified version of IRR.

 Formula provided

$$\left(\frac{\text{PV return phase}}{\text{PV investment phase}}\right)^{1/n} \times (1 + r_e) - 1$$

r_e = cost of capital

n = number of time periods

In the formula, the return phase is the phase during which the project is generating positive cash flows, and the investment phase covers the time periods that are generating negative cash flows.

The extent to which the MIRR exceeds the cost of capital is called the **return margin** and indicates the extent to which a new project is generating value.

In a **computer-based exam**, modified internal rate of return can be calculated using a spreadsheet formula. Like the formula for IRR, this should highlight the undiscounted cash flows for all years of the project including time 0. The formula is =MIRR (values, finance rate, reinvestment rate).

The finance rate is the cost of raising finance for a company and the reinvestment rate is the rate of return a company can obtain when reinvesting project inflows; the two rates will normally be the same (this has been the case in exam questions on this area).

For example, to identify the MIRR of the future cash flows from a project arising over five years (involving time periods 0-5) where the cost of capital to be applied to cash outflows (the finance rate) and cash inflows (reinvestment rate) is 10%, then the formula could be as follows:

=MIRR(A10:F10, 0.1, 0.1)

Exam focus point

When using the =MIRR function remember:

(a) To evaluate all **undiscounted** project cash flows **including cash flows at time 0**

(b) Not to use annuities (there **needs to be a separate** column for each time period if using the =MIRR formula).

(c) You will **need to insert the cost of capital** twice

Activity 3: MIRR

Using the MIRR formula or the spreadsheet formula =MIRR, calculate the modified IRR of Avanti's proposed investment.

Solution

Essential reading

See Chapter 3 Section 3 of the Essential reading for more on the logic of the MIRR approach; this is for your interest only.

The Essential reading is available as an Appendix of the digital edition of the Workbook.

3.3.1 Advantages of MIRR

MIRR makes a **more realistic assumption about the reinvestment rate**, and **does not give the multiple answers** that can sometimes arise with the conventional IRR.

> **PER alert**
>
> One of the optional performance objectives in your PER is the evaluation of the financial viability of a potential investment. This chapter covers some of the most popular methods of investment appraisal – NPV, IRR and MIRR – which you can regularly put into practice in the real world.

4 Risk and uncertainty

Before deciding to spend money on a project, managers will want to be able to make a judgement on the **possibility of receiving a return below the projected NPV**, ie the risk or uncertainty of the project.

Technically there is a difference between risk and uncertainty; **risk means that specific probabilities can be assigned** to a set of possible outcomes, while uncertainty applies when it is either not possible to identify all the possible outcomes or assign probabilities to them. In reality the two terms are often used **interchangeably**.

An analysis of risk or uncertainty may involve the use of a number of the following techniques.

4.1 Techniques from earlier exams

The techniques briefly described here should be familiar from your earlier exams.

Techniques	Description
Risk adjusted discount factor	Using a higher cost of capital if the project is high risk; this idea is revisited in **Chapter 7**.
Expected values	Using probabilities to calculate average expected NPV. Probabilities may be highly subjective.
Payback period	The period of time taken before the initial outlay is repaid. The quicker the payback, the less reliant a project is on the later, more uncertain, cash flows. Ignores timing of cash flows within the payback period and also the cash flows that arise after the payback period.
Discounted payback period	As above but uses the discounted cash flows and is a better method since it adjusts for time value.
Sensitivity analysis	An analysis of the percentage change in **one variable** (eg sales) that would be needed for the NPV of a project to fall to zero. Normally calculated as the NPV of the project divided by the NPV of the cash flows relating to the risky variable (eg sales).
Simulation	An analysis of how changes in **more than one variable** may affect the NPV of a project. The risk of a project can be measured by simulating the possible NPVs and weighting the outcomes by probabilities determined by management. This could be used to assess the probability, for example, of a project's NPV exceeding zero.

Essential reading

See Chapter 3 Section 4 of the Essential reading for a reminder on the basics of managing risk and uncertainty, if required.

The Essential reading is available as an appendix of the digital edition of the Workbook.

4.2 Advanced techniques (1) - project duration

KEY TERM

> **Project duration:** A measure of the average time over which a project delivers its value.

Project duration shows the reliance of a project on its later cash flows, which are less certain than earlier cash flows; it does this by weighting each year of the project by the % **of the present value of the cash inflows** received in that year.

Unlike payback (or discounted payback), this measure of uncertainty looks at **all of a project's life**.

Project duration (1)

A project with a three-year life, with all of the inflows being generated in the third year would have a three-year duration as follows:

Time	1	2	3
Present value of cash inflows ($'000)	0	0	2,400
% cash inflows received in each year	0	0	100%
Time period × % cash inflows	1 × 0	2 × 0	3 × 1

Project duration = 0 +0 + 3 = 3 years

4.2.1 Duration and project life

Although duration can (rarely) be the same as the project life (as in the above example), it will normally be different.

Project duration (2)

For example, if the above three-year project had an even spread of present value of cash inflows across the three years then duration would be:

Time	1	2	3
Present value of cash inflows ($'000)	800	800	800
% cash inflows received in each year	33.3%	33.3%	33.3%
Time period × % cash inflows	1 × 0.333	2 × 0.333	3 × 0.333

Project duration = 0.333 + 0.666 + 0.999 = approx **2 years**

4.2.2 Analysis of duration

Comparing the two examples above, the **second scenario** (duration two years) is preferable because there is less uncertainty attached to cash that is received sooner than there is to cash flows that are received later.

The **project duration** of the second scenario of two years is a measure of the **average time over which this project delivers its value,** ie it has the same duration as a project that delivers 100% of its (present value) cash inflows in two years' time.

The lower the project duration the lower the risk/uncertainty of the project.

4.2.3 Quick approach to calculating duration

A quicker approach to calculating duration is shown below, this avoids the need to work out the percentage **cash inflows** received each year:

Time	1	2	3	Total
Present value of cash inflows ($'000)	800	800	800	2,400
Time period x PV	1 × 800	2 × 800	3 × 800	

Project duration = (800 + 1,600 + 2,400)/PV of inflows of 2,400 = 2 years

Activity 4: Project duration

Calculate the project duration for Avanti, basing your calculations on the operational phase of the project (ie Time 1 onwards).

Project duration

Time	1	2	3	4	5	Total PV of inflows
PV ($'000)	(80)	897	586	3515	(196)	4,722

Solution

4.3 Advanced techniques (2) – value at risk (VaR)

A modern approach to quantifying risk involves estimating the likely change in the value of an investment by using the concept of a normal distribution. Some of the properties of a normal distribution are shown below (σ = standard deviation):

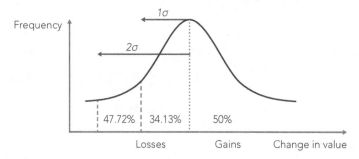

4.3.1 Value at risk

> **Value at risk (VaR):** The **maximum likely loss over a set period** (with only an x% chance of being exceeded).

Example

5% value at risk can be illustrated as follows:

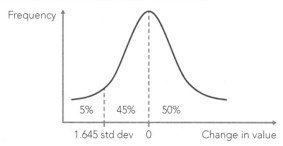

Using the extract from the normal distribution table shown (the full table is given in the exam and is available at the back of the Workbook), the number of standard deviations associated with 5% value at risk can be calculated by looking for the figure 0.45 (representing the 45% area in the diagram above).

Standard normal distribution table

$Z=\frac{(x-\mu)}{\sigma}$	0.00	0.01	0.02	0.03	0.04	0.05	0.06	0.07	0.08	0.09
0.0	.0000	.0040	.0080	.0120	.0160	.0199	.0239	.0279	.0319	.0359
0.1	.0398	.0438	.0478	.0517	.0557	.0596	.0636	.0675	.0714	.0753
0.2	.0793	.0832	.0871	.0910	.0948	.0987	.1026	.1064	.1103	.1141
0.3	.1179	.1217	.1255	.1293	.1331	.1368	.1406	.1443	.1480	.1517
0.4	.1554	.1591	.1628	.1664	.1700	.1736	.1772	.1808	.1844	.1879
0.5	.1915	.1950	.1985	.2019	.2054	.2088	.2123	.2157	.2190	.2224
0.6	.2257	.2291	.2324	.2357	.2389	.2422	.2454	.2486	.2517	.2549
0.7	.2580	.2611	.2642	.2673	.2704	.2734	.2764	.2794	.2823	.2852
0.8	.2881	.2910	.2939	.2967	.2995	.3023	.3051	.3078	.3106	.3133
0.9	.3159	.3186	.3212	.3238	.3264	.3289	.3315	.3340	.3365	.3389
1.0	.3413	.3438	.3461	.3485	.3508	.3531	.3554	.3577	.3599	.3621
1.1	.3643	.3665	.3686	.3708	.3729	.3749	.3770	.3790	.3810	.3830
1.2	.3849	.3869	.3888	.3907	.3925	.3944	.3962	.3980	.3997	.4015
1.3	.4032	.4049	.4066	.4082	.4099	.4115	.4131	.4147	.4162	.4177
1.4	.4192	.4207	.4222	.4236	.4251	.4265	.4279	.4292	.4306	.4319
1.5	.4332	.4345	.4357	.4370	.4382	.4394	.4406	.4418	.4429	.4441
1.6	.4452	.4463	.4474	.4484	.4495	.4505	.4515	.4525	.4535	.4545

The figures 0.4495 and 0.4505 are the closest we have to this and they represent 1.64 and 1.65 standard deviations respectively. So, for a figure of 0.45 we can say that halfway between 1.64 and 1.65, ie 1.645 standard deviations, is the correct answer.

So, the maximum reduction in value – which would only be exceeded 5% of the time – is 1.645 standard deviations.

4.3.2 Value at risk and time

Value at risk can be quantified for a project using a project's standard deviation.

Standard deviation relates to a period of time (eg a year), but the value at risk may be over a different time period (eg the life of a project).

In this context, the standard deviation may need to **be adjusted by multiplying by the square root of the time period.**

Formula to learn

95% value at risk = 1.645 × standard deviation of the project × $\sqrt{\text{time period of project}}$

For a five year project 5% value at risk is calculated as:

$$1.645 \times \text{project standard deviation} \times \sqrt{5}$$

Activity 5: Value at risk

A four year project has an NPV of $2 million and a standard deviation of $1 million per year.

Required

1   Analyse the project's value at risk at a 95% confidence level.

2   Analyse the project's value at risk at a 99% confidence level.

Solution

4.3.3 Drawbacks of value at risk

Value at risk is based on a normal distribution, which assumes that virtually all possible outcomes will be within three standard deviations of the mean and that success and failure are equally likely.

Neither is likely to be true for a one-off project.

Value at risk is also based around the calculation of a standard deviation and again this is hard to estimate in reality since it is based on forecasting the possible spread of the results of a project around an average.

5 Capital rationing (brought forward knowledge from Financial Management)

An assumption made in traditional investment appraisal is that capital will be available to finance any project that is wealth-creating ie generates a positive NPV. In reality, this may not be the case and only a limited amount of capital may be available. This is the issue of capital rationing.

5.1 Soft and hard capital rationing

If an organisation is in a capital rationing situation it will not be able to invest in all available projects (whether involving organic growth or acquisition) because there is not enough capital for all of the investments. Capital is **a limiting factor**.

Capital rationing may be necessary in a business due to **internal factors** (soft capital rationing) or **external factors** (hard capital rationing).

5.1.1 Soft capital rationing

Soft capital rationing may arise for one of the following reasons:

(a) Management may be **reluctant to issue additional share capital** because of concern that this may lead to outsiders gaining control of the business.

(b) Management may be **unwilling to issue additional share capital** if it will lead to a dilution of earnings per share.

(c) Management may **not want to raise additional debt capital** because they do not wish to be committed to large fixed interest payments.

(d) **Capital expenditure budgets** may restrict spending.

Note that whenever an organisation adopts a policy that restricts funds available for investment, such a policy may be less than optimal, as the organisation may reject projects with a positive NPV and forgo opportunities that would have enhanced the market value of the organisation.

5.1.2 Hard capital rationing

Hard capital rationing may arise for one of the following reasons:

(a) Raising money through the stock market may not be possible if **share prices are depressed**.

(b) There may be **restrictions on bank lending** due to loan covenants.

(c) Lending institutions may consider an organisation to be too **risky** to be granted further loan facilities.

(d) The **costs** associated with making small issues of capital may be too great.

5.2 Divisible and indivisible projects

(a) **Divisible projects** are those which can be undertaken completely or in fractions. Suppose that Project A is divisible and requires the investment of $15,000 to achieve an NPV of $4,000. $7,500 invested in Project A will earn an NPV of ½ × $4,000 = $2,000.

(b) **Indivisible projects** are those which must be undertaken completely or not at all. It is not possible to invest in a fraction of the project.

You may also encounter **mutually exclusive** projects when one, and only one, of two or more choices of project can be undertaken.

5.2.1 Single-period capital rationing with divisible projects

With single-period capital rationing, investment funds are a limiting factor in the current period. The total return will be maximised if management follows the decision rule of maximising the return per unit of the limiting factor. They should therefore select those projects whose cash **inflows have the highest present value per $1 of capital invested**. In other words, rank the projects according to their **profitability index**.

> ### Formula to learn
>
> The profitability index = Present value of cash inflows/Initial cash outflow.
>
> **The critical value of the PI is 1**. Any value above this indicates that the project has a positive net present value (ie the present value of the cash inflows is greater than the cash outflows); the higher the PI the higher the return delivered by a project per $1 invested.

5.2.2 Single-period capital rationing with non-divisible projects

The main problem if projects are non-divisible is that there is likely to be small amounts of unused capital with each combination of projects. The best way to deal with this situation is to use trial and error and test the NPV available for different combinations of projects. This can be a laborious process if there are a large number of projects available.

5.3 Multi-period capital rationing

Where capital rationing exists over a number of years, this is a signal that the company needs to broaden its capital base (if possible). If this is not possible, mathematical models can be used to find the optimal combination of projects to invest in. These will consider the timings of cash inflows and outflows, in the periods where a company faces capital rationing, from all possible project combinations and select the combination of projects that maximises NPV.

> ### Exam focus point
>
> Candidates only need to be aware of multi-period capital rationing, and will not have to apply models in the exam.

5.4 Practical methods of dealing with capital rationing

A company may be able to limit the effects of capital rationing and exploit new opportunities.

(a) It might **seek joint venture partners** with which to share projects.

(b) As an alternative to direct investment in a project, the company may be able to consider a **licensing** or **franchising agreement** with another enterprise, under which the licensor/franchisor company would receive royalties.

(c) It may be possible to **contract** out parts of a project to reduce the initial capital outlay required.

(d) The company may seek to **delay** one or more of the projects.

Chapter summary

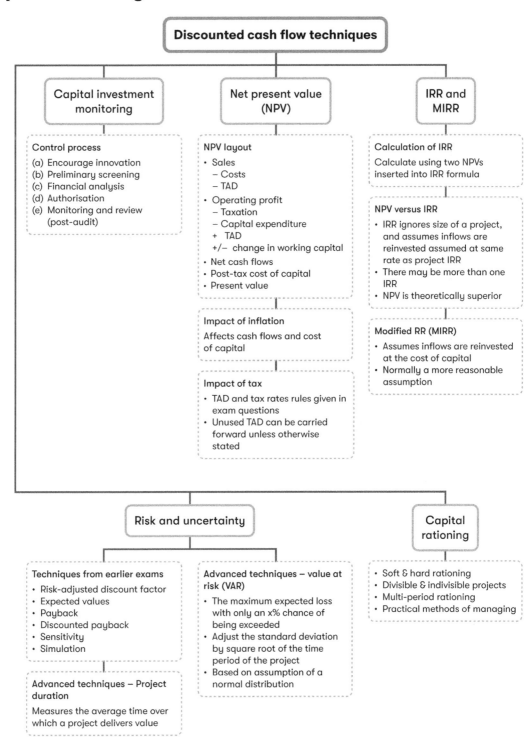

Discounted cash flow techniques

Capital investment monitoring

Control process
(a) Encourage innovation
(b) Preliminary screening
(c) Financial analysis
(d) Authorisation
(e) Monitoring and review (post-audit)

Net present value (NPV)

NPV layout
- Sales
  - Costs
  - TAD
- Operating profit
  - Taxation
  - Capital expenditure
  + TAD
  +/- change in working capital
- Net cash flows
- Post-tax cost of capital
- Present value

Impact of inflation
Affects cash flows and cost of capital

Impact of tax
- TAD and tax rates rules given in exam questions
- Unused TAD can be carried forward unless otherwise stated

IRR and MIRR

Calculation of IRR
Calculate using two NPVs inserted into IRR formula

NPV versus IRR
- IRR ignores size of a project, and assumes inflows are reinvested assumed at same rate as project IRR
- There may be more than one IRR
- NPV is theoretically superior

Modified RR (MIRR)
- Assumes inflows are reinvested at the cost of capital
- Normally a more reasonable assumption

Risk and uncertainty

Techniques from earlier exams
- Risk-adjusted discount factor
- Expected values
- Payback
- Discounted payback
- Sensitivity
- Simulation

Advanced techniques – Project duration
Measures the average time over which a project delivers value

Advanced techniques – value at risk (VAR)
- The maximum expected loss with only an x% chance of being exceeded
- Adjust the standard deviation by square root of the time period of the project
- Based on assumption of a normal distribution

Capital rationing

- Soft & hard rationing
- Divisible & indivisible projects
- Multi-period rationing
- Practical methods of managing

BPP
LEARNING
MEDIA

Knowledge diagnostic

1. Inflation

The formula for inflating the cost of capital only needs to be used if the cost of capital is given in 'real' terms; otherwise inflation can be assumed to be included in the cost of capital automatically.

2. Tax

Tax allowable depreciation should be included as a cost for the purposes of calculating the tax due; then it should be added back to the cash flows because it is not in itself a cash flow cost.

3. MIRR

Differs from IRR because of the assumption that cash inflows are reinvest at the cost of capital.

4. Project duration

A way of looking at the reliance of a project on later cash flows, unlike payback it looks at all years of a project.

5. Value at risk

A statistically complex technique that makes a crucial assumption that the normal distribution is valid to use; this may not be true.

6. Profitability index

Only valid for single-period capital rationing where projects are divisible.

Further study guidance

Question practice

Now try the following from the Further question practice bank (available in the digital edition of the workbook):

Q4 *CD*

Q5 *Bournelorth*

Further reading

There is a Technical Article available on ACCA's website, called 'Conditional Probability'.

We recommend you read this article as part of your preparation for the AFM exam.

Activity answers

Activity 1: Avanti

Time	0	1	2	3	4	5
Sales		1,100	2,500	2,800	3,000	
Direct costs		(750)	(1,100)	(1,500)	(1,600)	
Marketing		(170)	(250)	(200)	(200)	
Office overheads (40%)		(50)	(50)	(50)	(50)	
Net real operating flows		130 $\times 1.04$	1,100 $\times 1.04^2$	1,050 $\times 1.04^3$	1,150 $\times 1.04^4$	
Inflated at 4% (rounded)		**135**	**1,190**	**1,181**	**1,345**	
Tax allowable depn (TAD) (W1)		(135)	(131)	(99)	(195)	
Unused TAD from time 1			(40)			
Taxable profit		**0**	**1,019**	**1,082**	**1,150**	
Taxation at 30% in arrears			0	(306)	(325)	(345)
Land/buildings (–80k sunk cost)	(2,705)					
Fixture and fittings	(700)					
Resale value					4,000	
Add back TAD (used)		135	171	99	195	
		(175 – 40)	(131 + 40)			
Working capital cash flows (W2)	(165)	(225)	(64)	(52)	506	
Net nominal cash flows	**(3,570)**	**(90)**	**1,126**	**823**	**5,526**	**(345)**
Discount rate (W3)	1.0	0.893	0.797	0.712	0.636	0.567
Present values	(3,570)	(80)	897	586	3,515	(196)
NPV						**1,152**

Alternatively use the =NPV function for the net nominal cash flows in time periods 1-5 and then subtract the time 0 outlay to obtain the project NPV.

Workings

1   *Tax allowable depreciation (TAD)*

Time	0	1	2	3	4	5
Written down value: start of year		700	525	394	295	

Scrap value					(100)
					195
TAD (25% reducing balance)		175	131	99	195
					(balance)

2 **Working capital**

Time	0	1	2	3	4
Nominal sales		1,144	2,704	3,150	3,510
Working capital	165	390	454	506	0
Cash flow	(165)	(225)	(64)	(52)	506

3 **Nominal discount rate**

Nominal discount rate (1.077) × (1.04) = 1.12

Activity 2: IRR

$$IRR = 12 + \frac{1152}{1152-138}(20-12) = 21\%$$

Alternatively, using the =IRR function:

	A	B	C	D	E	F	G
1	Time	0	1	2	3	4	5
2	$'000	(3,570)	(90)	1,126	823	5,527	(345)
3	IRR	21%	Calculated as =IRR(B2:G2)				

Activity 3: MIRR

Time	0	1	2	3	4	5
Present values	(3,570)	(80)	897	586	3,515	(196)

The investment phase is any time period with a negative cash flow, and often this will only be the case for time 0 – however, here it is time periods 0, 1 and 5. The investment phase therefore has a present value of 3,570 + 80 + 196 = 3,846.

The returns phase is therefore time 2–4 and the sum of these present values is 4,998.

$$\left(\frac{4,998}{3,846}\right)^{1/5} \times (1 + 0.12) - 1 = 0.18$$

18.0% is the modified IRR

Alternatively using =MIRR:

	A	B	C	D	E	F	G
1	Time	0	1	2	3	4	5
2	Net nominal cash flows	(3,570)	(90)	1,126	823	5,527	(345)
3	MIRR	18.0%			Calculated as =MIRR(B2:G2,0.12,0.12)		

Activity 4: Project duration

Time	1	2	3	4	5
PV as % of inflows					
3,570 + 1,152 = 4,722	−80/4,722 = −0.02	897/4,722 = 0.19	586/4,722 = 0.12	3,515/4,722 = 0.74	−196/4,722 = −0.04

Project duration = (1 × −0.02) + (2 × 0.19) + (3 × 0.12) + (4 × 0.74) + (5 × −0.04) = −0.02 + 0.38 + 0.36 + 2.96 − 0.2 = **3.5**

Alternative solution, using quicker method:

PV of cash inflows = 4,722

Time	1	2	3	4	5
PV × time period	−80 × 1 = −80	897 × 2 = 1,794	586 × 3 = 1,758	3,515 × 4 = 14,060	−196 × 5 = −980

Project duration = (−80 + 1,794 + 1,758 + 14,060 − 980)/4,722 = **3.5**

This means that this project delivers its value over about 3.5 years, ie it has the same duration as a project that delivers 100% of its (present value) cash inflows in 3.5 years' time.

Activity 5: Value at risk

1   The VAR at 95% is 1.645 × 1,000,000 × $\sqrt{4}$ = $3,290,000, ie worst case NPV (only 5% chance of being worse) = $2m − $3.29m = −$1.29m

2   The VAR at 99% is calculated on the same basis but using 2.33 from the normal distribution table instead of 1.645. This results in a value at risk of $4.66m and a worst case NPV (only 1% chance of being exceeded) of $2m − $4.66m = −$2.66m

Skills checkpoint 1

Scepticism

Chapter overview

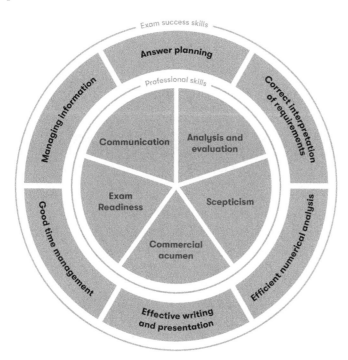

Introduction

Scepticism is one of the four professional skills that have been introduced to the AFM exam from 2022.

This skill will be examined in Section A of the exam, a compulsory 50 mark question, which tests all of the four professional skills for 10 marks in total.

This skill may also be examined in Section B, which consist of two compulsory scenario-based 25 mark questions each of which allocates 5 marks to professional skills. Each Section B question will contain a **minimum of two professional skills from Analysis and Evaluation, Scepticism and Commercial Acumen. Section B questions will state which of these professional skills are being tested.**

No Professional Skill will ever be worth more than five marks in a question.

As with the Technical marks **there will be slightly more marks available for candidates to score than the set amount.** For example, in a Section A question there are ten Professional Skills marks; however, those ten marks could be scored from a possible fourteen marks available. In a Section B question there are five Professional Skills marks; however, those five marks could be scored from a possible seven marks available.

AFM Professional Skill: Scepticism

How to score marks for Scepticism will depend on the nature of the question that is set.

Effective challenge and critical assessment of techniques used

The overall aim of the AFM syllabus is to create the ability to apply relevant knowledge, skills and professional judgement as expected of a senior financial advisor making decisions relating to the financial management of an organisation. As such, there is an expectation that candidates will be able to **critically assess** the techniques that they have used as part of an answer to a question.

The skill of scepticism requires candidates not only to understand the potential disadvantages or limitations of techniques but also to recognise that a technique may make assumptions that may not be valid.

For example, the use of a weighted average cost of capital to appraise an investment assumes that an investment will not result in a change of business or financial risk. It may follow that the usefulness of a technique, such as NPV, will be lessened because of the assumptions that are being made as the technique is being applied.

The skill of scepticism requires candidates to understand the **potential disadvantages or limitations of any of the techniques covered in the AFM syllabus** and to recognise that a technique will not always be appropriate for an organisation, or that care must be taken in applying the technique.

Effective challenge and critical assessment of information and assumptions provided

Information and assumptions provided in a question may sometimes be subject to challenge. However, to score a professional mark you cannot simply say that a piece of information may be wrong. Instead, you should explain **why the information or assumption may be subject to error**, or **the impact of the information or assumption being unreliable**.

If, for example, a rate of inflation is given in a net present value question then you may decide that this is a key assumption and if it is incorrect (eg if inflation is higher) you would need to consider **what impact this could have** on NPV and therefore **on the** investment **decision**.

Identification of missing or additional information, which may alter the decision reached

In some questions you may feel that useful information has not been provided and if so you can mention this to score marks for scepticism.

Missing or additional information needs to be important, practical and relevant so this is not an excuse to write an unrealistic list of extra information that is unlikely to be available to a company. You will need to **justify the need for this missing or additional information**.

For example, before investing in a project an evaluation may need to have been made of the potential impact of the investment on a company's capital structure and/or ability to pay dividends, because this may impact on the risk of a company (if the capital structure changes) or the returns to shareholders (if they are relying on dividend payments). If the question does not provide information on the impact of the investment on the company's capital structure/and or ability to pay dividends, it would be reasonable to state that this information should be provided before the investment decision is made.

Demonstration of the ability to probe into the reasons for issues and problems

Scepticism can also mean applying an enquiring mind and exploring the underlying reasons for a given situation.

This may involve **challenging opinions or assertions** made in a question.

For example, if the CEO has suggested that no debt finance should be used then the logic of this could be challenged. To score marks the basis for this challenge would have to be **explained**. You could refer to the company's gearing ratio, interest cover or asset backing as justification that the CEO's suggestion should be challenged.

Possible pitfall

Don't be sceptical about everything!

You should focus on one or two key issues and explain the basis for your scepticism and the potential impact of the issue.

Applying this professional skill

The AFM syllabus includes a large number of techniques which need to be studied and learned.

However, at Strategic Professional level you will be expected not only to be able to use a technique but also to be aware of what its drawbacks might be and in what circumstances its use may be inappropriate – ie to be sceptical.

The skill of **scepticism** can potentially be applied to any syllabus area in AFM, and can be developed by carefully studying the key assumptions and drawbacks in the techniques that you are studying.

Question practice

The solution to question 7 (Pandy), which is set as homework at the end of Chapter 4, gives an illustration of how this skill can be applied to score professional marks.

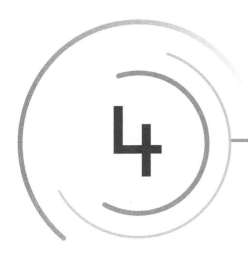

4

Application of option pricing theory to investment decisions

Learning objectives

On completion of this chapter, you should be able to:

	Syllabus reference no.
Apply the Black–Scholes option pricing model (BSOP) to financial product and to asset valuation:	B2(a)
• Determine and discuss, using published data, the five principal drivers of option value (value of the underlying, exercise price, time to expiry, volatility and the risk-free rate)	
• Discuss the underlying assumptions, structure, application and limitations of the BSOP model	
Evaluate embedded real options within a project, classifying them into one of the real option archetypes	B2(b)
Assess, calculate and advise on the value of options to delay, expand, redeploy and withdraw using the BSOP model	B2(c)

Exam context

This chapter continues to cover **Section B** of the syllabus: **'advanced investment appraisal'**; this syllabus section is covered in **Chapters 3–7**. Remember that **every exam will have questions that have a focus on syllabus Sections B and E.**

The formulae used in this chapter will initially look daunting but should, with practice, become manageable because they are given in the exam and have a **clear, specific use**. In fact, from the September 2022 exam onwards, ACCA have decided to provide **a spreadsheet to automate the calculations** when this topic is examined so you should not need to perform manual calculations.

Because the calculations are automated, it is correctly **identifying the variables that are input to the spreadsheet** and **identifying whether a real option is a call or a put option** that are the main challenges when applying this theory in the exam.

The discussion areas of the chapter (types of real options and the limitations of the theory) are **also important** so do not only over-focus on the mathematical content of this chapter.

Chapter overview

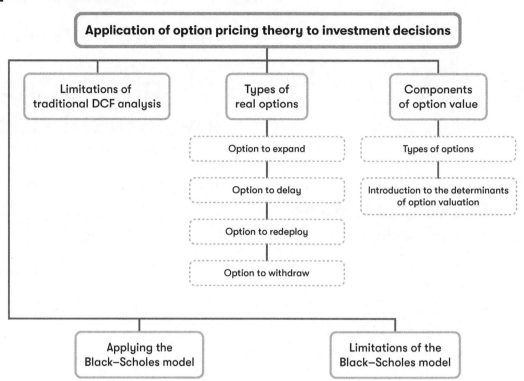

BPP LEARNING MEDIA

1 Limitations of traditional DCF analysis

NPV analysis does not recognise the value of investing in a project that can more easily adapt to changes in a company's environment after the decision to invest has been made. This **strategic flexibility** is valuable, and this value is often not captured by traditional NPV analysis. This can lead to some potentially value-adding investments being rejected.

It is possible to picture this strategic flexibility as a series of choices, or **options**, that are available to managers.

The Black-Scholes model is used to value **financial options** such as currency options (covered in Chapter 12) and interest options (covered in Chapter 13). In this chapter we will see how this model can be adapted to value the real choices, or **real options**, that an investment decision may (sometimes) possess.

Another benefit of this approach is that risks and uncertainties are viewed as opportunities, where upside outcomes can be exploited, and downside risk can be managed.

The value of a real option can then be added to the traditional NPV to give a revised and (arguably) more accurate assessment of the value created by a project.

2 Types of real options

Investment decisions need to be assessed to identify whether they contain 'real options'.

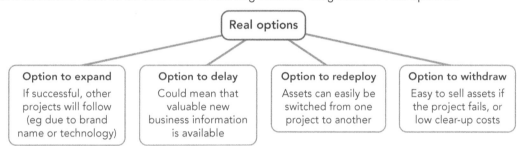

Making an investment now can, in addition to the cash inflows created by that investment, sometimes create **an opportunity for a company to expand** in the future. An **option to expand** can result from being able to apply a new technology or a brand name to other projects if the initial project is successful. It can also simply relate to the option to following on from a successful initial investment by further expansion in that same area. To be considered as an option to expand, the expansion opportunity would need to link to the initial investment ie the company would not be able to expand successfully **if it had not made the investment in the initial project.**

An **option to expand** involves choosing to **spend more money** to exploit upside risk.

Making an investment now can, in addition to the cash inflows created by that investment, sometimes create **an opportunity for a company to delay** further spending where an investment can potentially be delayed in a way that adds value to a project. For projects that have a series of clearly identifiable stages, managers may be able to consider the option to delay at each stage. **An option to delay will only exist if the project is protected**, for example by a patent or a license, so that competitors are unable to exploit the investment opportunity. For example, an option to wait may be considered to exist where an investment starts by establishing a patent, because after securing this a company can then wait to see how market conditions develop before deciding on when to start commercial production of a product.

An **option to delay** involves choosing to defer the decision to **spend more money**.

An investment can sometimes contain **an opportunity for a company to easily redeploy** assets to another use (eg the production of another product) if the initial investment is not successful. An **option to redeploy** involves choosing changing the use of assets to create different revenue streams, to manage downside risk.

An investment can sometimes contain a feature that gives a company a choice or **option to withdraw** from the market. This would mean that the project creates a right to selling a license or patent to a competitor, or to a joint venture partner. An **option to withdraw** involves choosing to raise money by abandoning the project, to manage downside risk.

Activity 1: Idea generation

Suntrack Co is considering an investment to manufacture solar panels for use by domestic households. Apart from the cash inflows that are expected, the project has the following features:

- The knowledge gained from the project is expected to result in a further expansion into solar panels for industrial companies in three years' time.
- A large energy company has offered to sign a deal with Suntrack to buy its facilities at a fixed price in two years' time.

A political election is expected next year that could result in a change in government. This will affect the likely growth of the solar panel industry.

Required

Identify which real options are present in the initial investment .

	Option Type			
	To expand	**To delay**	**To redeploy**	**To withdraw**
Solar panel investment				

PER alert

One of the optional performance objectives in your PER is to review the financial and strategic consequences of undertaking a particular investment decision. This chapter covers the concept of real options which attempts to quantify the strategic characteristics of investments.

3 Components of option value

3.1 Types of option

An option gives the holder the right (but not the obligation) to buy or sell an asset at a pre-agreed price; there are two main types of option.

Call option	Put option
Right to buy	Right to sell
(money is spent)	(money is received)

3.2 Introduction to the determinants of option valuation

There are two main components to the value of an option, **intrinsic value** and **time value**.

Intrinsic value: The difference between the current value of the asset and the exercise price of the option.

For example, consider a **call option** giving the holder the right to buy a share for $4 in three years' time, and the share price today is $5. The intrinsic value is the difference between the current share price of $5 and the exercise price of $4; so, the intrinsic value is $1.

This is sometimes referred to as an option being 'in-the-money'.

However, this option will be worth more than the intrinsic value because it will have a **time value**.

Time value: Reflects the possibility of an increase in intrinsic value between now and the expiry of the option; it is influenced by the variability in the value of the asset, the time until the option expires and interest rates.

Call option

Consider a **call option** giving the holder the right to buy a share for $4 in three years' time; the share price today is $5. In recent years the share price has been highly variable. Interest rates are currently high.

In the case of the call option, relevant factors affecting its (time) value are:

(a) **Variability**: this **adds to the value** of an option, because if the share price rises this will result in a gain for the option holder but if the share price falls below the exercise price of $4 the option holder does not make losses (because the option does not have to exercised).

(b) **Time until expiry of the option:** here three years. This gives considerable scope for variability as above. If this was longer the option would be more valuable because there would be greater potential for variability.

(c) **Interest rates**: if interest rates are **high** then it will less attractive to buy the share itself (because funds are earning an attractive rate of interest), so demand for options will be higher. So, the higher interest rates are then the higher the value of a call option.

Essential reading

See Chapter 4 Section 1 of the Essential reading for more reflections on this issue.

Chapter 11 also returns to this concept for a more detailed examination of the underlying determinants of option value.

The Essential reading is available as an Appendix of the digital edition of the Workbook.

3.2.1 Black-Scholes option pricing model (BSOP)

The full mechanics of the calculation of the value of options are covered below, using the BSOP model.

This model **incorporates the determinants of option value that have been discussed here** and is frequently examined.

4 Applying the Black–Scholes model

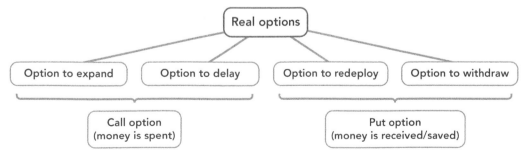

4.1 Call options

In the exam, you are provided with the following formulae to help to value **a call option**.

 Formula provided

Value of a **call option** at Time 0:

$$C_0 = P_aN(d_1) - P_eN(d_2)e^{-rt}$$

$N(d_x)$ is the cumulative value from the **normal distribution tables** for the value d_x

$$d_1 = \frac{\ln(P_a/P_e) + (r + 0.5s^2)t}{s\sqrt{t}}$$

$$d_2 = d_1 - s\sqrt{t}$$

P_a = Present value of the cash flows after exercising the option

P_e = Cost of the investment

r = risk-free rate of return

t = time to expiry of the option in years

s = standard deviation of the project

In fact, the calculations of C_0, d_1 and d_2 are performed **by a spreadsheet that will be provided** in any questions requiring the use of the BSOP model.

To use this spreadsheet, you will need to carefully input the variables determining the option value, let the spreadsheet perform its calculations and then interpret the result.

When you input the variables you should note the following:

- P_a is the present value of the cash flows generated **after the exercise of the option.** So, if you are told that the cost of exercising an option to expand in three years' time is say $60 million and that this follow-on project is expected to give an NPV in three years' time of $10 million, then the value of P_a is $70 million ($60m + $10m) discounted back by three years at the cost of capital that was used for the project.

- P_e is the cost of exercising the option. This is **not discounted back to a present value.** This is because in the formula valuing a call option (C_0) P_e is multiplied to e^{-rt};

$$C_0 = P_aN(d_1) - P_eN(d_2)e^{-rt}$$

- Which is a type of discount factor. So, if you are told that the cost of exercising an option to expand in three years' time is say $60 million and that this follow-on project is expected to give an NPV in three years' time of $10 million, then the value of P_e is $60 million.

- r is the **risk-free rate, this is not the same as the cost of capital** of the company

- t is the time to **expiry of the option, not of the project**. So, if you are considering an option to expand in three years' time, and this project lasts for 5 years then $t = 3$ (because this is when the option to expand must be exercised).

- s is standard deviation; you may have to calculate this as the **square root of the variance**

4.1.1 Spreadsheet provided

To calculate the value of an option you will insert the input variables into row 3 of the spreadsheet that will be provided in the exam.

Here is an example of a blank spreadsheet, ready to be completed:

◢	A	B	C	D	E	F
1						
2	Pa	Pe	r	t	s	
3						
4						
5	d1	#DIV/0!				
6	d2	#DIV/0!				
7	Nd1	#DIV/0!				
8	Nd2	#DIV/0!				
9	c	#DIV/0!				
10	p	#DIV/0!				

The cells marked as #DIV/0! cannot be overwritten and will provide the value of a call option C (cell B9) and a put option P (cell B10); the other values can be ignored.

4.1.2 Option to expand

An option to expand involves spending money, so it is a type of call option.

Activity 2: Valuing a call option

Project 1 has an NPV of –$10,000; it will **also** develop expertise so that Entraq would be ready to penetrate the European market with an improved product in four years' time. The expected cost at Time 4 of the investment is $600,000.

Currently the European project is valued at 0 NPV but management believe that economic conditions in four years' time may change and the NPV could be positive.

The standard deviation is 30%, the risk-free rate is 4% and the cost of capital is 10%.

Required

Evaluate the value of this option to expand.

Solution

Step 1   First identify the basic variables that are required in the spreadsheet.

$$C_0 = P_aN(d_1) - P_eN(d_2)e^{-rt}$$

Initial variables

P_a =	[ ]		r =	[ ]
			t =	[ ]
P_e =	[ ]		s =	[ ]

Step 2   Next interpret the output, the key point is to understand whether you are looking at a call or a put option because the calculations are done for you. Here we are looking at the value of a **call option (C)**.

	A	B	C	D	E
1					
2	Pa	Pe	r	t	s
3	409,800.000	600,000.000	0.040	4	0.30
4					
5	d1	-0.0688			
6	d2	-0.6688			
7	Nd1	0.4726			
8	Nd2	0.2518			
9	c	64,913.21			
10	p	166,399.49			

Step 3 Finally, assess the impact on the project evaluation

Impact on valuation of Project A =

4.1.3 Option to delay

An option to delay is also a call option (as ultimately it involves spending money) and will be valued in the same way as the option to expand.

4.2 Put options

In the exam, the same spreadsheet helps you to value **a put option.**

4.2.1 Option to withdraw

An option to withdraw involves receiving money, so it is a **put option**.

In the option pricing formula, the value of P_a is the present value of the estimated net cash inflows from the project **AFTER the exercise of the option to withdraw**.

 ### Activity 3: Valuing a put option

Company X is a considering an investment in a joint venture to develop high quality office blocks to be let out to blue chip corporate clients. This project has a 30-year life, and is expected to cost Company X $90 million and to generate an NPV of $10 million for Company X.

The project manager has argued that this understates the true value of the project because the NPV of $10 million ignores the option to sell Company X's share in the project back to its partner for $40 million at any time during the first ten years of the project.

The standard deviation is 45% p.a. and the risk-free rate is 5% p.a.

Required

Complete the evaluation of this option.

Solution

Step 1 First identify the basic variables that are needed.

$P_a =$		$r =$	
		$t =$	
$P_e =$		$s =$	

Step 2 Next interpret the output, the key point is to understand whether you are looking at a call or a put option because the calculations are done for you. Here we are looking at the value of a **put option (P)**.

◢	A	B	C	D	E
1					
2	Pa	Pe	r	t	s
3	66.700	40.000	0.050	10	0.45
4					
5	d1	1.4222			
6	d2	-0.0008			
7	Nd1	0.9225			
8	Nd2	0.4997			
9	c	49.41			
10	p	6.97			

Step 3 Finally, assess the impact on the project evaluation.

Put option value =	$6.97m

– the project's NPV is understated by this value.

If this option can be exercised **at any point** up to the end of the ten-year period then the option would be worth more than this since it could be exercised if the project is failing. However, the Black-Scholes model **assumes that the option is exercised on a specific date**, ie at the end of ten years.

4.2.2 Option to redeploy

An option to redeploy is also a put option and will be valued in the same way.

5 Limitations of the Black–Scholes model

The most significant limitation of the Black–Scholes model is the **estimation of the standard deviation** of the asset. Historical deviation is often a poor guide to expected deviation in the future, so in reality the standard deviation is based on judgement.

The formulae also **assume that the options are 'European'**, ie exercisable on a fixed date. An alternative model (the binomial model) can be used to value 'American' style options which are exercisable over a range of dates; this model is beyond the scope of this syllabus. If using the BSOP model to value an American style option in the exam then you should note that the BSOP model will **undervalue American style options** because it does not take into account this time flexibility (this is the case in the preceding activity).

Other assumptions include:

(a) The risk-free interest rate is assumed to be constant and known.

(b) The model assumes that the return on the underlying asset follows a normal distribution.

(c) The model assumes that the volatility of the project is known and remains constant throughout its life.

Chapter summary

Application of option pricing theory to investment decisions

Limitations of traditional DCF analysis

- Ignores the value of real options/strategic flexibility
- Leads to potentially lucrative investments being rejected

Types of real options

Option to expand
- Eg if successful, technology or brand name used in other projects
- Call option

Option to delay
- Eg so that valuable new business information is available
- Call option

Option to redeploy
- Eg assets can easily be switched from one project to another
- Put option

Option to withdraw
- Eg easy to sell assets if the project fails, or low clear up costs
- Put option

Components of option value

Types of options
- Call option
- Put option

Introduction to the determinants of option valuation
- Intrinsic value
  - Current asset price versus exercise price
- Time value
  - Variability
  - Time to expiry
  - Interest rates

Applying the Black–Scholes model

- P_e is not discounted
- r is the risk-free rate
- t is the time to expiry of option
- Standard deviation is the square root of the variance
- Steps in valuing a call option:
  (a) Identify input variables
  (b) Calculate d1 then d2
  (c) Use normal distribution tables to calculate N(d1) and N(d2)
  (d) Complete the call option formula
- A call option needs to be valued before a put option can be valued

Limitations of the Black–Scholes model

- Estimation of standard deviation
- Assumed to be exercised on a fixed date (European style)

Knowledge diagnostic

1. **Call option**

   This is an option to buy; options to expand and options to delay are call options.

2. **Put option**

   This is an option to sell; options to redeploy and options to withdraw are put options.

3. **Impact of high volatility**

   Higher volatility normally decreases value, but in the context of option valuation it increases the value of both put and call options.

4. **Standard deviation**

   You may have to calculate this as the square root of the variance.

5. **Drawbacks of BSOP**

   Assumes that options are exercised on a fixed date, and that standard deviation can be estimated.

Further study guidance

Question practice

Now try the following from the Further question practice bank (available in the digital edition of the workbook):

Q6 *Four Seasons*

Q7 *Pandy*

Further reading

There is a Technical Article available on ACCA's website, called 'Investment appraisal and real options'.

We recommend you read this article as part of your preparation for the AFM exam.

Activity answers

Activity 1: Idea generation

	Option Type			
	To expand	**To delay**	**To redeploy**	**To withdraw**
Solar panel investment	The opportunity to invest in commercial solar panels is dependent on the initial investment and represents an opportunity to expand.	Better information on which to make this decision will be available after the election, however this is available regardless of whether the investment is made or not, so there may well be an argument to delay but this is not the same thing as the project possessing an option to delay.	No information to suggest this.	The ability to sell to an energy company is an option to withdraw.

Activity 2: Valuing a call option

Steps are as follows:

Step 1 First identify the basic variables that are required in the spreadsheet.

$$C_0 = P_aN(d_1) - P_eN(d_2)e^{-rt}$$

Initial variables

P_a =	*$409,800		r =	0.04 (risk free rate)
	*$600,000 discounted back to time 0 at 10% =		t =	4 (expiry of option)
P_e =	$600,000		s =	0.3

If P_a had been given in present value terms then you would not have discounted this value.

Step 2 Next interpret the output, the key point is to understand whether you are looking at a call or a put option because the calculations are done for you. Here we are looking at the value of a **call option (C)**.

	A	B	C	D	E
1					
2	Pa	Pe	r	t	s
3	409,800.000	600,000.000	0.040	4	0.30
4					
5	d1	-0.0688			
6	d2	-0.6688			
7	Nd1	0.4726			
8	Nd2	0.2518			
9	c	64,913.21			
10	p	166,399.49			

Step 3 Finally, assess the impact on the project evaluation

Impact on valuation of Project A =

Project A now becomes a +NPV project ($64,913 – $10,000 = $54,913)

We can now see the value of the real options approach. Here a project originally showed a negative NPV of $10,000 and would therefore be rejected. However, by valuing a real option associated with the project we can see that the project now has a positive NPV and can therefore be justified.

Activity 3: Valuing a put option

Step 1 First identify the basic variables that are needed.

PV of the inflows from the project = outlay $90m + NPV $10m = $100m

$P_a =$	$66.7m*	$r =$	0.05	
		$t =$	10	
$P_e =$	$40m	$s =$	0.45	

*This is the PV of the cash inflows from the project AFTER the exercise of the option. Assuming that this is in 10 years' time, then 20 years of the project remain so Pa is estimated as 20/30 × 100 = $66.7m

Step 2 Next interpret the output, the key point is to understand whether you are looking at a call or a put option because the calculations are done for you. Here we are looking at the value of a **put option (P)**.

	A	B	C	D	E
1					
2	Pa	Pe	r	t	s
3	66.700	40.000	0.050	10	0.45
4					
5	d1	1.4222			
6	d2	-0.0008			
7	Nd1	0.9225			
8	Nd2	0.4997			
9	c	49.41			
10	p	6.97			

Step 3 Finally, assess the impact on the project evaluation.

Put option value =	$6.97m

– the project's NPV is understated by this value.

If this option can be exercised **at any point** up to the end of the ten-year period then the option would be worth more than this since it could be exercised if the project is failing. However, the Black-Scholes model **assumes that the option is exercised on a specific date,** ie at the end of ten years.

International investment and financing decisions

Learning objectives

On completion of this chapter, you should be able to:

	Syllabus reference no.
Assess the impact upon the value of a project of alternative exchange rate assumptions	B5(a)
Forecast project or company free cash flows in any specified currency and determine the project's net present value or firm value under differing exchange rate, fiscal and transaction cost assumptions	B5(b)
Evaluate the significance of exchange controls for a given investment decision and strategies for dealing with restricted remittance	B5(c)
Assess the impact of a project on a firm's exposure to translation, transaction (covered in Chapter 11) and economic risk	B5(d)
Assess and advise upon the costs of alternative sources of finance available within the international equity and bond markets	B5(e)

Exam context

This chapter continues to cover **Section B** of the syllabus: 'advanced investment appraisal'; this syllabus section is covered in **Chapters 3–7**.

Every exam will have questions that have a focus on syllabus Sections B and E.

This chapter builds on Chapter 4 and places **investment appraisal in an international context**, which is how investment appraisal is often examined.

Companies that undertake overseas projects are exposed to exchange rate risks as well as other risks, such as exchange control, taxation and political risks. In this chapter we look at capital budgeting techniques for multinational companies that incorporate these additional complexities in the decision-making process. **International investment questions are commonly examined.**

The availability of a variety of international financing sources to multinational companies is also considered.

Chapter overview

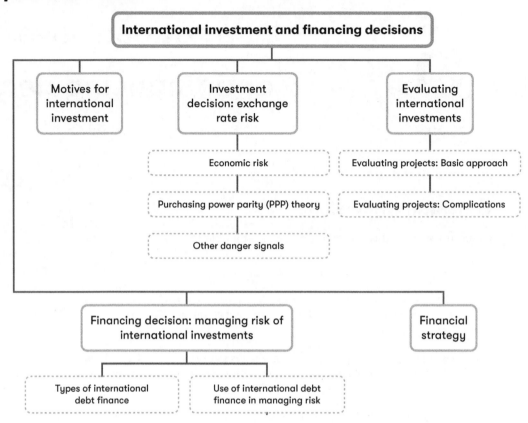

BPP LEARNING MEDIA

1 Motives for international investment

There are many possible motives for investing outside a company's domestic market, including:

	Explanation
Company	Expansion strategy may create economies of scale.
Country	Access cheap labour and government grants. Local investment may be needed to overcome trade barriers.
Customer	Locate close to international customers so that shorter lead times can be offered.
Competition	Some international markets may have weaker competition.

2 Investment decision: exchange rate risk

As with any investment, international investments will need to be carefully scrutinised to identify relevant **business risks** (and potentially financial risks) and to put in place appropriate risk management strategies (as discussed in Chapter 2).

International investments will create a variety of transactions (eg purchases or sales) that are denominated in a foreign currency. It is often necessary for the parent company to convert the home currency in order to provide the necessary currency to meet foreign obligations. This necessity gives rise to **transaction risk**. The cost of foreign obligations could rise as a result of a weaker domestic currency or the domestic value of foreign revenues could depreciate as a result of a stronger home currency. Even when foreign subsidiaries operate independently of the parent company, without relying on the parent company as a source of cash, they will ultimately remit dividends to the parent in the home currency. Once again, this will require a conversion from foreign to home currency. Chapter 12 covers the management of transaction risk.

Some risks that are especially important for **international investments** are considered here, starting with **long-term exchange rate risk or economic risk**.

2.1 Economic risk

> **Economic risk:** The risk that the present value of a company's future cash flows might be reduced by adverse exchange rate movements.

In this chapter we will normally assume that the **domestic currency is $s** and that the domestic country is the USA, and the foreign currency is the peso and the foreign country is country Z.

If there is a **long-term decline** in the **value of the foreign currency** after an international investment has been made then the **net present value of the project** in the domestic currency ($s) **may fall**. This is an aspect of **economic risk.**

So, before an international investment proceeds, **the risk of the foreign currency falling in value should be carefully assessed.**

> **Exam focus point**
>
> You need to be aware that even companies that do not trade internationally are exposed to economic risk if exchange rate movements benefit international rivals (or if exchange rate movements cause a rise in the cost of goods supplied to them by foreign suppliers).

2.2 Purchasing power parity (PPP) theory

One of the causes of a long-term decline in the value of a foreign currency is if the rate of inflation in the foreign country, Country Z, is higher than it is in the USA.

PPP theory suggests that the impact of higher inflation is to **decrease the purchasing power of the foreign currency (peso)** which over time will **reduce its value** on foreign currency markets.

PPP is often used in exams to forecast exchange rate movements, based on predicted future inflation rates; the forecast exchange rates are then used to appraise international investment decisions.

Formula provided

$$S_1 = S_0 \times \frac{(1 + h_c)}{(1 + h_b)}$$

S_1 = exchange rate in 1 year, S_0 = exchange rate today

h_c = inflation in foreign country, h_b = inflation in **base currency country**

Activity 1: PPP theory

The exchange rate in 20X7 is 1.5 peso to the $. Inflation for the next two years is forecast at 2.1% in the USA and 2.5% in Country Z, and then for the following two years inflation is forecast at 1% in the USA and 3% in Country Z.

Required

What is the forecast spot rate in each of the next three years for the peso to the $? (Work to three decimal places.)

Solution

2.2.1 PPP and the international Fisher effect

If an exam question provides interest rates instead of inflation rates, the PPP formula can still be used (inserting interest rates instead of inflation rates) on the assumption that interest rate differentials between economies of similar risk are simply a reflection of different expectations of inflation. The idea that if long-term $ interest rates are higher this is an indication that $ inflation will be higher is **the international Fisher effect** because it is an extension of the Fisher formula (introduced in Chapter 3 Section 2.2).

2.2.2 PPP and base currency

Care must be taken in using PPP theory because the formula requires you to specify which country is the base country or base currency (h_b = inflation in base currency).

The **base currency is the currency that is quoted to 1 unit**, ie in the previous activity the base currency is the $ because exchange rates are quoted in terms of the value of $1.

2.2.3 PPP and economic risk

In the previous activity, the peso was weakening because of **higher inflation** in Country Z. This means that cash inflows in pesos will be worth less in $s and will result in a lower project NPV in $s.

It is also possible that **higher inflation will increase the cash inflows in pesos** from an investment in Country Z. If so, there is a possibility that there will be no impact on the overall $NPV as the higher cash inflows **compensate** for the worsening exchange rate.

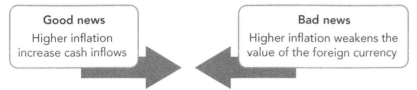

Good news
Higher inflation increase cash inflows

Bad news
Higher inflation weakens the value of the foreign currency

So, **if cash inflows are affected by inflation in exactly the same way as the exchange rate** a weaker exchange rate due to higher foreign inflation **may not matter**.

In reality project cash flows from an international (or domestic) project are likely to inflate at different rates so some overall impact on the project NPV from inflation is likely.

2.3 Other danger signals

Apart from inflation, there are other **danger signals** in a country that is being considered for an international investment, that indicate that a **fall in the value of the foreign currency** (here the peso) is likely.

Danger signals	Explanation
Weak economic growth	This will reduce investment inflows into the foreign country (Country Z), and reduce the demand for the foreign currency (peso).
High balance of payments deficit	If imports exceed exports for a long period in the foreign country, this will increase the supply of the foreign currency (peso) on the foreign exchange markets (as a result of paying for imported goods and services) and can decrease its value.
High government deficit	Debt repayments increase the supply of the foreign currency (peso) on the foreign exchange markets. Again, this can decrease its value.

Essential reading

See Chapter 5 Section 1 of the Essential reading, available as an Appendix of the digital edition of the Workbook, for a broader discussion of economic risk. In addition, Section 2 gives more background on Purchasing Power Parity theory.

The Essential reading is available as an Appendix of the digital edition of the Workbook.

3 Evaluating international investments

3.1 Evaluating projects: basic approach

International investment appraisal questions will normally require you to estimate the **overseas cash flows** of a project and then to use a **forecast exchange rate** to convert these into the domestic currency before discounting at a **suitable (domestic) cost of capital**.

```
┌─────────────────────────────────────────────────────┐
│ Forecast foreign (peso) cash flows including inflation │
└─────────────────────────────────────────────────────┘
                          │
                          ▼
┌─────────────────────────────────────────────────────────────┐
│ Forecast exchange rates and convert into domestic currency ($s) │
└─────────────────────────────────────────────────────────────┘
                          │
                          ▼
┌──────────────────────────────────────────────────────────────────────────┐
│ Finally include any other domestic ($) cash flows and discount at a domestic cost of capital │
└──────────────────────────────────────────────────────────────────────────┘
```

Activity 2: Technique demonstration

KStat Co, an accountancy services company based in the USA, is evaluating an investment project overseas – in Country Z, a politically stable country. The project will cost an initial 2.5 million peso and it is expected to earn **nominal** (ie already inflated) cash flows as follows.

Year	1	2	3	4
Cash flow (peso '000)	750	950	1,250	1,350

(1) The expected inflation rate in Country Z is 3% a year, and 5% in the USA

(2) The current spot rate is 2 peso per $1.

(3) The company requires a return from this project of 16%.

Ignore tax.

Required

Calculate the $ net present value of the project.

Time	0	1	2	3	4
Cash flow (peso '000)	(2,500)	750	950	1,250	1,350
Exchange rate (see workings)					
Cash flow ($'000)					
Discount at 16%	1.000	0.862	0.743	0.641	0.552
Present value					

Total NPV =

Solution

3.2 Evaluating projects – complications

In **international** investment appraisal questions, in addition to exchange rate forecasting and the issues covered in Chapter 3, you may also have to deal with:

(a) Overseas tax issues

(b) Intercompany transactions

(c) Exchange controls

This will mean that the proforma we developed in Chapter 3 for NPV questions will have to be adapted to deal with the extra complications of international NPV.

In the following proforma, the overseas currency is the peso and is denoted by P, and $s are the domestic currency.

Time	0	1	2	3	4
Revenue less all operating costs and TADs in pesos		X	X	X	X
Taxation in pesos		(X)	(X)	(X)	(X)
Capital expenditure in pesos	(X)				
Add back TAD	–	X	X	X	X
Net cash flows in pesos	(X)	X	X	X	X
Forecast exchange rate	X	X	X	X	X
Net cash flows in $s	(X)	X	X	X	X
Extra domestic tax in $s		(X)	(X)	(X)	(X)
Profits on intercompany transactions		X	X	X	X
Other local $ cash flows	–	(X)	(X)	(X)	(X)
Tax paid or saved on local $ cash flows		X	X	X	X
Net cash flows in $s	(X)	X	X	X	X
Discount factors @					
Post-tax cost of capital	X	X	X	X	X
Present value in $s	(X)	X	X	X	X

Note. As with any investment, whether international or not, the =NPV spreadsheet function can be used to estimate the present value of the cash flows from time 1 onwards and then the outlay at time 0 is deducted to calculate the NPV.

3.2.1 Taxation

To prevent 'double taxation', most governments give a tax credit for foreign tax paid on overseas profits (this is double tax relief, or DTR).

The home country will only charge the company the **difference between the tax paid overseas and the tax due in the home country**. This extra tax will appear as an extra cash flow in the project NPV.

3.2.2 Intercompany transactions

Companies may charge their overseas subsidiaries for royalties and components supplied. These charges will affect the taxable profit, and therefore the tax paid, in the foreign country. Domestic tax may also be payable on the **profits from these transactions**.

Activity 3: Extra complications

This **builds on the data from Activity 2, but introduces some new information**.

Tax in Country Z is 20%, and in the USA it is 30%. Tax is payable in the same year that profits are earned.

Tax allowable depreciation of 100,000 peso per year (straight-line) are available.

KStat Co will charge its overseas subsidiary 25,000 peso per year for the provision of internal services.

$15,000 per year in extra administration costs will be incurred to support the new subsidiary.

Required

Complete the table to calculate the revised **$ net present value** of the project.

Time	0 '000s peso	1 '000s peso	2 '000s peso	3 '000s peso	4 '000s peso
Operating cash flows		750	950	1,250	1,350
Tax allowable depreciation		(100)	(100)	(100)	(100)
Intercompany transactions					
Taxable profit in pesos		625	825	1,125	1,225
Taxation in pesos (20%)					
Capital expenditure in pesos	(2,500)				
Add back TAD					
Net cash flows in pesos	(2,500)	600	760	1,000	1,080
Forecast exchange rate	2.000	1.9619	1.9245	1.8878	1.8518
Net cash flows in $'000	(1,250)	306	395	530	583
Extra tax in US in $'000 (extra 10%)					
Intercompany transactions					
Other US cash flows					
Taxable profit in $'000					
Tax paid or saved on US cash flows					
Net cash flows in $'000	(1,250)	273	351	469	516
DF @ US rate 16%	1.0	0.862	0.743	0.641	0.552
Present value in $'000	(1,250)	235	261	301	285

Net present value = $(168) in '000

Solution

3.2.3 Exchange controls

Another potential problem is that some countries impose delays on the payment of a dividend from an overseas investment. These exchange controls create liquidity problems and add to exchange rate risk because the exchange rate may have worsened by the time that dividends are permitted.

The impact of the delay in the timing of remittances may have to be incorporated into the international project appraisal.

Multinational companies have used many different strategies to overcome exchange controls, the most common of which are:

Strategies for dealing with exchange controls	Explanation
Transfer pricing	A higher transfer price may be imposed for internally supplied goods and services.
Other charges	A parent company can charge a royalty for granting a subsidiary the right to make goods protected by patents. Management charges may be levied by the parent company for costs incurred.
Loans	If the parent company makes a loan to a subsidiary, a higher rate of interest on a loan may be charged.

Essential reading

See Chapter 5 Section 3 of the Essential reading, available in Appendix 2 of the digital edition of the Workbook, for further discussion of basic approaches to international investment appraisal. Section 4 also provides a numerical illustration to reinforce the impact of exchange controls, if required.

The Essential reading is available as an Appendix of the digital edition of the Workbook.

PER alert

One of the optional performance objectives in your PER is to evaluate projects and to advise on their costs and benefits. This chapter covers how to evaluate **international** project appraisal decisions.

4 Financing decision: managing risk of international investments

The question of **how much debt** a company should employ in its capital structure is one of the themes of the next chapter. However, here we note that the use of **international debt finance** in the context of international investment decisions.

4.1 Types of international debt finance

Types of international debt finance	Discussion
Loan from a foreign bank	Depending on the profile of the company in the foreign currency this may be slow to organise and potentially expensive.
Eurobond	Large companies with excellent credit ratings use **the euromarkets**, to borrow in any foreign currency using unregulated markets organised by merchant banks. The eurobond (or international bond) market **is much bigger than the market for domestic bonds**.
Syndicated loan	A syndicated loan is a loan put together by a group of lenders (a 'syndicate') for a single borrower. Banks may be unwilling (due to risk) or unable to provide the total loan individually but may be willing to work as part of a syndicate to supply the requested funds. The efficiency of the syndicated loans market means that large loans can be put together very quickly.

4.2 Use of international debt finance in managing risk

International debt finance may be helpful in managing some of the risks associated with international investments.

Types of international debt finance	Discussion
Economic risk	As discussed a foreign subsidiary can be financed with a loan in the currency of the country in which the subsidiary operates (subject to thin capitalisation rules as discussed in Chapter 16 Section 4). This creates a matching effect.
Political risk	Reduces taxable profit, reducing exposure to increases in corporation tax.
Translation risk exchange rate change causing a fall in the book value of foreign assets or an increase in the book value of liabilities	Translation risk does not involve cash flows, so there is doubt as to whether it matters. However, if write-offs result in changes to gearing (using book values) that affect a borrowing covenant there may be real economic consequences from translation risk. Also, if it affects reported profits it may cause a change in the share price. It could also signal a direction of movement in exchange rates and therefore indicate cash problems in future. Using international debt finance reduces the net assets in foreign currency resulting from an overseas investment and reduces translation risk.

Activity 4: Translation risk

It is now November 20X7; QWE is a public listed company supermarket based in France. Its forecast statement of financial position for 31 December 20X7 is given below.

	€m
Assets	14,000
Equity	5,650
Floating rate debt	2,000
Current liabilities	6,350
	14,000

This does not take into account an investment of $1,000m which is about to be made. The current exchange rate is 1 euro = $1.1 (ie 1.1 $/€), but this could rise to 1 euro = $1.40 (1.4 $/€) by the end of the year.

Required

1   Prepare a revised forecast statement of financial position, assuming that the project is funded using long-term debt finance in euros under both exchange rate forecasts.

Exchange rate	1 euro = $1.1	Exchange rate	1 euro = $1.4
	€m		€m
Assets		Assets	
Equity (balance)		Equity	
Floating rate debt		Floating rate debt	
Current liabilities		Current liabilities	

2   Prepare the same calculations assuming that the project is funded using $ debt.

Exchange rate	1 euro = $1.1	Exchange rate	1 euro = $1.4
	€m		€m
Assets		Assets	
Equity (balance)		Equity	
Floating rate debt		Floating rate debt	
Current liabilities		Current liabilities	

Solution

Essential reading

See Chapter 5 Section 5 of the Essential reading, available as an Appendix of the digital edition of the Workbook, for further discussion of IRP theory. Section 6 also gives some further background on eurobonds.

The Essential reading is available as an Appendix of the digital edition of the Workbook.

PER alert

As part of the fulfilment of the performance objective 'evaluate potential business/investment opportunities and the required finance options' you are expected to be able to identify and apply different finance options to single and combined entities in domestic and multinational business markets. This section has looked at the financing options available to multinationals which you can put to good use if you work in such an environment.

5 Financial strategy

A firm that is planning a strategy of international expansion, does not only have to consider **new 'direct' investments**, for example in manufacturing facilities. This may be a sensible approach because it does allow a firm to retain control over its value chain, but it may be slow to achieve, expensive to maintain and slow to yield satisfactory results. So other forms of expansion may be preferable.

(a) A firm might **take over or merge** with established firms abroad. This provides a means of **purchasing market information, market share** and **distribution channels**. If speed of entry into the overseas market is a high priority, then acquisition may be preferred to a start-up. However, the better acquisitions may only be available at a **premium**.

(b) **A joint venture with a local overseas partner** might be entered into. This will allow resources and competences to be shared. Depending on government regulations, joint ventures may be the **only**, or the preferred, means of access to a particular market.

Essential reading

See Chapter 5 Section 7 of the Essential reading for further discussion of alternatives to international investment.

The Essential reading is available as an Appendix of the digital edition of the Workbook.

Chapter summary

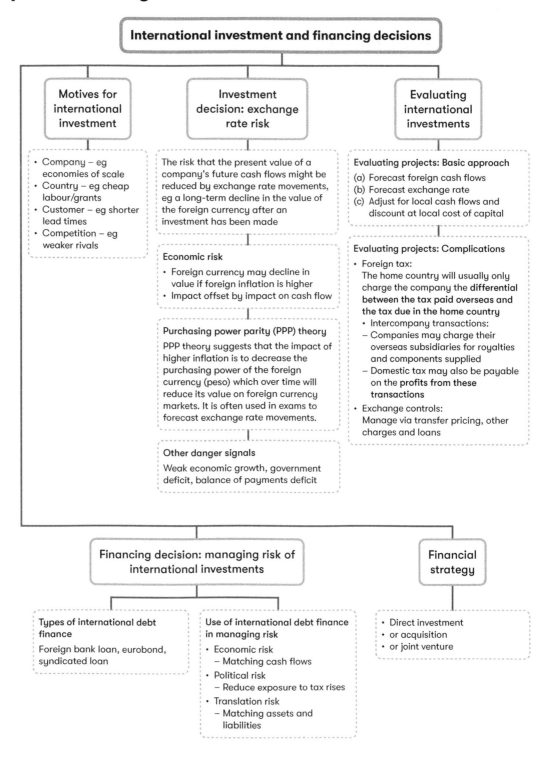

International investment and financing decisions

Motives for international investment

- Company – eg economies of scale
- Country – eg cheap labour/grants
- Customer – eg shorter lead times
- Competition – eg weaker rivals

Investment decision: exchange rate risk

The risk that the present value of a company's future cash flows might be reduced by exchange rate movements, eg a long-term decline in the value of the foreign currency after an investment has been made

Economic risk

- Foreign currency may decline in value if foreign inflation is higher
- Impact offset by impact on cash flow

Purchasing power parity (PPP) theory

PPP theory suggests that the impact of higher inflation is to decrease the purchasing power of the foreign currency (peso) which over time will reduce its value on foreign currency markets. It is often used in exams to forecast exchange rate movements.

Other danger signals

Weak economic growth, government deficit, balance of payments deficit

Evaluating international investments

Evaluating projects: Basic approach

(a) Forecast foreign cash flows
(b) Forecast exchange rate
(c) Adjust for local cash flows and discount at local cost of capital

Evaluating projects: Complications

- Foreign tax:
  The home country will usually only charge the company the **differential between the tax paid overseas and the tax due in the home country**
  - Intercompany transactions:
    – Companies may charge their overseas subsidiaries for royalties and components supplied
    – Domestic tax may also be payable on the **profits from these transactions**
- Exchange controls:
  Manage via transfer pricing, other charges and loans

Financing decision: managing risk of international investments

Types of international debt finance

Foreign bank loan, eurobond, syndicated loan

Use of international debt finance in managing risk

- Economic risk
  – Matching cash flows
- Political risk
  – Reduce exposure to tax rises
- Translation risk
  – Matching assets and liabilities

Financial strategy

- Direct investment
- or acquisition
- or joint venture

Knowledge diagnostic

1. Purchasing power parity theory

Explains exchange rate movements by looking at inflation rate differentials.

2. Economic risk

Damage to a company's market (present) value created by long-term exchange rate movements. In the context of international investment this means a weakening of the value of the foreign currency.

3. Eurobond (or international bond)

A bond issued in a currency outside the currency of origin.

4. Translation risk

Damage to book value of equity created by exchange rate movements. In the context of international investment this means a weakening of the value of the foreign currency.

5. Syndicated loan

A loan put together by a group of lenders (a 'syndicate') for a single borrower.

Further study guidance

Question practice

Now try the following from the Further question practice bank (available in the digital edition of the workbook):

Further reading

Q8 *Novoroast*

Q9 *PMU*

Own research

A practical, and amusing, example of purchasing power parity is the Big Mac index (Economist, 2021). Under purchasing power parity, movements in countries' exchange rates should in the long term mean that the prices of an identical basket of goods or services are equalised. The McDonald's Big Mac represents this basket. The index compares local Big Mac prices with the price of Big Macs in America. This comparison is used to forecast what exchange rates should be, and this is then compared with the actual exchange rates to decide which currencies are over- and undervalued.

This index can be found here:

https://www.economist.com/big-mac-index

Activity answers

Activity 1: PPP theory

Year 1 = 1.5 × 1.025/1.021 = 1.506

Year 2 = 1.506 × 1.025/1.021 = 1.512

Year 3 = 1.512 × 1.030/1.010 = 1.542

This is potentially bad news for a US firm because the strengthening dollar indicates a **fall in the value of the foreign currency (the peso).**

Activity 2: Technique demonstration

The first step is to calculate the expected exchange rate between the peso and the $ at the end of each year. This can be estimated using purchasing power parity theory.

It is assumed that expected inflation remains constant.

Formula: Forecast rate = Spot rate × (1 + foreign inflation) / (1 + base country inflation)

The expected spot rate at the end of each year can now be found.

Year		Peso / $
0		2.0000
1	2.000 × 1.03/1.05 =	1.9619
2	1.9619 × 1.03/1.05 =	1.9245
3	1.9245 × 1.03/1.05 =	1.8878
4	1.8878 × 1.03/1.05 =	1.8518

The $ NPV can now be found.

Discounting annual $ cash flows at 16%

Time	0	1	2	3	4
Cash flow (peso '000)	(2,500)	750	950	1,250	1,350
Exchange rate (see workings)	2.0000	1.9619	1.9245	1.8878	1.8518
Cash flow ($'000)	(1,250)	382	494	662	729
Discount at 16%	1.000	0.862	0.743	0.641	0.552
Present value	(1,250)	329	367	424	402

Total NPV = +$272(000)

Alternatively, the =NPV spreadsheet function can be used to estimate the present value of the Time 1–4 cash flows, and then the outlay at time 0 is deducted to calculate the NPV.

Activity 3: Extra complications

'000 peso	0	1	2	3	4
Operating cash flows		750	950	1,250	1,350
TAD		(100)	(100)	(100)	(100)
Intercompany transactions		(25)	(25)	(25)	(25)
Taxable profit		625	825	1,125	1,225
Taxation (20%)		(125)	(165)	(225)	(245)

'000 peso	0	1	2	3	4
Capital expenditure	(2,500)				
Add back TAD		100	100	100	100
Net cash flows	(2,500)	600	760	1,000	1,080
Forecast exchange rate	2.0000	1.9619	1.9245	1.8878	1.8518
Net cash flows in $'000s	(1,250)	306	395	530	583
Extra tax in US in $'000s (extra 10%)		(32)	(43)	(60)	(66)
Intercompany transactions		13	13	13	14
Other US cash flows		(15)	(15)	(15)	(15)
Taxable profit in $s		(2)	(2)	(2)	(1)
Tax paid or saved on US cash flows (at 30%)		1	1	1	0
		(2 × 0.3 = 0.6 rounded to 1)			(1 × 0.3 = 0.3 rounded to 0)
Net cash flows in $'000s	(1,250)	273	351	469	516
DF @ US rate 16%	1.000	0.862	0.743	0.641	0.552
Present value in $'000s	(1,250)	235	261	301	285

Net present value = $(168) in '000s, ie reject project

Alternatively, the =NPV spreadsheet function can be used to estimate the present value of the time 1-4 cash flows, and then the outlay at time 0 is deducted to calculate the NPV.

Workings

1 **Extra US tax**

'000 peso	0	1	2	3	4
Taxable profit		625	825	1,125	1,225
Overseas tax paid		(125)	(165)	(225)	(245)
Extra US tax (30% is 50% above 20%)		(62.5)	(82.5)	(112.5)	(122.5)
In $s (dividing by exchange rate)		(32)	(43)	(60)	(66)

Or

2 **Extra US tax**

'000 peso	0	1	2	3	4
Taxable profit		625	825	1,125	1,225
Extra tax in US (extra 10%) in pesos		(62.5)	(82.5)	(112.5)	(122.5)
In $s (dividing by exchange rate)		(32)	(43)	(60)	(66)

Activity 4: Translation risk

1 Revised forecast statement of financial position

Exchange rate	1.1 $/€	Exchange rate	1.4 $/€
	€m		€m
Assets	14,909	Assets	14,714
Equity (balance)	5,650	Equity	5,455
Floating rate debt	2,909	Floating rate debt	2,909
Current liabilities	6,350	Current liabilities	6,350
	14,909		14,714

2 Project is funded using $ debt

Exchange rate	1.1 $/€	Exchange rate	1.4 $/€
	€m		€m
Assets	14,909	Assets	14,714
Equity (balance)	5,650	Equity	5,650
Floating rate debt	2,909	Floating rate debt	2,714
Current liabilities	6,350	Current liabilities	6,350
	14,909		14,714

Using overseas debt means that if the local exchange rate falls, the decline in the value of the overseas assets is matched by a decline in the value of the liabilities – if local debt finance is used this does not happen and the book value of equity is damaged.

Skills checkpoint 2

Analysis and evaluation

Chapter overview

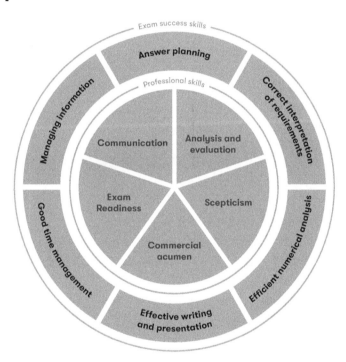

Introduction

'Analysis and evaluation' is one of the four professional skills that have been introduced to the AFM exam.

This skill will be examined in Section A of the exam, a compulsory 50 mark question, which tests all of the four professional skills for 10 marks in total.

This skill may also be examined in Section B, which consist of two compulsory scenario-based 25 mark questions each of which allocates 5 marks to professional skills. Each Section B question will contain a **minimum of two professional skills from Analysis and Evaluation, Scepticism and Commercial Acumen. Section B questions will state which of these professional skills are being tested.**

No Professional Skill will ever be worth more than five marks in a question.

As with the Technical marks **there will be slightly more marks available for candidates to score than the set amount.** For example, in a Section A question there are ten Professional Skills marks; however, those ten marks could be scored from a possible fourteen marks available. In a Section B question there are five Professional Skills marks; however, those five marks could be scored from a possible seven marks available.

AFM Professional Skill: Analysis and Evaluation

How to score marks for this professional skill will depend on the nature of the question that is set.

Appropriate use of data to determine suitable calculations

Some questions will require you to judge which technique to use. This issue often arises in syllabus Section C – Acquisitions and Mergers, where you may need to assess from the scenario what type of valuation is required and what techniques can be used given the details that are provided in the scenario.

In syllabus Section B, investment appraisal questions will also sometimes be formulated so that you will have to infer that specific techniques (such as adjusted present value) are required as the question may not always specifically tell you to use these techniques.

Appropriate use of data to support discussion & draw appropriate conclusions

Analysis is performed in order to arrive at a thorough and comprehensive evaluation of a matter. You may need to explain the meaning of numbers and use these to help to draw reasonable conclusions.

For example, if an internal rate of return of a project is 10% and the company has a cost of capital of 12% then you would need to explain the meaning of the IRR and why it suggests that the project is not viable.

Reasoned judgement when considering key matters

Some questions will require you to consider the impact of decisions on relevant stakeholders that have been mentioned in a question.

For example, if a project has a positive NPV but is severely impacting on other stakeholders through pollution of the local environment then it would be valid to discuss this issue as part of coming to a conclusion on whether or not to proceed with the project.

Ability to consider relevant factors applicable to a company's situation

This will mean making your points relevant by applying your points to the scenario.

Each point you make should ideally be linked back to the scenario and why it matters in the context of the scenario (and the question's requirement).

A common complaint from the ACCA examining team is that 'less satisfactory answers tended to give more general responses rather than answers specific to the scenario'.

Ability to evaluate information objectively to make a recommendation

Information should be evaluated **objectively with a view to balancing the costs, risks, benefits and opportunities**, before recommending **appropriate solutions or decisions that are logical** given the appraisal that has been made. This may involve deciding what issues to prioritise.

Even if you have a strong feeling that a particular course of action should be taken you can score analysis and evaluation marks by showing awareness of possible **problems** that may arise if that course of action is taken.

Possible pitfalls

Avoid writing at great length on a single issue

Try to make your points **concise** to ensure that you produce your answer in the time allowed.

For example, explain what you mean in one (or two) sentence(s) and then in the next sentence analyse it by explaining why it matters in the given scenario. This should result in a series of concise paragraphs containing points that address the specific content of the scenario.

Avoid writing about issues that are not relevant to the scenario

Focus on the requirement, underlining key verb or verbs to ensure you answer the question that has been set and that your analysis is relevant to this requirement.

In fact, many exam questions contain more than one requirement – so focus on the verbs in each sub-requirement and analyse them to determine exactly what your answer should address, and what areas of analysis would not be relevant.

Applying this professional skill

AFM is positioned as a Masters-level exam. It is not easy to 'analyse and evaluate', but it is important to realise that this is a **fundamental skill** that is being tested at this stage in your qualification.

To help to develop this skill, throughout your studies whenever you are tackling questions you will need to practice:

- Assimilating information from a scenario quickly and effectively. There is guidance on the general exam success skills of **'managing information'** and **'interpreting question requirements'** in the **introduction section at the start of this workbook** (exam success skills 1 and 2); and

- **Spending sufficient time** (about 20% of the time available for a question) **on planning** your answer to allow you to understand the key issues within a scenario. There is guidance on this general exam success skills of 'answer planning' and 'time management' in the introduction section at the start of this workbook (exam success skill 3 and 6).

Question practice

The solution to question 10 (Fubuki), which is set as homework at the end of the next chapter, gives an illustration of how points can be 'analysed and evaluated' in the context of a scenario to score professional marks.

6

Cost of capital and changing risk

Learning objectives

On completion of this chapter, you should be able to:

	Syllabus reference no.
Calculate the cost of capital of an organisation, including the cost of equity and cost of debt, based on the range of equity and debt sources of finance. Discuss the appropriateness of using the cost of capital (see Chapter 2) to establish project and organisational value, and discuss its relationship to such value	B3(c)
Calculate and evaluate **project-specific cost of equity and cost of capital,** including their impact on the overall cost of capital of an organisation. Demonstrate detailed knowledge of business and financial risk, the capital asset pricing model and relationship between equity and asset betas	B3(d)
Assess the impact of financing and capital structure on an organisation with respect to: • Modigliani and Miller propositions, before and after tax • Static trade-off theory • Pecking order propositions • Agency effects	B3(h)
Apply the **adjusted present value** technique to the appraisal of investment decisions that entail significant alterations in the financial structure of the organisation, including their fiscal and transaction costs implications	B3(i)
Assess the impact of a significant capital investment project upon the reported financial position and performance of the organisation, taking into account alternative financial strategies (see Chapter 14)	B3(j)

Exam context

This chapter continues **Section B** of the syllabus: **'advanced investment appraisal'**. Remember, every exam will have questions that have a focus on syllabus sections B and E.

This chapter builds on Chapter 1 (which looked at practical factors affecting gearing) and Chapter 2 (which introduced cost of capital calculations). Here we look at the theories concerning capital structure, and use these to consider the implication of the changing financial risk and changing business risk on project evaluation. This links to the previous chapter, because international investment appraisal often involves a significant amount of debt finance.

Chapter overview

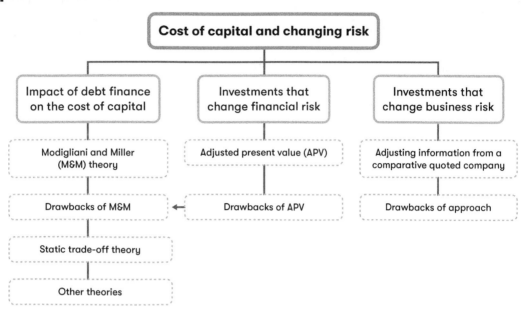

1 The impact of debt finance on the cost of capital

As noted earlier, the cost of debt is cheaper than the cost of equity because debtholders face less risk, so it is sensible for companies with stable cash flows to use some debt finance. Here we review **key theories** that address the issue of how much debt should be used.

1.1 Modigliani and Miller (M&M) theory

Modigliani and Miller (M&M) demonstrated that, ignoring tax, the use of debt simply transfers more risk to shareholders, and that this **makes equity more expensive** so that the use of **debt does not reduce finance costs, ie does not reduce the WACC.**

M&M then introduced the effect of corporation tax to demonstrate that if debt **also** saves corporation tax (as discussed in Chapter 2), then this **extra effect** means that **the WACC will fall.** This suggests that a company should use as much debt finance as it can.

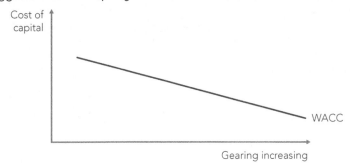

1.1.1 Relationship between WACC and value

As you would expect, a fall in the WACC benefits shareholders. This is because the **present value** of the cash flows generated by a company to its investors (shareholders and debtholders) will be **higher if it is discounted at a lower rate**. In an efficient market this would imply that the market value of equity plus debt will rise as the WACC falls.

 Activity 1: Idea generation

1   Discuss the implication of M&M theory (with tax) for the use of a company's existing WACC to evaluate a project that will be financed mainly by debt.

2   Discuss what will happen to the cost of equity (Ke) as the level of debt rises.

Solution

1.2 Revised formula for K_e

M&M's formula for the K_e of a geared company reflects the effects of using debt finance ie the benefit of the tax relief and the extra financial risk that it brings.

Formula provided

$$K_e = K_e^i + (1 - T)(K_e^i - K_d)\frac{V_d}{V_e}$$

K_e = cost of equity of a geared company

K_e^i = cost of equity of an ungeared company

K_d = cost of debt (pre - tax)

V_d, V_e = market value of debt and equity

Activity 2: M&M cost of equity demonstration

An ungeared company with a cost of equity of 12% is considering adjusting its gearing by taking out a loan at 6% and using it to buy back equity. After the buyback the ratio of the market value of debt to the market value of equity will be 1:1. Corporation tax is 30%.

$$WACC = \left(\frac{V_e}{V_e + V_d}\right)K_e + \left(\frac{V_d}{V_e + V_d}\right)K_d(1 - T)$$

Required

1 Calculate the new Ke, after the buyback.

2 Calculate and comment on the WACC after the buyback.

Solution

1.3 Drawbacks of M&M

A key assumption of M&M theory is that capital markets are perfect, ie a company will always be able to raise finance to fund good projects. In reality, this is not true.

Capital market imperfections	Explanation
Direct financial distress costs	The legal and administrative costs associated with the bankruptcy or reorganisation of the firm.
Indirect financial distress costs	(a) A **higher cost of debt** due to a firm's high risk of default. (b) **Lost sales** due to customers having concerns that a firm with high gearing may be at risk of failure and so will not be able to provide after sales service or to honour product guarantees. (c) Managers and employees will try **drastic actions** to save the firm that might result in some long-term problems eg closing down plants, downsizing, drastic cost cuts and selling off valuable assets; these actions will ultimately damage the value of the firm. (d) **Higher prices** or shorter payment terms **from suppliers** who will have concerns about the risk that a firm with high gearing may not be able to pay its suppliers.

1.4 Static trade-off theory

Myers (Ryan 2007, p.208) argues that these imperfections (static) mean that the level of gearing that is appropriate for a business depends on its **specific business context**.

This suggests that a company should gear up to take advantage of any tax benefits available, but only to the extent that the **marginal benefits exceed** the **marginal costs** of **financial distress**.

After this point, the market value of the firm will start to fall and its WACC will start to rise.

Mature, asset intensive, industries tend to have high gearing because they are at low risk of default and so financial distress costs are likely to be outweighed by the value of tax saved from interest payments

Companies with **fewer tangible assets** or facing **more volatile cash flows** (young, high tech, high fixed costs) tend to have lower gearing because financial distress costs are likely to be higher than the present value of tax saved from interest payments

This theory supports the idea outlined in Chapter 1 that the level of gearing that is appropriate for a business depends on the type of industry that it is in and the stage of its life cycle.

1.5 Other theories

Pecking order theory suggests that, partly due to issue costs, the preferred 'pecking order' for financing is as follows: 1, retained earnings; 2, debt; 3, new equity.

Agency theory suggests that if a company is mainly equity financed there is less pressure on cash flow, and managers will often embark on 'vanity projects' such as ill-judged acquisitions. Higher gearing creates a discipline that can effectively deal with this agency problem.

Essential reading

See Chapter 6 Section 1 of the Essential reading, which recaps on the different capital structure theories in greater detail, this will be useful if you were exempt from the Financial Management exam.

The Essential reading is available as an Appendix of the digital edition of the Workbook.

2 Investments that change financial risk

2.1 When NOT to use the WACC

We noted in Chapter 2 that the current WACC cannot be used as a discount rate at which to appraise projects if:

(a) A project causes a company to change its existing capital structure (financial risk).

(b) A project incurs higher than normal business risk (covered in the next section).

Where the financial risk or business risk of an extra project is different from normal, there is an argument for a cost of capital to be calculated for that particular project; this is called a **project-specific cost of capital**.

2.2 Changing financial risk – adjusted present value (APV)

Modigliani and Miller's theory on gearing tells us that the impact of debt finance is purely to save tax. If so, then the value of this can be quantified and added as an adjustment to the present value of a project.

If a question shows an investment has been funded by an unusually high level of debt or asks for project appraisal using 'the adjusted present value method', you must apply the following steps.

Step 1 Calculate project NPV **as if ungeared,** ie K_e^i

Step 2 **Adjust** for the impact of **financing** (eg present value of tax saved, benefit of any loan subsidy)

Step 3 Subtract the cost of **issuing** new finance

2.2.1 Points to note

Be careful which discount factors you use in APV:

Step 1 Calculate the project NPV using an ungeared cost of equity (K_e^i) calculated either by using the M&M formula or an asset beta (see next section). These cash flows are risky.

Step 2 Add the **PV of the tax saved at the required return on debt** (K_d pre-tax).

This reflects the low risk of the tax savings.

If you are told in an exam question that a **subsidised loan** is offered, then this clearly adds some extra value to the APV. This should be factored into Step 2 and calculated as the **present value of the net interest savings** due to the subsidy, discounted at the normal pre-tax K_d (again because it is low risk).

Formula provided

For ungearing the cost of equity in Step 1:

$$K_e = K_e^i + (1 - T)(K_e^i - K_d)\frac{V_d}{V_e}$$

K_e = cost of equity of a geared company

K_e^i = cost of equity of an ungeared company

Activity 3: APV demonstration

Epsilon plc is considering a project that would involve investment of $11 million now and would yield $2.9 million per year (after tax) for each of the next five years.

$8 million of the project will be financed by a loan, at an interest rate of 5%. The costs of raising this loan are estimated at $200,000 (net of tax).

The company's **existing** K_e is 12% and corporation tax is 30%. Epsilon currently has a ratio of 1:2 for market value of debt to market value of equity.

Required

Review the illustration of the use of the M&M formula for calculating the ungeared cost of equity, and then complete the boxes to calculate the project APV.

Solution

$$K_e = K_e^i + (1 - T)(K_e^i - K_d)\frac{V_d}{V_e}$$

$$12 = K_e^i + (0.7)(K_e^i - 5)\frac{1}{2}$$

So $K_e = K_e^i + (0.35)(K_e^i - 5)$

So $12 = K_e^i + 0.35K_e^i - 1.75$

So $13.75 = 1.35K_e^i$

$$K_e^i = 13.75/1.35 = 10.19\%$$

This is the cost of equity ungeared.

Round this down to **10%** to use the discount tables in Step 1 of APV.

Step 1   Base case NPV at **ungeared** cost of equity:

Time	0	1-5
Project cash flows $m		
Df 10%	1.0	
Present value		
Overall NPV of project as if ungeared		

Step 2

Annual interest paid $m		×		=	

Time	1–5				
Tax saved on interest $m		×		=	
Df at return on debt					
Present value					

Step 3 Issue costs $m = ($0.2m)

APV $m

Step 1 + Step 2 + Step 3 =

+ [   ] − [   ] = [   ]

2.3 APV in an international context

Because international investments often include significant levels of debt (as discussed in the previous chapter), APV may be applied in an international context. The steps will be the same.

2.4 Drawbacks of APV

APV is an M&M theory and suffers from the drawbacks of M&M described in Section 1.3.

Essential reading

See Chapter 6 Section 2 of the Essential reading, which provides a numerical illustration of the impact of a loan subsidy on the APV approach.

The Essential reading is available as an Appendix of the digital edition of the Workbook.

---

3 Investments that change business risk

3.1 Adjusting information from a comparative quoted company (CQC)

For projects with **different business risk** (compared to current operations) it is inappropriate to use the existing WACC to calculate a project NPV; instead a marginal cost of capital (using the CAPM) should be used.

When a company is moving into a new business area it can use the beta of a company in that sector (a comparable quoted company, CQC) and ungear their cost of equity **or** their equity beta to establish the **business risk** of this new area.

This ungeared cost of equity or ungeared beta can then be adjusted again to reflect the debt level of the company making the investment so that it reflects the appropriate level of financial risk when evaluating an investment.

This involves three steps:

Step 1 Ungear the cost of equity or ungear the equity beta relating to the comparable company.

Step 2 Regear the cost of equity or asset beta with the capital structure to be used in the new investment.

Step 3 Use the regeared cost of equity to calculate a revised WACC to use in the appraisal of the project.

Activity 4: Business risk – two approaches

Stetson plc is a **passenger airline** which has a debt:equity ratio of 1:1. It wishes to expand into **air freight**. It has identified that the beta of a highly geared parcel delivery company (Company X) is 1.8 and its K_e is 18.4% - **these are influenced by its gearing of 2:1 debt to equity**. Assume that debt has a beta of 0.

Risk-free rate = 4%   Market rate = 12%   Tax = 30%

Required

Calculate the cost of capital that Stetson should use to appraise this investment by:

1   Ungearing and regearing the beta approach covered above:

   Required

   Step 1: Find a company's equity beta in the area you are moving into and ungear the beta

   Step 2: Regear the beta

   Step 3: Use the regeared beta to calculate an appropriate cost of capital

Steps	Workings
Step 1	
Step 2	
Step 3	

Formula (given in the exam)

$$\beta a = \left(\frac{V_e}{(V_e + V_d(1 - T))}\right)\beta e + \left(\frac{V_d(1-T)}{(V_e + V_d(1 - T))}\right)\beta d$$

2   Ungearing and regearing the cost of equity using the M&M K_e formula covered in the previous section:

Required

Step 1: Find a company's Ke in the area you are moving into and ungear it

Step 2: Then regear the Ke with your own gearing

Step 3: Use the revised Ke to calculate an appropriate cost of capital: (identical to Step 3 in the first part of this question)

Steps	Workings
Step 1	
Step 2	
Step 3	

Formula (given in the exam)

$$\beta_a = \left[\frac{V_e}{(V_e + V_d(1-T))}\beta_e\right] + \left[\frac{V_d(1-T)}{(V_e + V_d(1-T))}\beta_d\right]$$

$$K_e = K_e^i + (1-T)(K_e^i - K_d)\frac{V_d}{V_e}$$

3.2 Drawbacks of approach

3.2.1 Finding a suitable CQC

The key problem with using the geared and ungeared beta formula for calculating a firm's equity beta from data about other firms is that it is **difficult to identify a comparative company with identical operating characteristics to use as a benchmark**.

For example, there may be differences between firms caused by different cost structures (eg the ratio of fixed costs to variable costs), and the type of products and markets of a comparative company business is unlikely to be a perfect match to a proposed project.

3.2.2 Other issues

In addition, there are technical flaws in the models used (either adjusting beta factors or using M&M theory to adjust the cost of equity) which have been reviewed in earlier sections.

 Essential reading

See Chapter 6 Section 3 of the Essential reading, which provides another numerical illustration of this area.

The Essential reading is available as an Appendix of the digital edition of the Workbook.

Chapter summary

Cost of capital and changing risk

Impact of debt finance on the cost of capital

Modigliani and Miller (M&M) theory

- Modigliani & Miller
  - In a zero tax world, debt is cheaper (lower risk) but its use makes equity more expensive (higher financial risk) so the WACC is unchanged
  - With tax, debt brings the benefit of tax savings and a company should **maximise its use of debt finance** to drive down its WACC
- **A lower WACC increases the value of the company to its investors**

Drawbacks of M&M

- A key assumption of M&M theory is that capital markets are perfect eg a company will always be able to raise finance to fund good projects
- Capital market imperfections
  - **Direct financial distress costs** – managing the insolvency process
  - **Indirect financial distress costs** – costs of higher debt payments, loss of sales/higher costs from suppliers

Static trade-off theory

- The level of gearing that is appropriate for a business depends on its **specific business context.**
- **Mature, asset intensive, industries tend to have high gearing** because they are at low risk of default and so financial distress costs are likely to be outweighed by the value of tax saved from interest payments

Other theories

- Pecking order theory suggests the preferred order for financing is: 1, retained earnings; 2, debt; 3, equity.
- Agency theory: equity finance facilitates the agency problem

Investments that change financial risk

Adjusted present value (APV)

Step 1 – calculate the base case NPV as if ungeared using an asset beta or using the M&M formula for K_e

Step 2 – add the PV of the tax saved as a result of the debt & benefit of subsidy (use K_d)

Step 3 – subtract the cost of issuing new finance

Drawbacks of APV

Investments that change business risk

Adjusting information from a comparative quoted company

Step 1 – ungear the cost of equity or equity beta relating to the comparable company

Step 2 – regear the cost of equity or asset beta with the capital structure to be used in the new investment

Step 3 – use the cost of equity to calculate a revised WACC to use in the appraisal of the project

Drawbacks of approach

- Difficult to identify a comparative company with identical operating characteristics to use as a benchmark
- Technical flaws in the models used (adjusting beta factors or using M&M theory to adjust the cost of equity)

Knowledge diagnostic

1. Modigliani and Miller theory with tax

In the absence of financial distress costs, the use of debt finance will drive down WACC and increase value for investors.

2. Static trade-off theory

The level of gearing depends on the business context.

3. Current WACC is sometimes not appropriate as a cost of capital

If financial or business risk change.

4. APV

M&M technique: discount the project as if ungeared and adjust for financing effects separately.

5. Asset and equity betas

An asset beta is an ungeared beta, an equity beta is geared.

6. Change in business risk

Use a comparable company (if available) to act as a benchmark for risk of new business and adjust for the impact of differences in gearing.

Further study guidance

Question practice

Now try the following from the Further question practice bank (available in the digital edition of the workbook):

Q10 Fubuki (a past exam question from 2010)

Activity answers

Activity 1: Idea generation

1 The existing WACC could not be used because this would ignore the benefit of using debt finance.

2 K_e would rise because the use of debt makes equity more risky (higher financial risk, dividends become more volatile). Note that the WACC would still fall.

Activity 2: M&M cost of equity demonstration

1 $K_e = 12 + (1 - 0.3)(12 - 6) \times 1/1 = 12 + 4.2 = 16.2\%$

2 WACC $= (0.5 \times 16.2) + (0.5 \times 6 \times (1 - 0.3)) = 8.1 + 2.1 = \textbf{10.2\%}$

The use of debt will bring benefit to the company because the lower WACC will enable future investments to bring greater wealth to the company's shareholders.

Activity 3: APV demonstration

$$K_e = K_e^i + (1 - T)(K_e^i - K_d)\frac{V_d}{V_e}$$

$$12 = K_e^i + (0.7)(K_e^i - 5)\frac{1}{2}$$

So $K_e = K_e^i + (0.35)(K_e^i - 5)$

So $12 = K_e^i + 0.35K_e^i - 1.75$

So $13.75 = 1.35K_e^i$

$$K_e^i = 13.75/1.35 = 10.19\%$$

This is the cost of equity ungeared.

Round this down to **10%** to use the discount tables in Step 1 of APV.

Step 1 Base case NPV at **ungeared** cost of equity:

Time	0	1-5
Project cash flows $m	(11.0)	2.900
Df 10%	1.0	3.791
Present value	(11.0)	10.994
Overall NPV of project as if ungeared	($0.006)m	

Step 2

Annual interest paid $m	$8m	×	0.05	=	$0.4m
Time	1–5				
Tax saved on interest $m	$0.4m	×	0.3	=	$0.12m
Df at return on debt (5%)	4.329				
Present value	$0.519m				

Step 3 Issue costs $m = ($0.2m)

APV $m

Step 1 + Step 2 + Step 3 = –0.006 + 0.519 – 0.2 = +$0.313m

Therefore accept

Activity 4: Business risk – two approaches

1   Ungearing and regearing the beta approach:

Steps	Workings
Step 1	Beta of parcel delivery company = 1.8 Ungeared this becomes: $\beta_a = 1.8 \times 1/24 = 0.75$
Step 2	**Regear to reflect Stetson's gearing** $$0.75 = \beta_e \times 1/1.7$$ so $$\beta_e = 0.75/(1/1.7) = 1.275$$
Step 3	Ke = 4 + (8)1.275 = 14.2% WACC = (14.2 × 1/2) + (4% × 0.7 × 1/2) = 7.1 + 1.4 = 8.5% This WACC reflects the business and financial risk of the new investment.

2   Ungearing and regearing the cost of equity using the M&M K_e formula:

Steps	Workings
Step 1	Ke = 18.4% Ungeared this becomes: $$18.4\% = K_e^i + 0.7(K_e^i-4) \times 2/1$$ so $$18.4\% = K_e^i + 1.4K_e^i - 5.6$$ So $$24\% = 2.4K_e^i$$ So $$K_e^i = 24/2.4 = 10\%$$
Step 2	**Regear to reflect Stetson's gearing** Ke = 10 + 0.7 × (10-4) × 1/1= 14.2%
Step 3	WACC = (14.2 × 1/2) + (4% × 0.7 × 1/2) = 7.1 + 1.4 = 8.5% This WACC reflects the business and financial risk of the new investment.

7 Financing and credit risk

Learning objectives

On completion of this chapter, you should be able to:

	Syllabus reference no.
Identify and assess the **appropriateness of the range of sources of finance available to an organisation** including equity, debt, hybrids, lease finance, venture capital, business angel finance, private equity, asset securitisation and sale (see Chapter 16), Islamic finance and security token offerings. Include assessment of the financial position, financial risk and the value of an organisation (see Chapter 14)	B3(a)
Discuss the role of, and developments in, Islamic financing as a growing source of finance for organisations; explaining its rationale, benefits and deficiencies	B3(b)
Assess an organisation's debt exposure to interest rate changes using the simple Macaulay **duration** and modified duration methods	B3(e)
Discuss the benefits and limitations of duration including the impact of convexity	B3(f)
Assess the company's exposure to credit risk, including: • The role of, and the risk models used by, the principal rating agencies • Estimate the likely credit spread over risk free • Estimate the organisation's current cost of debt capital using the appropriate term structure of interest rates and credit spread	B3(g)

Exam context

This chapter completes **Section B** of the syllabus: '**advanced investment appraisal**'. Remember every exam will have questions that have a focus on syllabus Sections B and E (treasury and advanced risk management techniques).

This chapter builds on Chapter 2 (which introduced the concept of credit ratings/spreads), and Chapter 4 (which introduced the Black–Scholes option pricing model).

Here we consider a range of general financing issues. There are two **main themes**. First, the use of bond finance and how yield curves and credit ratings can be used to estimate the cost of debt. Second, emerging sources of finance which should build on your knowledge of sources of finance, from your earlier studies.

Chapter overview

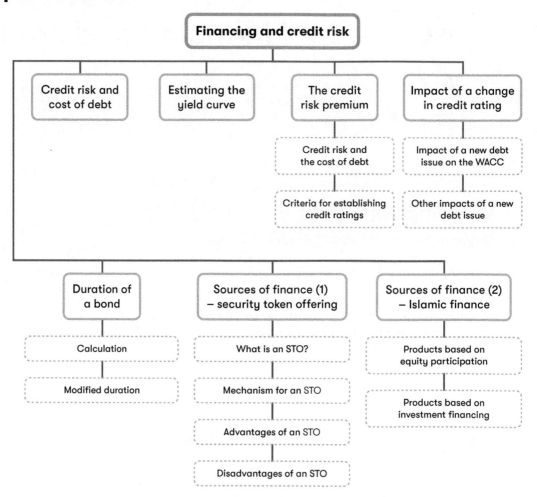

BPP
LEARNING
MEDIA

1 Credit risk and the cost of debt

One of the drawbacks of M&M theory is that it fails to recognise that a significant increase in gearing will alter the credit rating of a company, which can impact on the cost of capital and therefore on shareholder wealth.

As we have seen in Chapter 2, the yield expected on a bond will depend on two factors:

(a)   The risk-free rate derived from the **yield curve; estimating the yield curve** is discussed in **Section 2**.

(b)   The **credit risk premium** – derived from a bond's credit rating; this is discussed in **Section 3**.

2 Estimating the yield curve

Chapter 2 introduced the yield curve, which shows how the yield on government bonds varies according to the term of the borrowing.

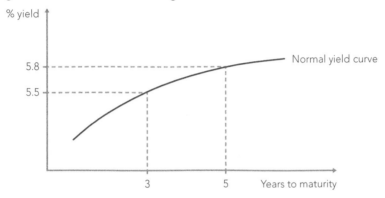

The yield curve can be calculated **by comparing government bonds with different prices and maturities**.

If an exam question provides the coupon interest rate being paid by a government bond and its market price then you can calculate the **required yield in each year** by comparing the market price of the bond to the interest and capital repayments from the bond.

Estimating yield

Estimating required yield in Year 1

If we know that a government bond with a coupon rate of 4% and one year to maturity is trading at $99.50, then we can estimate the required yield in Year 1 as follows:

$$\text{Amount invested today} = \$99.50$$
$$\text{Amount due to be received in one year} = (\$4.00 \text{ interest} + \$100.00 \text{ capital}) = \$104.00$$
$$\text{Return on investment} = \left(\frac{104}{99.5} - 1\right) \times 100 = 4.5\%$$

The yield in a specific year can also be estimated using an equation, this is more useful in the exam.

This approach identifies the expected return (or expected yield) that is required to discount the future cash flow from the bond ($104) back to the given market price, or present value (here $99.50), as follows:

$$\$99.5 = \$104 \times (1 + r)^{-1}$$
$$\text{So } \$99.5/\$104 = (1 + r)^{-1}$$
$$\text{So } 0.957 = (1 + r)^{-1}$$
$$\text{Given that } (1 + r)^{-1} = 1/(1 + r), \text{ then: } 1/0.957 = 1 + r$$
$$\text{So } 1 + r = 1.045$$
$$\text{So } r = 0.045 \text{ or } 4.5\%$$

Estimating required yield in Year 2

If we are then told that another government bond with a coupon rate of 3.5% and **two years** to maturity is trading at $97.2, then we can estimate the required yield in Year 2 using the same equation-based approach as:

$$\$97.2 = \$3.5 \times (1 + r1)^{-1} + \$103.5 \times (1 + r_2)^{-2}$$

(where and are the yields in Year 1 and Year 2)

We know the required yield for cash flows in Year 1 is 4.5% or 0.045 (see earlier) so:

$$\$97.2 = \$3.5 \times (1 + 0.045)^{-1} + \$103.5 \times (1 + r_2)^{-2}$$
$$\text{So} \quad (\$97.2 - \$3.35)/\$103.5 = (1 + r_2)^{-2}$$
$$\text{So} \quad 0.907 = (1 + r_2)^{-2}$$
$$\text{So} \quad 1/0.907 = (1 + r_2)^2 = 1.1025$$
$$\text{So} \quad (1 + r_2) = \sqrt{1.1025} = 1.05$$
$$\text{So} \quad r_2 = 0.05 \text{ or } 5.0\%$$

There is the required yield for cash flows received in Year 2.

Activity 1: Yield curve

A government bond with a coupon rate of 4.5% and **three years** to maturity is trading at $97.4.

Required

Using the above information and the information provided in the previous illustration (ie expected yield in Year 1 is 4.5% and in Year 2 is 5%), estimate the required yield in Year 3.

Solution

---

3 The credit risk premium

3.1 Credit risk and the cost of debt

As we have seen in Chapter 2, the credit risk premium is the extra return (or **credit spread**) required by investors above the risk-free rate that is required to compensate for the risk of a bond.

Building blocks of the cost of debt	%
Yield curve benchmark	From previous section
Credit spread on debt	Given in an exam question
Required yield on debt (pre-tax)	Yield curve + credit spread
Cost of debt post-tax	Required yield × (1 − tax rate)

Example of credit ratings (recap)

Standard & Poor's	Definition
AAA, AA+, AAA−, AA, AA−, A+	Excellent quality, lowest default risk
A, A−, BBB+	Good quality, low default risk
BBB, BBB−, BB+	Medium rating
BB or below	Junk bonds (speculative, high default risk)

3.2 Criteria for establishing credit ratings

The issuer of debt will pay for a credit rating; this will involve the disclosure of confidential information to a credit rating agency. The criteria for rating debt encompasses the following:

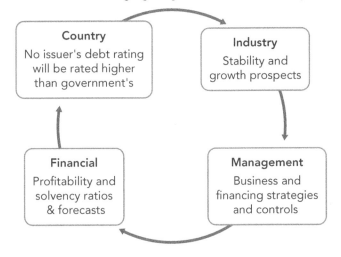

Essential reading

See Chapter 7 Section 1 of the Essential reading, which provides further background on the calculation of credit ratings.

The Essential reading is available as an Appendix of the digital edition of the Workbook.

4 Impact of a change in credit rating

4.1 Impact of a new debt issue on the WACC

One reason that a company's credit rating can worsen is due to the issue of new debt; this can have a number of potential impacts on the weighted average cost of capital:

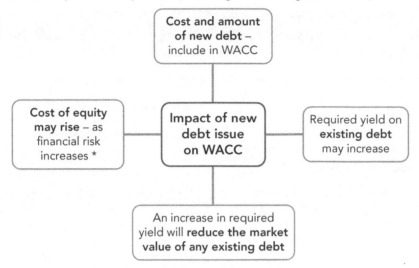

* Exam questions often specify that the impact of the new debt issue on the value or cost of equity is not known, or can be assumed to be insignificant. If so, there is no need to adjust the cost of equity using the M&M cost of equity formula from Chapter 6.

Activity 2: Impact of a change in credit rating

Currently Tetron Co has debt finance with a market value of $10 million which is **due to mature in one year**. Tetron also has $90 million of equity (market value), and a cost of equity of 8%.

Tetron Co is considering the issue of $5 million of new of debt with a **maturity of three years**. Tetron is worried that the extra debt will worsen its credit rating from its current AAA to A and that this will increase its WACC. Tax is at 20%.

The impact of the new debt issue on the value (and cost) of equity is hard to predict and can be assumed to be insignificant.

Relevant data	1 year	3 year
AAA	10	18
A	60	75
Yield curve rate	4.4	5.5

Required

Complete the following evaluation of the impact of a worsening of Tetron's credit rating from AAA to A as a result of the new debt issue, by filling in the boxes.

Solution

(1) **Tetron's current WACC**

Current required return on debt =	
Current WACC =	

$$\text{WACC} = \left(\frac{V_e}{V_e + V_d}\right) K_e + \left(\frac{V_d}{V_e + V_d}\right) K_d(1 - T)$$

(2) **New required yield on debt at a credit rating of A**

Current debt finance (1 year to maturity)	
New debt finance (3 years to maturity)	

(3) **New market value of debt**

Current debt finance (one year to maturity) Repays $10m + $0.45 = $10.45m in 1 year	Time $m df 5% Present value	
New debt finance (three years to maturity)	$5 million as given	

(4) **Revised WACC**

Revised WACC =	

4.2 Other impacts of a new debt issue

Additional debt may have other restrictive covenants which may restrict a company from buying or selling assets, this may restrict a company from being able to maximise returns to shareholders.

Debt repayment covenants require a company to build up a fund over time which will be enough to redeem the debt at the end of its life. These may make it harder to pay dividends to shareholders.

If the WACC rises (which does not necessarily happen as shown in Activity 2), this will reduce the value of a company to its investors.

5 Duration of a bond

We have seen, in Chapter 3, the concept of duration in the context of project appraisal to give a measure of the average amount of time over which a project delivers its value. Duration is also known as Macaulay duration.

The same concept can be applied to a bond, where it helps to explain the risk of a bond to investors.

5.1 Calculation

The average amount of time taken to recover the cash flow from a bond is **not only affected by its maturity date** – it is also affected by the **size of the interest** (coupon) **payments**, eg a 5% bond maturing in three years will not give cash back as quickly as a 10% three-year bond.

Duration measures the weighted average number of years over which a bond delivers its returns.

As we have seen, duration is calculated by multiplying the present value of cash inflows to the time period of that inflow and then dividing by the total present value of the cash inflows.

Duration allows bonds of **different maturities** and **coupon rates** to be directly compared.

The illustration below is a recap of the calculation of duration.

Illustration 1: Bond duration

A company has a 5% bond in issue with a nominal value of $100 and is redeemable at nominal value in three years' time. The required yield is 4%.

Required

Calculate the duration of Bond A.

Solution

Time	1	2	3	Total
Cash	5	5	105	
DF 4%	0.962	0.925	0.889	
PV	4.8	4.6	93.3	102.7
PV × year	4.8	9.2	279.9	293.9

293.9/102.7 = **2.86 years**

5.1.1 Influences on duration

Duration will be higher if the bond has:

(a)   A long time to maturity

(b)   A low coupon rate

5.2 Modified duration

Modified duration is a useful measure of the risk of a bond to an investor.

Modified duration is calculated as:

Formula to learn

$$\frac{\text{(Macaulay) duration}}{1 + \text{yield}}$$

Modified duration

From the previous illustration the modified duration of Bond A is 2.86/1.04 = 2.75.

If the modified duration is 2.75 then, if required yields rise by 1%, the bond price will fall by 2.75%.

This is a **useful measure of the price sensitivity (risk) of a bond to changes in interest rates**.

5.2.1 Convexity and modified duration

A limitation of modified duration is that it assumes a linear relationship between the yield and the price. In fact, the actual relationship between price and yield is given by the curve below.

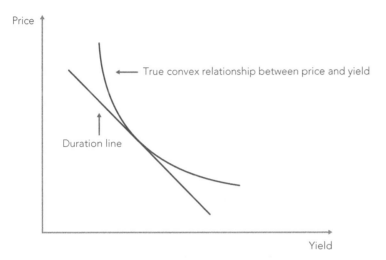

The impact of **convexity** (ie a non-linear relationship) will be that the modified duration will tend to overstate the fall in a bond's price and understate the rise. Therefore, modified duration should be treated with caution in your predictions of interest rate/price relationships.

The problem of convexity only becomes an issue with more substantial fluctuations in the yield.

Essential reading

See Chapter 7 Section 2 of the Essential reading, which provides a further example of bond duration.

The Essential reading is available as an Appendix of the digital edition of the Workbook.

6 Sources of finance (1) – Security token offering (STO)

6.1 What is an STO?

A security token offering (STO) is a relatively new way for organisations to raise capital. Like an Initial Public Offering (IPO), an STO raises finance from investors. However, there are two key differences:

(a) Instead of receiving shares, an investor receives a new type of coin or token

(b) Payment is made in a cryptocurrency such as bitcoin or ether

6.1.1 Types of tokens/coins

Type of token	Explanation
Investment tokens	Equity tokens which offer a share in the company
Asset tokens	Represent a physical asset or product, eg allowing investors to purchase difficult-to-store physical assets such as gold online.
Utility tokens	Provide users with access to a product or service, eg Filecoin raised over $250 million; its tokens give access to its decentralised cloud storage service.

The future value of these tokens depends on the success of the venture.

6.1.2 Regulatory status

The attitude of regulators to STOs differs around the world; in some countries (China and South Korea) STOs are banned.

In general, regulators are **less concerned** with STOs that **do not** offer investors the reasonable expectation of profit eg where an STO aims to simply develop technology or where investors receive utility tokens to exchange for future services (these STOs currently tend to be outside the definition of a 'security' and therefore are not normally of interest to regulators).

STOs that in some way offer **future income streams** are likely to be **judged to be securities** (eg equity tokens or tokens that can also serve as a 'payment voucher' for an underlying service). These STOs are likely to have to fulfil the related regulatory criteria for an issue of securities (full prospectus etc). There may also be a risk that if this has not been done then fines may be levied (which may be severe), or the regulator puts a stop to the STO.

Increasingly regulators are viewing STOs as offering **future income streams,** and so they are **judging them to be securities.** This means that STOs are likely to have to fulfil the related regulatory criteria for an issue of securities (eg production of a full prospectus). This has led to a moderation in the use of STOs.

6.2 Mechanism for an STO

One of the attractions of an unregulated STO is its simplicity, the issuer raises money by issuing a '**white paper**' providing details of the concept that the venture intends to build, and details of the tokens that will be issued in exchange for cryptocurrency.

The white paper is available via the venture's website, which also provides the mechanism for payment of cryptocurrency to the venture's account (typically bitcoin or ether). It is now more common for payments to be made into an escrow account (an account established by an independent third party), to provide greater assurance of the venture's validity.

Most STO sites include instructions for how investors should go about buying their bitcoins or ether – the assumption being that they don't already own any cryptocurrency (ACCA, 2018).

6.3 Advantages of an STO

Since 2017, there has been a dramatic increase in STO activity, due to:

(a) Its speed and ease of use as a source of finance for new ideas, compared to traditional methods

(b) Investor interest, often based on a speculative expectation of rapid, high returns

(c) The sale of utility tokens creates a source of finance and also an established user base, which will make it easier for a company to further develop their product.

6.4 Disadvantages of an STO

6.4.1 To investors

Type of risk	Explanation
Fraud risk	STOs tend to be launched by start-ups. Organisation details are often vague with just a website, and no specific geographic location. White papers may make wild claims about the potential for the project being financed.
Valuation risk	Valuation of tokens is highly speculative, in addition the entities involved are generally start-ups.
Security risk	If a token repository is hacked and tokens stolen, investors typically have no recourse.

6.4.2 To the issuer

Type of risk	Explanation
Value of cryptocurrency	For example, the value of bitcoin fell by over 50% between mid-April 2021 and mid-June 2021.
Risk of money laundering	The anonymity of transactions makes STOs a target for investment from funds belonging to organised crime.
Risk to investor	As discussed earlier, this may reduce the availability of funds and the price that investors are willing to pay.
Risk of regulation	This is illustrated by Protostarr, which abandoned its STO in 2017 after being contacted by the US SEC to discuss its status.

Essential reading

See Chapter 7 Section 3 of the Essential reading for a recap of the variety of types of finance that are available; most of this is a recap from the Financial Management exam.

The Essential reading is available as an Appendix of the digital edition of the Workbook.

7 Sources of finance (2) – Islamic finance

The justification for the use of Islamic finance may be either religious or commercial reasons; here we focus on **commercial reasons**:

- **Availability of finance**. The impact of the credit crash on Islamic nations, eg wealthy Gulf countries, has been less than in many other parts of the world. The Gulf countries own approximately 45% of the world's oil and gas reserves.
- Islamic finance may also appeal due to its **more prudent investment and risk philosophy**. Conventional banks aims to profit by taking in money deposits in return for the payment of interest (or **riba**) and then lending money out in return for the payment of a higher level of interest. **Islamic finance does not permit the charging of interest** and invests under arrangements which share the profits and losses of the enterprises.

7.1 Products based on equity participation

To tap into the **Islamic equity markets**, a company must be sharia compliant. To achieve this, there are two key screening tests:

(a) **Does the company engage in business practices that are contrary to Islamic law**, eg alcohol, tobacco, gambling, money lending and armaments are not acceptable.

(b) Does the company pass **key financial tests**, eg **a low debt–equity ratio** (less than approx 33%); in theory any interest-based transaction is not permitted, but in reality it is accepted that this is not realistic.

To establish social justice, Islam requires that investors and entrepreneurs share risk and reward; there are two main products that are **offered by Islamic banks** that facilitate this (remember that Islamic banks cannot lend money out in a conventional way in exchange for interest repayments). Despite being offered by banks, both products actually create **equity participation**.

Mudaraba

Profits are shared according to a pre-agreed contract. There are no dividends paid. **Losses are solely attributable to the provider of capital, eg a bank**. The entrepreneur (the mudarib) takes sole responsibility for running the business, because they have the expertise in doing so – if losses are made the entrepreneur loses their time and effort.

Mudaraba contracts can either be **restricted** (to a particular project) or **unrestricted** (funds can be used in any project).

Musharaka

Profits are shared according to a pre-agreed contract. There are no dividends paid. Losses are shared according to capital contribution. **Both the organisation/investment manager and finance provider participate in managing and running the joint venture**.

Profits are normally shared in a proportion that takes into account the capital contribution **and** the expertise being contributed by the bank and the entrepreneur/joint venture partners. Losses are shared in proportion to the % capital being contributed by each party.

Under a diminishing musharaka agreement the mudarib pays increasingly greater amounts to increase their ownership over time, so that eventually the mudarib owns the whole venture or asset.

7.1.1 Sukuk bonds

The other key product that allows equity participation is a **sukuk bond.** Although these are often referred to as Islamic bonds, the sukuk holders share risks and rewards, **so this arrangement is more like equity**. The sukuk holder shares in the risk and rewards of ownership of a **specific asset, project or joint venture**.

Sukuks require the creation of a **special purpose vehicle (SPV)** which acquires the assets. This adds to the costs of the bond-issuing process, but they are often registered in tax-efficient jurisdictions, eg Bahrain.

The **prospectus** for a sukuk **must clearly disclose its purpose, its risk and the Islamic contract on which it is based** (mudaraba, musharaka, ijara (see below)) – all of which will be crucial in obtaining sharia compliance (which must be disclosed in the prospectus too).

7.2 Product based on investment financing (ie no equity participation)

Debt-based finance is also possible but, even here, **no interest can be charged**; the products ensure both parties involved **share risk** (eg late payment fees can be applied by the bank but any such fees must be given to charity), and **no money is actually loaned** (the finance is linked to an **asset being purchased** on behalf of the client).

Type of contract	Explanation
Murabaha	The financial institution purchases the asset and sells it to the business or individual. There is a pre-agreed mark-up to be paid, in recognition of the convenience of paying later, for an asset that is transferred immediately. No interest is charged.
Ijara	The financial institution purchases the asset for the business to use, with lease payments, period and payment terms being agreed at the start of the contract. The financial institution is still the owner of the asset and incurs the risk of ownership. **This means that the financial institution will be responsible for major maintenance and insurance**, which is different from a conventional finance lease.
Salam	A commodity is sold for future delivery; cash is received from the financial institution **in advance** (at a discount) and delivery arrangements are determined immediately. Note that Sharia scholars have concerns about derivatives products (eg futures) because they are not based on real economic activity (unless they are held to delivery).
Istisna	For funding large, long-term construction projects. The financial institution funds a project; the client pays an initial deposit, followed by instalments during the course of construction. At the completion, ownership of the property passes to the client.

Essential reading

See Chapter 7 Section 4 of the Essential reading, which considers the pros and cons of Islamic finance.

The Essential reading is available as an Appendix of the digital edition of the Workbook.

Activity 3: Islamic finance

Why might a bank prefer to advance funds based on a Musharaka contract instead of a Mudaraba contract?

Solution

Chapter summary

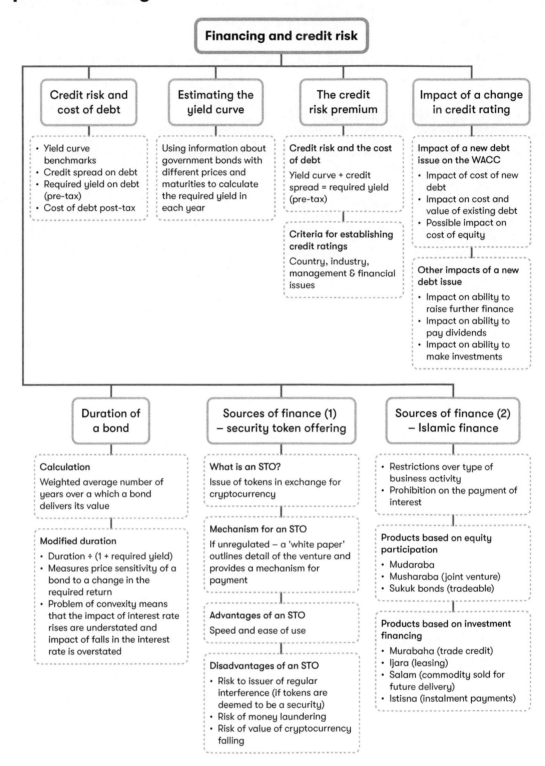

Financing and credit risk

Credit risk and cost of debt
- Yield curve benchmarks
- Credit spread on debt
- Required yield on debt (pre-tax)
- Cost of debt post-tax

Estimating the yield curve

Using information about government bonds with different prices and maturities to calculate the required yield in each year

The credit risk premium

Credit risk and the cost of debt

Yield curve + credit spread = required yield (pre-tax)

Criteria for establishing credit ratings

Country, industry, management & financial issues

Impact of a change in credit rating

Impact of a new debt issue on the WACC
- Impact of cost of new debt
- Impact on cost and value of existing debt
- Possible impact on cost of equity

Other impacts of a new debt issue
- Impact on ability to raise further finance
- Impact on ability to pay dividends
- Impact on ability to make investments

Duration of a bond

Calculation

Weighted average number of years over a which a bond delivers its value

Modified duration
- Duration ÷ (1 + required yield)
- Measures price sensitivity of a bond to a change in the required return
- Problem of convexity means that the impact of interest rate rises are understated and impact of falls in the interest rate is overstated

Sources of finance (1) – security token offering

What is an STO?

Issue of tokens in exchange for cryptocurrency

Mechanism for an STO

If unregulated – a 'white paper' outlines detail of the venture and provides a mechanism for payment

Advantages of an STO

Speed and ease of use

Disadvantages of an STO
- Risk to issuer of regular interference (if tokens are deemed to be a security)
- Risk of money laundering
- Risk of value of cryptocurrency falling

Sources of finance (2) – Islamic finance
- Restrictions over type of business activity
- Prohibition on the payment of interest

Products based on equity participation
- Mudaraba
- Musharaba (joint venture)
- Sukuk bonds (tradeable)

Products based on investment financing
- Murabaha (trade credit)
- Ijara (leasing)
- Salam (commodity sold for future delivery)
- Istisna (instalment payments)

Knowledge diagnostic

1. Credit ratings

Determined by country, industry, management and financing factors.

2. Impact of worsening credit ratings

Worsening credit ratings will increase the cost of debt on new and existing debt (will also affect the value of existing debt).

3. Duration of a bond

This shows the period of time over which a bond delivers its value. The higher duration is, the greater the risk to the investor.

4. Modified duration

This shows the impact of a 1% change in interest rates on bond value.

5. Types of token or coin

Tokens can be investment, asset or utility tokens.

6. Islamic finance

Share risk and return between the entrepreneur and the finance provider.

Further study guidance

Question practice

Now try the following from the Further question practice bank (available in the digital edition of the workbook):

Q11 Levante (a past exam question from 2011)

Q12 AWP Co

Further reading

There is a Technical Article available on ACCA's website, called 'Aspects of Islamic finance' which has been written by a member of the AFM examining team.

Another useful Technical Article available on ACCA's website is called 'Bond valuation and bond yields', again this has been written by a member of the AFM examining team.

We recommend that you read these articles as part of your preparation for the AFM exam.

Activity answers

Activity 1: Yield curve

If a government bond with a coupon rate of 4.5% and **three years** to maturity is trading at $97.4, then we can estimate the required yield in Year 3 as:

$97.4 = $4.5\% \times (1 + r_1)^{-1} + $4.5 \times (1 + r_2)^{-2} + $104.5 \times (1 + r_3)^{-3}$

We know that the required yield for cash flows in one year is 4.5% from the earlier illustration, and in Year 2 is 5% so this becomes:

$$\$97.4 = \$4.31 + \$4.08 + \$104.5 \times (1 + r_3)^{-3}$$
$$\text{So } (\$97.4 - 4.31 - \$4.08)/\$104.5 = (1 + r_3)^{-3}$$
$$\text{So } 0.852 = (1 + r_3)^{-3}$$
$$\text{Given that } (1 + r)^{-3} = 1/(1 + r)^3 \text{ then: } 1/0.852 = (1 + r_3)^3$$
$$\text{Then } (1 + r_3) = \sqrt[3]{1.174} = 1.055$$
$$\text{So } r_3 = 0.055 \text{ or } 5.5\%.$$

This is the required yield in Year 3.

Activity 2: Impact of a change in credit rating

(1) **Tetron's current WACC**

Current required return on debt =	4.4% + 0.10% = 4.5% (pre-tax)
Current WACC =	(90/100) 8% + (10/100) 4.5% (1 - 0.2) = 7.56%

$$\text{WACC} = \left(\frac{V_e}{V_e + V_d}\right) K_e + \left(\frac{V_d}{V_e + V_d}\right) K_d (1 - T)$$

(2) **New required yield on debt at a credit rating of A**

Current debt finance (1 year to maturity)	4.4 + 0.6 = 5.0% pre-tax
New debt finance (3 years to maturity)	5.5 + 0.75 = 6.25% pre-tax

(3) **New market value of debt**

Current debt finance (one year to maturity) Repays $10m + $0.45 = $10.45m in 1 year	Time $m df **5%** Present value	1 10.45 **0.952** $9.95m
New debt finance (three years to maturity)	$5 million as given	

(4) **Revised WACC**

Revised WACC =	(90/104.95) 8% + (9.95/104.95) 5% (1 - 0.2) + (5/104.95) 6.25% (1 - 0.2) = 6.86 + 0.38 + 0.24 = 7.48%

BPP LEARNING MEDIA

Working

Impact of new debt issue

Ve = $90 million

Existing debt = $9.95 million costing 5% pre-tax

New debt = $5 million costing 6.25%

Total capital = $90m + $9.95m + $5m = $104.95m

Despite the change in credit rating the impact of the new debt issue, in this example, is to decrease the WACC.

Activity 3: Islamic finance

With a Mudaraba contract, any profits would be shared with the bank according to a pre-agreed arrangement when the contract is constructed. Losses, however, would be borne solely by the bank as the provider of the finance. The bank would not be involved in the executive decision-making process. In effect, the bank's role in the relationship would be similar to an equity holder holding a small number of shares in a large organisation.

With a Musharaka contract, the profits would still be shared according to a pre-agreed arrangement similar to a Mudaraba contract, but losses would also be shared according to the capital or other assets and services contributed by both parties involved in the arrangement. Within a Musharaka contract, the bank can also take the role of an active partner and participate in the executive decision-making process. In effect, the role adopted by the bank would be similar to that of a venture capitalist.

A bank may prefer the Musharaka contract because it may be of the opinion that it needs to be involved with the project and monitor performance closely due to the inherent risk and uncertainty of the venture, and also to ensure that the revenues, expenditure and time schedules are maintained within initially agreed parameters. In this way, it may be able to monitor and control agency related issues more effectively.

8

Valuation for acquisitions and mergers

Learning objectives

On completion of this chapter, you should be able to:

	Syllabus reference no.
Advise on the value of an organisation using its free cash flow and free cash flow to equity under alternative horizon and growth assumptions	B4(c)
Explain the role of option pricing models, such as the BSOP model, in the assessment of the value of equity, the value of debt and of default risk	B4(d)
Discuss the problem of overvaluation	C2(a)
Estimate the potential near-term and continuing growth levels of a corporation's earnings using both internal and external measures	C2(b)
Discuss, assess and advise on the value created from an acquisition or merger of both quoted and unquoted entities (taking into account the changes in the risk profile of the acquirer and target entities) using models such as: • 'Book value-plus' models • Market-based models • Cash flow models, including free cash	C2(c)
Apply appropriate models eg risk adjusted cost of capital, APV and changing P/E multipliers resulting from the acquisition or merger	C2(d)
Demonstrate **an understanding** of the procedure for valuing high growth start-ups	C2(e)

Exam context

This chapter mainly focuses on Section C of the syllabus 'acquisitions and mergers', although it also covers some remaining areas of syllabus Section B.

The techniques that are covered in this chapter are used to ensure that the decision to **invest** by acquisition is carefully analysed and results in an outcome that benefits shareholders. Valuation questions are common in both Section A and Section B of the AFM exam.

Valuation techniques will require you to make estimates/assumptions. In the exam, it is accepted that a business does not have a single 'precise' valuation, and markers will reward a variety of **logical, justified approaches,** so there is **often not a 'single' correct answer**.

Chapter overview

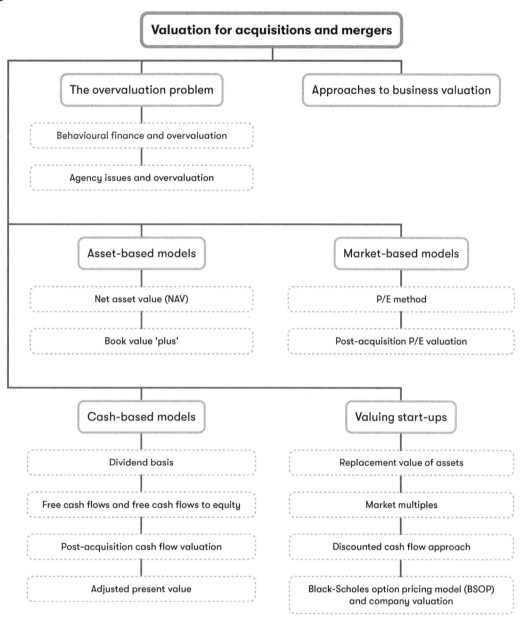

1 The overvaluation problem

When a company acquires a target company, it will pay a 'bid premium' above the target's current market value. Where this premium is **excessive**, this creates a problem of **overvaluation**.

Many studies suggest that the **target company** shareholders **enjoy the benefit** of the 'bid premium' but the shareholders **of the acquirer** often do not benefit as a result of **overvaluation**.

1.1 Behavioural finance and overvaluation

A number of **behavioural** factors may explain why acquisitions are often overvalued.

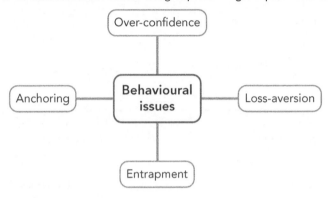

1.1.1 Overconfidence and confirmation bias

People tend to overestimate their capabilities. If this is happening at board level it may lead **the board to overestimate their ability to turn around a firm** and to produce higher returns than its previous management.

Overconfidence can result from managers paying more attention to evidence supporting the logic of an acquisition than they will to evidence that questions this logic. This is **confirmation bias**.

1.1.2 Loss aversion

Many takeover bids are contested, ie more than one company is involved in bidding for a firm. In this situation there is a likelihood that the bid price will be pushed to excessively high levels. This can be explained in psychological terms in that there is a stronger desire to possess something because there is a threat of it being taken away from you. This is sometimes called **loss aversion**.

1.1.3 Entrapment

Where a strategy is failing, managers may become unwilling to move away from it because of their personal commitment to it (for example, it may have been their idea). This **entrapment** may mean that they commit even more funds (eg buying another company even if this means paying a price that is excessive) in an increasingly desperate attempt to turn around failing businesses.

Entrapment can help to explain excessive prices being paid to acquire companies that are **seen as crucial** to helping to turn around a failing strategy.

1.1.4 Anchoring

If valuing an unlisted company, the bidder may be strongly influenced by that company's initial **asking price**, ie this **becomes a (biased) reference point** for the valuation (however irrational it is).

1.2 Agency issues and overvaluation

Managers may follow their own self-interest, instead of focusing on shareholders. For example, managers may look to make large acquisitions (and may pay too much for them) primarily to reduce the vulnerability of their company to being taken-over (Ryan 2007).

2 Approaches to business valuation

Overvaluation may also arise due to a miscalculation of the value of an acquisition.

To ensure that a company does not overpay for a target, it is important that careful analysis is undertaken to establish a realistic valuation for a potential acquisition.

There are **three basic approaches** to valuation:

- **Asset-based models**

These models attempt to value the assets that are being acquired as a result of the acquisition.

- **Market-based models**

These models use market data to value the acquisition.

- **Cash-based models**

These models are based on a discounted value of the future cash flows relating to an acquisition.

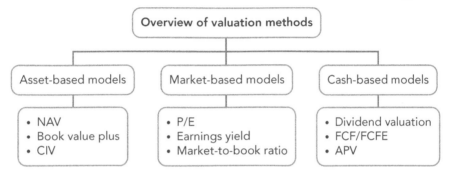

An acquisition may potentially have an impact on both the **financial and the business risk** of the acquirer. This impact needs to be incorporated into the analysis of the valuation of an acquisition.

> **PER alert**
>
> One of the performance objectives in your PER is to 'select investment or merger or acquisition opportunities using appropriate appraisal techniques'.

3 Asset–based models

3.1 Net asset value (NAV)

Asset-based methods use the **statement of financial position** as the starting point in the valuation process.

This values a target company by comparing its assets to its liabilities, which gives an estimate of the funds that would be available to the target's shareholders if it entered voluntary liquidation. For an unquoted company, this value would need to **at least** be matched by a bidder, and this value is often used as a **starting point** for negotiating the acquisition price.

Activity 1: Asset valuation

Transit Co's latest statement of financial position is shown below:

	$m
Non-current assets	1,350
Current assets	1,030
Total assets	**2,380**
Share capital	240
Retained earnings	860
Total equity	**1,100**
Current liabilities	700
Non-current liabilities	580
Total liabilities	**1,280**
Total equity plus liabilities	**2,380**

Required

Which of the following is the correct asset valuation of Transit Co's equity?

O $2,380 million

O $1,680 million

O $1,100 million

O $240 million

Solution

The target company's net asset value may need to be adjusted if an exam questions tells you that the **realisable value** of assets differs from their book value.

3.1.1 Drawbacks of NAV approach

This technique is sometimes used to estimate a minimum **value for an unquoted company that is in financial difficulties or is difficult to sell** (if a company is **listed** then its minimum value is its current **share price**).

This technique ignores:

- The value of future profits
- The value of intangibles

However, both of these drawbacks can be addressed.

3.2 Book value 'plus'

Because this valuation of a target company ignores the profit of the target company a **premium** is normally negotiated, based either on a multiple of the firm's profits or an **estimated value of the company's intangible assets**. This is called a **'book value plus'** model.

3.2.1 Intangible assets

In many firms **intangible assets** are of enormous value; a company's knowledge base, its network of contacts with suppliers and customers, and the trust associated with its brand name are often significant sources of value.

Calculated Intangible Value (CIV) assesses whether a company is achieving an above-average return on its tangible assets. This figure is then used in determining the present value attributable to intangible assets.

CIV involves the following steps:

(a) Estimate the profit that would be **expected** from an entity's tangible asset base using an **industry average** expected return.

(b) Calculate the present value of any *excess* profits that have been made in the recent past, using the **WACC** as the discount factor.

Activity 2: (continuation of Activity 1) CIV

Transit Co's average pre-tax earnings for the last three years has been $400 million, and its average year end asset base for the last three years has been $2,000 million.

The average (pre-tax) return on tangible assets in this sector has been 12%, corporate income tax is 25% and Transit Co's weighted average cost of capital is estimated to be 10%.

Required

Using CIV, calculate the value of Transit Co's intangible assets:

1 Estimate the profit that would be **expected** from an entity's tangible asset base using an **industry average** expected return.

2 Calculate the present value of any *excess* profits that have been made in the recent past, using the **WACC** as the discount factor.

Solution

3.2.2 Drawbacks of CIV approach

(a) It uses the **average industry return** on assets as a basis for computing excess returns; the industry average may be distorted by extreme values.

(b) CIV assumes that **past profitability** is a sound basis for evaluating the **current value** of intangibles – this will not be true if, for example, a brand has recently been weakened by a corporate scandal or changes in legislation.

(c) CIV also assumes that there will be **no growth** in value of the excess profits being created by intangible assets.

Essential reading

See Chapter 8 Section 1 of the Essential reading, which provides some further thoughts on asset-based approaches.

The Essential reading is available as an Appendix of the digital edition of the Workbook.

4 Market-based models

A sensible starting point for valuing a listed company is the **market value** of its shares.

If the stock market is **efficient** the market price will reflect the market's assessment of the company's future cash flows and risk (both business risk and financial risk).

It follows that the relationship between a company's share price and its earnings figure, ie its **P/E ratio**, also indicates the market's assessment of a company or a sector's future cash flows and risk (both business and financial risk).

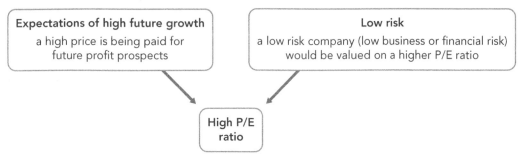

Expectations of high future growth	Low risk
a high price is being paid for future profit prospects	a low risk company (low business or financial risk) would be valued on a higher P/E ratio

↓ High P/E ratio ↓

4.1 P/E method

Market-based value = earnings of target × appropriate P/E ratio

Shows the **current profitability** of the company	Reflects the **growth prospects/risk** of a company

Activity 3: Technique demonstration

Groady plc wants to acquire an Italian company, Bergerbo S.p.A., a company in the **same industry**.

BERGERBO S.P.A. SUMMARISED STATEMENT OF PROFIT OR LOSS FOR THE YEAR ENDING 31 DECEMBER 20X3

	€m
PBIT	9.8
Interest expense	2.3
Taxable profit	7.5
Taxation (25%)	1.9
Profit after tax	5.6
Dividend	5.0
Retained earnings	0.6

Bergerbo's P/E ratio is 16.0

Required

If Groady's P/E is currently 21.2 and it anticipates turning Bergerbo around so that it shares Groady's growth prospects, calculate the value of Bergerbo in €m.

Solution

4.1.1 Problems with this method

Choice of which P/E ratio to use

Care has to be taken that the P/E ratio used reflects the **business and financial risk (ie capital structure) of the company that is being valued**. This is quite difficult to achieve in practice.

Also, the P/E ratio will normally be **reduced** if the company that is being valued is **unlisted**. Listed companies have a higher value, mainly due to the greater ease in selling shares in a listed company. The P/E ratio of an unlisted company's shares will be 30%–50% lower compared to the P/E ratio of a similar public company.

Care has to be taken that the P/E ratio used reflects the **business and financial risk (ie capital structure) of the company that is being valued**. This is quite difficult to achieve in practice.

Earnings calculation

The earnings of the target company may need to be adjusted if it includes one-off items that will tend not to recur, or if it is affected by directors' salaries which might be adjusted after a takeover.

Historic earnings will not reflect the potential future synergies that may arise from an acquisition. Earnings may need to be adjusted to reflect such synergies.

Finally, the latest earnings figures might have been manipulated upwards by the target company if it has been looking to be bought by another company.

Stock market efficiency

Behavioural finance (see Section 1) suggests that stock market prices may not be efficient because they are affected by psychological factors, so P/E ratios may be distorted by swings in market sentiment.

Using your judgement

In practice, using the P/E ratio approach may require you to **make a number of judgements** concerning the growth prospects and risk of the company that is being valued and therefore which P/E ratio is appropriate to use. There may be arguments for increasing the P/E ratio to reflect expectations of higher growth or lower risk as a result of an acquisition (or for decreasing the P/E ratio to reflect expectations of lower growth or higher risk as a result of an acquisition). In the exam you should make and **state your assumptions clearly**, and **you should not worry about coming up with a precise valuation** because, in reality, valuations **are not a precise science** and are affected by bargaining skills, psychological factors and financial pressures.

4.2 Post-acquisition P/E valuation

Where an acquisition affects the growth prospects of the **bidding company** too, the P/E ratio of the **bidding company** will change. In this case, the P/E approach needs to be adapted.

4.2.1 Maximum to pay for an acquisition

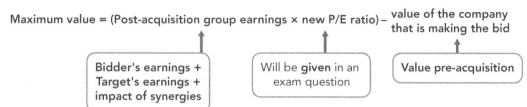

Maximum value = (Post-acquisition group earnings × new P/E ratio) − value of the company that is making the bid

Bidder's earnings + Target's earnings + impact of synergies

Will be **given** in an exam question

Value pre-acquisition

The post-acquisition value of the group can be compared to the pre-acquisition value of the bidding company (ie the acquirer); **the difference gives the maximum that the company should pay for the acquisition.**

Activity 4: Post-acquisition values

Macleanstein Inc is considering making a bid for 100% of Thomasina Inc's equity capital. Thomasina has a P/E ratio of 14 and earnings of $500 million.

It is expected that $150 million in annual synergy savings will be made as a result of the takeover and the P/E ratio of the combined company is estimated to be 16.

Macleanstein currently has a P/E ratio of 17 and earnings of $750 million.

Required

1   What is the maximum amount that Macleanstein should pay for Thomasina?

2   What is the minimum bid that Thomasina's shareholders should be prepared to accept?

Solution

4.2.2 Calculation of value added by the acquisition

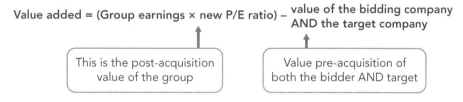

Value added = (Group earnings × new P/E ratio) − value of the bidding company AND the target company

This is the post-acquisition value of the group

Value pre-acquisition of both the bidder AND target

Post-acquisition values

Using the previous activity:

Current value of Macleanstein = $750m × 17 = $12,750m

Current value of Thomasina = $500m × 14 = $7,000m

Group post-acquisition earnings = $750m + $500m + $150m = $1,400m

Value added = ($1,400m × 16) - ($12,750m + $7,000m) = **$2,650m**

Essential reading

See Chapter 8 Section 2 of the Essential reading, which provides background on other, less important, earnings based methods.

The Essential reading is available as an Appendix of the digital edition of the Workbook.

5 Cash-based models

The final set of valuation models are based on the concept of valuing a company using its forecast cash flows discounted at a rate that reflects that company's business and financial risk. These models are often seen as the most elegant and theoretically sound methods of business valuation and can be adapted to deal with acquisitions that change financial or business risk.

5.1 Dividend basis

The simplest cash flow valuation model is the **dividend valuation model (DVM)**. This is based on the theory that an equilibrium price for any share is the **future expected stream of income** from the share **discounted** at a suitable cost of capital.

Formula provided

$$\text{Value per share} = P_0 = \frac{d_0(1 + g)}{r_e - g}$$

d_0 = current dividend

r_e = cost of equity **of the target**

g = annual dividend growth rate

The formula calculates the value of a share as the present value of a **constantly growing future dividend**. The anticipated dividends are based on existing management policies, so this technique is most relevant to **minority shareholders** (who are not able to change these policies).

5.1.1 Estimating dividend growth

There are two methods for estimating annual dividend growth:

- Analysing historic dividend growth
- Analysing re-investment levels

You will have seen these methods before in the Financial Management exam, they are briefly recapped in the following illustrations.

Formula provided

g = br

b = balance of earnings reinvested

r = return on investment

 Illustration 1: Historic dividend growth

AB Co has just paid a dividend of 40p per share; this has grown from 30p four years ago.

Required

What is the estimated rate of dividend growth?

Solution

$30 \times (1 + g)^4 = 40$

$30 \times (1 + g)^4 = 40/30 = 1.3333$

$30 \times 1 + g = $ 4th root of $1.3333 = 1.0746$

$g = 0.0746$ or 7.46%

 Illustration 2: Reinvestment levels

RS Co has just paid a dividend per share of 30p. This was 60% of earnings per share. Estimated return on equity = 20%.

Required

What is the estimated rate of dividend growth?

Solution

b = balance of earnings reinvested

$b = 1 - 0.6 = 0.4$

$r = 0.2$

$g = 0.4 \times 0.2 = 0.08$ or 8%

5.1.2 Other issues

When using the dividend valuation model to value an **unlisted company** it may be necessary to use the **beta of a similar listed company** to help to calculate a K_e. This beta will need to be ungeared and then regeared to reflect differences in gearing (see Chapter 6).

5.1.3 Drawbacks

(a) It is difficult to estimate future dividend growth.

(b) It creates zero values for zero dividend companies and negative values for high growth companies (if g is greater than r_e).

(c) It is inaccurate to assume that growth will be constant.

5.1.4 Non-constant growth

The DVM model can be adapted to value dividends that are forecast to go through **two phases**:

Phase 1 (eg next two years)	Phase 2 (eg Year 3 onwards)
Growth is forecast at an unusually high (or low) rate	Growth returns to a constant rate
Use a normal NPV approach to calculate the present value of the dividends in this phase.	(a) Use the formula to assess the NPV of the constant growth phase; however the time periods need to be adapted eg: $$P_0 = \frac{d_0(1 + g)}{r_e - g}$$ is adapted to $$P_2 = \frac{d_2(1 + g)}{r_e - g}$$ (b) Then adjust the value given above by discounting back to a present value (here using a T2 discount rate).

Activity 5: Non-constant growth

Hitman Co's latest dividend was $5 million. It is estimated to have a cost of equity of 8%.

Required

Use the DVM to value Hitman Co, assuming 3% growth for the next three years and 2% growth after this.

Solution

Phase 1 (3% growth per year)

Time	1	2	3
Dividend $m			
DF @ 8%	0.926	0.857	0.794
PV			

Total = [   ]

Phase 2 (2% growth)

$$P_0 = \frac{d_0(1 + g)}{r_e - g} \text{ is adapted to } P_3 = \frac{d_3(1 + g)}{r_e - g}$$

P3 = [   ] / [   ] = [   ]

Then discounting back to a present value (at a Time 3 discount factor of 0.794) =

[   ] × [   ] = [   ]

Total Phase 1 + Phase 2

= [   ] + [   ] = [   ]

5.1.5 Earnings growth

Note that the techniques that have been covered for estimating dividend growth (historic method and current reinvestment method) can also be used to evaluate forecasts of a company's earnings growth.

5.2 Free cash flows and free cash flows to equity

KEY TERM

Free cash flow (FCF): The cash available for payment to investors (shareholders and debt holders), also called free cash flow to firm.

Free cash flow to equity (FCFE): The cash available for payment to shareholders, also called dividend capacity.

This method can **build in the extra cash flows** (synergies) resulting from a change in management control, and **when** the synergies are expected to be received. There are two approaches which can be used.

Free cash flow (FCF) method	Free cash flow to equity (FCFE) method
PBIT	PBIT
less	less
tax, investment in assets	**interest,** tax, debt repayment, investment in assets
plus	plus
depreciation, any new capital raised	depreciation, any new capital raised

Approach 1	Approach 2
(a) Identify the **FCF** of the target company **(before interest)**	(a) Identify the **FCFE** of the target company **(after interest)**
(b) Discount at **WACC**	(b) Discount at an appropriate cost of equity, K_e.
(c) This calculates the NPV of the cash flows **before** allowing for interest payments	(c) This calculates the NPV of the **equity**
(d) **Subtract the value of debt from Step 3 to obtain the value of the equity.**	

Activity 6: FCF and FCFE method

Wmart Co plans to make a bid for the entire share capital of Ada Co, a company in **the same industry**. It is expected that a bid of $75 million for the entire share capital of Ada Co will be successful. The acquisition will generate the following **after-tax operating** cash flows (ie pre-interest) over the next few years by:

Year	1	2	3	4 onwards
$m	5.6	7.4	8.3	12.1

Both companies have similar gearing levels of 16.7% (debt as a % of total finance). Ada Co has a $15 million bank loan paying a fixed rate of 5.75%. Wmart Co has an equity beta of 2.178, the risk-free rate is 5.75% and the market rate is 10%.

Corporation tax is at 30%.

Required

Assess whether the acquisition will enhance shareholder wealth in Wmart Co. (Use both Approach 1 and Approach 2.)

Solution

5.3 Post-acquisition cash flow valuation

Where an acquisition affects the growth prospects or risk of the **bidding company** too, this approach needs to be adapted.

Where an acquisition alters the bidding firm's **business risk** there is an impact on the **existing value** of the acquirer as a result of the change in risk, so the following approach needs to be used.

Step 1 Calculate the asset beta of both companies

Step 2 Calculate the average asset beta for the group post-acquisition

Step 3 Regear the beta to reflect the gearing of the group post-acquisition

Step 4 Estimate the post-acquisition value of the group's equity using a cash flow valuation approach

Step 5 Subtract the existing value of the bidder to determine the maximum value to pay for the target

Step 6 Subtract the pre-acquisition value of both companies to calculate the value created by the acquisition (ie the value of the synergies

Activity 7: Technique demonstration

Salsa Co plans to make a bid for the entire share capital of Enco Co, a company in a **different industry**. It is expected that a bid of £80 million for the entire share capital of Enco Co will be successful. This will be entirely financed by new debt at 6.8%.

After the acquisition the post-tax operating cash flows of Salsa's existing business will be:

Time	1	2	3	4	5
£m	24.12	25.57	27.10	28.72	30.45

After the acquisition the post-tax operating cash flows of Enco's existing business will be:

Time	1	2	3	4	5
£m	6.06	6.30	6.56	6.84	7.13

After the acquisition, £6.5 million of land will be sold and there will be synergies of £5 million post-tax p.a. Before the acquisition, Salsa had £45 million of debt finance (costing 5.6% pre-tax) and 40 million shares worth £9 each and an equity beta of 1.19.

As a consequence of the acquisition, the credit rating of Salsa will fall and the interest paid on **existing** debt will rise by 1.2% to 6.8%.

Enco has an equity beta of 2.2, its existing share price is £1 and it has 62.4 million shares in issue; it also has £5 million of existing debt that would be taken over by Salsa Co. The risk-free rate is 4.5% and the market rate is 8%; corporation tax is 30%.

Required

Evaluate the impact on shareholder wealth, assuming that cash flows after Year 5 will grow at 2% p.a. (assume that the beta of debt is zero).

Solution

Important Note

In fact, this approach is slightly inaccurate because the weightings used in Step 3 do not reflect the value of the company post-acquisition; a computer model can solve this, so this is not something you will have to deal with in the exam.

5.4 Adjusted present value

Adjusted present value (APV) has been **covered numerically in Chapter 6**.

APV can also be used to **value acquisitions that change the gearing of the bidding company**. One reason that this could happen is that the acquisition is a bid that is financed by **borrowing** (see Chapter 10).

This technique values the enterprise (ie debt plus equity) and the amount of debt needs to be subtracted in order to value the equity in the target company.

Step 1   Base case

Calculate the present value of the target's future cash flows **as if ungeared** (at an **ungeared cost of equity**)

Step 2   Financing effects

Add the PV of the **tax saved** as a result of the **debt used** (using all of the debt involved in the acquisition ie the debt of the target company plus any debt used to buy the target company)

Step 3   Issue costs

Subtract the **cost of issuing new finance**

6 Valuing start-ups

Start-ups companies are often characterised by:

(a) Having no track record

(b) Ongoing losses due to high set-up costs and little if any revenue

(c) Facing unknown market acceptance, unknown product demand and growth prospects

Given the lack of profitability, and the difficulties in forecasting growth prospects, valuation of start-ups is difficult. There are a number of possible approaches.

6.1 Replacement value of assets

Value could be assessed by estimating how much it would cost for an investor to create the assets of the company from scratch; this could also consider the cost of R&D spending, patent protection etc. Although this would not capture the value of a firm's intangible assets (ie brand value, intellectual capital), there are ways of valuing intangible assets as discussed earlier.

However, such approaches would not capture the potential value resulting from the **potential future growth** of a start-up, and this is likely to represent the main part of a start-up's value.

6.2 Market multiples

It is possible to use **ratios based on acquisitions of similar companies** (in terms of their growth potential and stage of development) to create a valuation.

For example, **the ratio of amount paid compared to sales** in recent acquisitions could be used to value a start-up.

If a start-up has reached the stage when it is making positive EBITDA then **the amount paid compared to EBITDA** in recent acquisitions can help to place a value on a start-up.

However, similar acquisitions may be difficult to identify, which may make this approach difficult to apply.

6.3 Discounted cash flow approach

The validity of this approach will depend on the ability of the analyst to forecast future growth.

Where this is felt to be possible, **a higher discount rate** will be used to value the cash flows to reflect the higher risk associated with start-ups.

6.4 Black-Scholes option pricing model (BSOP) and company valuation

The BSOP model was introduced in Chapter 4; this can also be applied to company valuation and the assessment of default risk, although in these contexts you will **not have to perform any calculations**.

This approach is mainly useful for a start-up firm that is high risk and difficult to value using normal techniques.

The value of a firm can be thought of in these terms:

(a) If the firm fails to generate enough value to repay its loans, then its value = 0; shareholders have the **option** to let the company die at this point.

(b) If the firm does generate enough value, then the extra value over and above the debt belongs to the shareholders.

(c) In this case shareholders can pay off the debt (this is the **exercise price**) and continue in their **ownership** of the company (ie just as the exercise of a **call option** results in the ownership of an asset).

(d) BSOP can be applied because shareholders have a **call option** on the business. The protection of limited liability creates the same effect as a call option because there is an upside if the firm is successful, but shareholders lose nothing other than their initial investment if it fails.

(e) The value of a company can be calculated as the **value of a call option**.

A problem with this technique is that it is difficult to estimate the standard deviation of cash flows for a company that does not have a trading record (although it could be based on other start-up companies).

6.4.1 BSOP and default risk

The BSOP model can also be used to assess the probability of asset values falling to a level that would trigger default. This can be assessed by looking at the past levels of volatility of a firm's asset values and assessing the number of standard deviations that this fall would represent.

Within the BSOP model, $N(d_2)$ depicts the probability that the call option will be in-the-money (ie have intrinsic value for the equity holders).

If $N(d_2)$ depicts the probability that the company has not failed and the loan will not be in default, then $1 - N(d2)$ depicts the probability of default.

The probability of default is used in the BSOP model to calculate the market value of debt.

If the present value of the repayments on the debt is less than the market value, this shows the expected loss to the lender on holding the debt. If the expected loss and default risk are known then the recoverability of the debt in the event of default can be estimated.

This section is not examinable numerically.

Essential reading

Review Chapter 7 Section 1.2 of the Essential reading to recap on the relationship between expected loss, default risk and recoverability. See Chapter 8 Section 3 of the Essential reading for further thoughts on the use of the BSOP model in these contexts.

The Essential reading is available as an Appendix of the digital edition of the Workbook.

Chapter summary

```
                    ┌─────────────────────────────────────────┐
                    │   Valuation for acquisitions and mergers  │
                    └─────────────────────────────────────────┘
```

The overvaluation problem

Behavioural finance and overvaluation
- Overconfidence and confirmation bias
- Loss aversion
- Entrapment
- Anchoring

Agency issues and overvaluation
Management self-interest

Approaches to business valuation

There are three basic approaches to valuation:
- Asset-based models
  - These models attempt to value the assets that are being acquired as a result of the acquisition.
- Market-based models
  - These models use market data to value the acquisition.
- Cash-based models
  - These models are based on a discounted value of the future cash flows relating to an acquisition.

Asset-based models

Net asset value (NAV)
- Ignores futures profits
- Ignores value of intangibles

Book value 'plus'
- Multiple of profit, or
- Valuation of intangibles
- CIV values excess profits using WACC, assumes no growth

Market-based models

P/E method
- Earnings of target × P/E ratio
- P/E ratio may need adjusting
- Assumes efficient market

Post-acquisition P/E valuation
- Earnings of group × P/E ratio
- Subtract value of bidder = max price to pay; or
- Subtract value of bidder + target = value created

Cash-based models

Dividend basis
- Constant growth model
- Adapt to two phases of growth
- Most suitable for minority shareholders

Free cash flows and free cash flows to equity
- FCFE discounted at cost of equity = value of equity
- FCF discounted at WACC = value of company
- Then subtract value of debt to obtain value of equity

Post-acquisition cash flow valuation
- Cash-based equity valuation
- Subtract value of bidder = max price to pay, or
- Subtract value of bidder + target = value created
- If business risk changes: Calculate average asset beta of target and bidder and regear for post-acquisition gearing.

Adjusted present value
- Value cash flows at ungeared cost of equity
- Value tax saved on debt at required return on debt
- Adjust for issue costs

Valuing start-ups

- Start-up companies are often characterised by:
  – Having no track record
  – Ongoing losses
  – Facing unknown market acceptance/product demand/growth prospects.
- Thus, valuation of start-ups is difficult.
- There are a number of possible approaches, namely:
  - Replacement of value assets
  - Market multiples
  - Discounted cash flow approach

BSOP and company valuation

Values equity as a call option, because there is an upside if the firm is successful, but shareholders lose nothing other than their initial investment if it fails

BSOP and default risk

If $N(d_2)$ is the probability that the call option is in-the-money (ie the company has not failed), then $1 - N(d_2)$ depicts the probability of default

Knowledge diagnostic

1. Overvaluation problem

A significant problem in acquisitions, can be explained by behavioural or agency factors.

2. Calculated intangible values

This assesses the excess profits post-tax being made, and values these as a constant cash flow using the company's WACC.

3. P/E ratio

This indicates the growth potential of a company.

4. Post-acquisition valuations

This approach is useful where the acquisition has an underlying impact on the growth or risk of the **bidding company** (the acquirer).

5. Free cash flow

The cash flows available for all investors (whether equity or debt holders) ie before interest but after tax.

6. Free cash flow to equity

The cash flows available for equity investors only, ie after interest and tax.

BPP
LEARNING
MEDIA

Further study guidance

Question practice

Now try the following from the Further question practice bank (available in the digital edition of the workbook):

Q13 *Mercury Training*

Q14 *Kodiak Company*

Further reading

There is a Technical Article on behavioural finance available on ACCA's website, called 'Patterns of behaviour' which has been written by a member of the AFM examining team. This article was recommended reading in Chapter 2, but if you have not had a chance to read it then please look at it now.

Activity answers

Activity 1: Asset valuation

The correct answer is: $1,100 million

The value of the net assets is $2,380 – $1,280 = **$1,100m** (which is also the book value of equity).

Note on incorrect answers:

- $2,380 million – this is the total value of assets, ie ignores liabilities
- $1,680 million – this is total assets less current liabilities, ie ignores non-current liabilities

Activity 2: (continuation of Activity 1) CIV

CIV involves the following steps:

First, estimate the profit that would be **expected** from an entity's tangible asset base using an **industry average** expected return

12% of $2,000m = $240m

Next calculate the present value of any *excess* profits that have been made in the recent past, using the **WACC** as the discount factor.

So, Transit is making excess pre-tax profits of $400m – $240m = $160m

Post-tax this is $160 × (1 – 0.25) = $120m

$120m discounted to infinity at 10% = $120m × 1/0.1 = **$1,200m**

This is an estimated of the value of Transit Co's intangible assets.

So, the revised asset value is $1,100m (from Activity 1) + $1,200m = **$2,300m**

Activity 3: Technique demonstration

Groady's P/E ratio is higher, indicating higher growth prospects.

If Bergerbo can be turned around and will share these growth prospects, then its earnings of €5.6 million will have a total value of **€118.7 million** (5.6 × 21.2).

Activity 4: Post-acquisition values

1   **Maximum amount to be paid**

    Macleanstein must consider the synergies to be made from the combination when determining the maximum amount to pay.

    Value of Thomasina to Macleanstein = value of combined company – current value of Macleanstein

    Earnings of combined company = (500m + 750m + 150m) = $1,400m

    Current value of Macleanstein = 17 × $750m = $12,750m

    Max price = $9,650m ($1,400m × 16) – $12,750m

2   **Minimum amount that Thomasina's shareholders should accept**

    = current value of Thomasina's equity

    = 14 × $500m = $7,000m

    The final amount paid will probably fall between these two extremes.

Activity 5: Non-constant growth

Phase 1 (3% growth per year)

Time	1	2	3
Dividend $m	5.15	5.30	5.46
DF @ 8%	0.926	0.857	0.794
PV	4.77	4.54	4.34

Total = **$13.65 million**

Phase 2 (2% growth)

$$P_0 = \frac{d_0(1 + g)}{r_e - g} \text{ is adapted to } P_3 = \frac{d_3(1 + g)}{r_e - g}$$

P3 = (5.46 × 1.02)/(0.08 - 0.02) = $92.83m

Then discounting back to a present value (at a Time 3 discount factor of 0.794) =
$92.83 × 0.794 = $73.71m

Total Phase 1 + Phase 2

= $13.65m + $73.71m = $87.36m

Activity 6: FCF and FCFE method

Approach 1

Time	1	2	3	4 onwards
$m	5.6	7.4	8.3	12.1
Annuity (1/0.13)				7.692
Value **at Time 3**				93.1
@ 13%	0.885	0.783	0.693	0.693
PV	5.0	5.8	5.8	64.5
Total PV	81.1			
Less debt	(15.0)			
Value of equity	**66.1**			

This suggests that the target is not worth $75 million.

Working

K_e (using CAPM) = 5.75 + 2.178 (10 − 5.75) = 15.0%

K_d = 5.75% × 0.7 = 4.03%

WACC = (15 × **0.833**) + (**4.03** × 0.167) = 13.2% (rounded to 13%)

Approach 2

Interest p.a. = $0.6m after tax ($15m × 0.0575 × 0.7)

Time	1	2	3	4 onwards
$m after interest	5.0	6.8	7.7	11.5
Annuity (1/0.15)				6.667
Value at Time 3				76.7
K_e = 15%	0.870	0.756	0.658	0.658
PV	4.4	5.1	5.1	50.5
Value of equity	65.1			

(As in Approach 1 but small rounding difference, as 13.0% was used in A1 in instead of 13.2%)

Activity 7: Technique demonstration

(1) **Asset beta calculations assuming a debt beta of zero**

Value of Salsa = £9 × 40m = £360m pre-acquisition

Value of Enco = £1 × 62.4m = £62.4m pre-acquisition

Total = £360m + £62.4m = £422.4m

Degearing Salsa's beta: (360/(360 + 45 (1 − 0.3)) 1.19 **= 1.09**

Degearing Enco's beta: (62.4/(62.4 + 5 (1 − 0.3)) 2.2 **= 2.08**

Post-acquisition asset beta: (1.09 × 360/422.4) + (2.08 × 62.4/422.4) **= 1.24**

(2) **Regear the beta using pre-acquisition equity and debt weightings, including the £80 million of extra debt**

(ie total debt = 80 + 45 + 5 = 130)

1.24/(422.4/(422.4 + 130 × (1 − 0.3))) = 1.51

so = 4.5 + (1.51 × 3.5) = 9.79%

(3) **Post-acquisition WACC**

(9.79 × 422.4/552.4) + (6.8 × 130/552.4 × (1 − 0.3)) = 8.6%

7.49 + 1.12 = 8.6%

(4) **Post-acquisition NPV**

Time	1	2	3	4	5	After Year 5
Free cash flows	35.18	36.87	38.66	40.56	42.58	43.43
Annuity (1/(0.086 − 0.02))						15.15
Value as at time 5						657.96
df at 8.6%	0.921	0.848	0.781	0.719	0.662	0.662
NPV	32.40	31.27	30.19	29.16	28.19	435.57
Total	586.71					
Land	6.5					
Total	593.21					

Subtract debt:

Salsa debt	45
Enco debt	5
New debt (this reflects the price currently being paid for the acquisition)	80
Total debt	130

Total value of equity post-acquisition = £593.21m − £130m = **£463.21m**

(5) **Subtract value of bidder to establish the maximum value to pay**

Value of Salsa was initially £360m (40m × £9).

The maximum **extra** that could be paid for Enco = Salsa's post-acquisition value £463.21m (which includes £80m already being paid for Enco) minus £360m (Salsa's pre-acquisition value) = **£103.21m.**

So the maximum price for Enco is £103.21m + £80m = £183.21m (which is a premium of £120.81 million above Enco's current value of £62.4 million).

(6) **Subtract value of bidder and target to establish the value created**

Total value created = £463.21m post acquisition value after paying for the acquisition + £80m paid for acquisition − £360m (Salsa pre-acquisition value) − £62.4m (Enco's value pre-acquisition) = **£120.81m**

This can be analysed as follows:

Enco has benefitted by £80m - £62.4m = £17.6m

Salsa has benefitted by £463.21m - £360m = £103.21m

Acquisitions: strategic issues and regulation

Learning objectives

On completion of this chapter, you should be able to:

	Syllabus reference no.
Discuss the arguments for and against the use of acquisitions as a method of corporate expansion	C1(a)
Evaluate the corporate and **competitive nature** of a given acquisition proposal	C1(b)
Advise upon the **criteria for choosing an appropriate target** for acquisition	C1(c)
Compare the various explanations for the high failure rate for acquisitions in enhancing shareholder value – also covered in Chapter 8	C1(d)
Evaluate, from a given context, the potential for synergy separately classified as: • Revenue synergy • Cost synergy • Financial synergy	C1(e)
Evaluate the use of the **reverse takeover** as a method of acquisition and as a way of obtaining a stock market listing	C1(f)
Demonstrate an understanding of the principal factors influencing the development of the regulatory framework for mergers and acquisitions globally and, in particular, be able to compare and contrast the shareholder vs the stakeholder models of regulation	C3(a)
Identify the main regulatory issues in the context of a given offer and: • Assess whether the offer is likely to be in the shareholders' best interests • Advise the directors of a target company on the most appropriate defence if a specific offer is to be treated as hostile	C3(b)

Exam context

This chapter continues Section C of the syllabus 'acquisitions and mergers'.

The acquisition decision is not only about 'the numbers', ie the valuation process. The M in AFM stands for 'management' and this is the focus of this chapter, ie how to manage the strategic and regulatory aspects of an acquisition.

These areas are likely to be examined in conjunction with the valuation techniques covered in the previous chapter.

Chapter overview

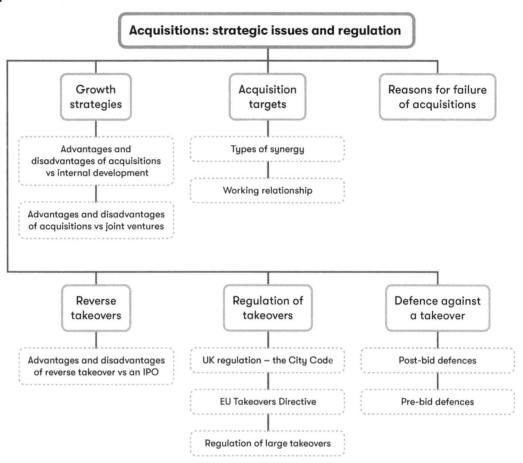

1 Growth strategies

To achieve its growth objectives, a company has three strategies that it can use, including:

- Internal development (organic growth)
- Acquisitions/mergers
- Joint ventures

Different forms of expansion have already been identified and discussed in Chapter 5.

Here we briefly recap on this focusing mainly on acquisitions; note that these are general points and may or may not be relevant to the issues facing a company in an exam question.

1.1 Advantages and disadvantages of acquisitions vs internal development

Advantages of acquisitions	Disadvantages of acquisitions
Speed An acquisition allows a company to reach a certain optimal level of production much quicker than through organic growth.	**Acquisition premium** When a company acquires another company, it normally pays a premium over its present market value. Too large a premium may render the acquisition unprofitable. However, this may be offset by a takeover target being undervalued.
Benefit of synergies An acquisition may create synergies (extra cash flows). These are discussed later.	**Lack of control over value chain** Assets or staff may prove to be lower quality than expected.
Acquisition of intangible assets A firm through an acquisition will acquire not only tangible assets but also intangible assets, such as brand recognition, reputation, customer loyalty and intellectual property, which are more difficult to achieve with organic growth.	**Integration problems** Many acquisitions are beset with problems of integration, as each company has its own culture, history and ways of operating, and there may exist aspects that have been kept hidden from outsiders. These are discussed later.

1.2 Advantages and disadvantages of acquisitions vs joint ventures

Advantages of acquisitions	Disadvantages of acquisitions
Reliability Joint venture partners may prove to be unreliable or vulnerable to take-over by a rival.	**Cost and risk** Acquisitions will involve a higher capital outlay and will expose a company to higher risk as a result.
Managerial autonomy Decision making may be restricted by the need to take account of the views of all the joint venture partners. There may be problems in agreeing on partners' percentage ownership, transfer prices etc.	**Access to overseas markets** When a company wants to expand its operations in an overseas market, a joint venture may be the only option of breaking into the overseas market.

Essential reading

See Chapter 9 Section 1 of the Essential reading for further discussion of types of acquisitions.

The Essential reading is available as an Appendix of the digital edition of the Workbook.

2 Acquisition targets

A company's strategic planning should give a focus for selecting an acquisition target.

The strategic plan might be to diversify, or to find new geographical markets, or to find firms that have new skills/products/key technology, or simply to identify firms that are poorly managed and to turn them around and sell them on at a higher price.

The criteria that should be used to assess whether a target is appropriate will **depend on the motive** for the acquisition.

For example, if the strategic plan is to acquire and turn around companies that are undervalued then the key criteria will be whether a target firm's share price is below the estimated value of the company **when acquired** – which is true of companies which have assets that are not exploited.

Having identified the general type of target, two areas of particular importance are:

(a) Are there **potential synergies** with the target (covered in Section 2.1)?

(b) Is there a likelihood of a **good working relationship** with the target (covered in Section 2.2)?

> **Synergies:** Extra benefits resulting from an acquisition either from higher cash inflows and/or lower risk.

2.1 Types of synergy

> **Revenue synergy:** Higher revenues may be due to sharing customer contacts and distribution networks or increased market power.
>
> **Cost synergy:** This may result from being able to negotiate better terms from suppliers, sharing production facilities or sharing Head Office functions.
>
> **Financial synergy:** Occurs where combining two companies results in improvements to their financial activities.

Examples of financial synergy include:

- A reduction in **risk** due to diversification (this assumes shareholders are not already well diversified)
- A reduction in the **tax** paid by two firms combined (losses in one firm reduce the tax paid by the other)
- The negotiation of **better rates of interest** with a bank due to higher bargaining power
- When a firm with excess **cash** acquires a firm with promising projects but with insufficient capital to finance them

2.2 Working relationship

Possible issues that impede a good working relationship between the acquired company and its new owner include language, culture and strategic values. These issues should be examined as part of a **due diligence** investigation prior to a takeover being finalised.

2.2.1 Due diligence

Prior to takeover bid, investigations should be undertaken to assess the target. Three types are common:

- **Legal due diligence** – checks for any legal concerns, for example any pending litigation and are there concerns about the costs of complying with the local regulatory environment.
- **Financial due diligence** – focuses on verifying the financial information provided (eg updated financial forecasts).
- **Commercial due diligence** – considers, for example, an assessment of competitors and a fuller analysis of the assumptions that lie behind the business plan.

3 Reasons for failure of acquisitions

Overvaluation has been discussed in the previous chapter. Other potential reasons for the failure of acquisitions are discussed here.

Risk	Explanation
Clash of cultures	Especially if the two firms follow different business strategies
Uncertainty among staff	Lay-offs expected, the best staff often leave
Uncertainty among customers	Customers fear post-acquisition problems and sales fall
Unanticipated problems	Information systems may be more difficult to integrate than expected, assets or staff may prove to be lower quality than expected
Paying too high a price for the target	Managers' desire to grow may stem less from a desire to benefit shareholders and more from a desire to empire-build or to make the company less of a takeover target; so they may overpay to acquire the target

To minimise these risks a firm should have a **clear post-integration strategy**. This should include:

(a) **C**ontrol of key factors – eg new capex approval centralised

(b) **R**eporting relationships – appoint new management and establish reporting lines quickly

(c) **O**bjectives and plans – to reassure staff and customers

(d) **O**rganisation structure – integrating business processes to maximise synergies

(e) **P**osition audit of the acquired company – build understanding of the issues faced by the target via regular online employee surveys and strategy discussion forums with front line staff and managers.

> **PER alert**
>
> One of the performance objectives in your PER is to 'review the financial and strategic consequences of an investment decision'. This chapter evaluates mergers and acquisitions as a method of corporate expansion and also looks at the potential corporate consequences of such activity. This information will be invaluable in practice, as it gives you an idea of the issues that might arise when considering the viability of mergers and acquisitions.

4 Reverse takeovers

> **Reverse takeover:** A situation where a smaller quoted company (S Co) takes over a larger unquoted company (L Co) by a share-for-share exchange.

To acquire L Co, a large number of S Co shares will have to be issued to L Co's shareholders. This will mean that **L Co will hold the majority of shares and will therefore have control of the company**.

The company will then often be renamed, and it is normal for the larger company (L Co) to impose its own name on the new entity.

Eddie Stobart

In 2007, Eddie Stobart, a well-known UK road haulage company, used a reverse takeover **to obtain a listing on the London Stock Exchange**. This deal combined Eddie Stobart's road transport, warehouse and rail freight operations with Westbury (a property and logistics group).

Eddie Stobart's owners, William Stobart and Andrew Tinkler, were appointed chief executive and chief operating officer of the new company. They owned 28.5% of the new company following the merger.

The merged group was renamed **Stobart** and took up Westbury's share listing.

4.1 Advantages and disadvantages of a reverse takeover vs an IPO

A reverse takeover is a route to a company obtaining a stock market listing. Compared to an initial public offering (IPO), a reverse takeover has a number of potential advantages and disadvantages:

Advantages of reverse takeovers	Disadvantages of reverse takeovers
Speed An IPO typically takes between one and two years. By contrast, a reverse takeover can be completed in a matter of months.	**Risk** There is the risk that the listed company being used to facilitate a reverse takeover may have some liabilities that are not clear from its financial statements.
Cost Unlike an IPO, a reverse takeover will not incur advertising and underwriting costs. In addition, a reverse takeover results in two companies combining together, with the possibility of **synergies** (see earlier) resulting from this combination.	**Lack of expertise** Running a listed company requires an understanding of the regulatory procedures required to comply with stock market rules. There is the risk that the unlisted company that is engineering the reverse takeover does not have a full understanding of these requirements.
Availability In a downturn, it may be difficult to stimulate investor appetite for an IPO. This is not an issue for a reverse takeover.	**Share price decrease** If the shareholders in the listed company sell their shares after the reverse takeover then this could lead to a sharp drop in the share price.

5 Regulation of takeovers

Takeover regulation in the UK (and the US) is based on a **market-based or shareholder-based model** and is designed to protect **a wide and dispersed shareholder base**.

In the UK and the US companies normally have wide share ownership so the emphasis is on agency problems and the protection of the widely distributed shareholder base.

In Europe most large companies are **not** listed on a stock market and are often **dominated by a single shareholder** with more than 25% of the shares (often a corporate investor or the founding family). Banks are powerful shareholders and generally have a seat on the boards of large companies.

Regulations in Europe have been developed to control the power of these powerful stakeholder groups, which is sometimes referred to as a **stakeholder-based system**.

European regulations on takeovers have generally in the past relied on legal regulations that seek to **protect a broader group of stakeholders**, such as creditors, employees and the wider national interest.

5.1 UK regulation – the City Code

This is a voluntary code that aims to protect the interests of shareholders during the bid process. Although it is voluntary, any listed company not complying may have its membership of the London Stock Exchange suspended. **The details** of this code do not have to be memorised, but awareness of its existence and purpose is examinable.

Here are a few of the key rules in the UK's City Code (for full details see www.thetakeoverpanel.org.uk).

(a) **Rules 2.2, 2.4, 2.6.** Any companies that are identified as potential bidders have a 28-day period within which they must either announce a firm intention to bid or state that they do not intend to make a bid (in which case they cannot make another bid for a six-month period without the consent of the board of the target company).

(b) **Rule 2.5.** Where a bid involves an element of cash, the bidding company must obtain confirmation by a third party that it can obtain these resources.

(c) **Rule 3.** The board of an offeree company must obtain competent independent advice on any offer and the substance of such advice must be made known to its shareholders. If the board disagrees with the advice this must be explained to shareholders.

(d) **Rule 9.** An offer must be made for all other shares if the % shareholding rises above **30%**, at not less than the highest price paid by the bidding company in last year.

(e) **Rule 31.** After a formal offer there is a 14-day deadline for the defence document to be published, and a 46-day deadline for the offer to be improved and finalised. Offers are normally conditional on more than 50% of the shares being secured.

(f) **Rule 35.** If a bid fails then the bidder cannot make another bid for another 12 months.

Activity 1: Homework exercise

What is the purpose of the types of regulations listed above?

Solution

5.2 EU Takeovers Directive

The Takeovers Directive was introduced by the EU in 2006 in order to achieve harmonisation and convergence of the shareholder-based and stakeholder systems. In terms of approach, it has mainly led to the **convergence** of the **European system** and the **UK and US** one, by adopting many of the elements of the **City Code**. Its key points included:

(a) **The mandatory bid rule**

The aim of this rule is to protect minority shareholders by providing them with the opportunity to exit the company at a fair price once the bidder has accumulated a certain percentage of the shares. In the UK, this threshold is specified by the City Code for Takeovers and Mergers and is at 30%.

The mandatory bid rule is based on the grounds that once the bidder obtains control it may exploit its position at the expense of minority shareholders. This is why the mandatory bid rule normally also specifies the price that is to be paid for the shares.

The bidder is normally required to offer to the remaining shareholders a price not lower than the highest price for the shares already acquired during a specified period prior to the bid.

(b) **The principle of equal treatment**

In general terms, the principle of equal treatment requires the bidder to offer to minority shareholders the same terms as those offered to earlier shareholders from whom the controlling block was acquired.

(c) **Squeeze-out rights**

Squeeze-out rights give the bidder who has acquired a specific percentage of the equity (usually 90%) the right to force minority shareholders to sell their shares.

The rule enables the bidder to acquire 100% of the equity once the threshold percentage has been reached and eliminates potential problems that could be caused by minority shareholders.

However, in two key areas the original wording of the European code was **significantly diluted in the final draft:**

(a) **Board neutrality and anti-takeover measures (Article 9)**

Seeking to address the agency issue where management may be tempted to act in their own interests at the expense of the interests of the shareholders, it was originally proposed that the board would not be permitted to carry out post-bid aggressive defensive tactics (such as selling the company's main assets, known as a 'crown jewels' defence, or entering into special arrangements giving rights to existing shareholders to buy shares at a low price, known as poison pill defence), without the prior authority of the shareholders.

However, this has become an **optional provision** for member countries – because there is the argument that the shareholders may have limited experience so managers are better placed to act in the shareholders' best interest.

(b) **The break-through rule (Article 11)**

The effect of the break-through rule is to enable a bidder with 75% of the capital carrying voting rights to break through the company's multiple voting rights and exercise control as if one-share-one-vote existed.

Again, this has become an **optional provision** for member countries.

5.3 Regulation of large takeovers

It is likely that any acquisition that is likely to lead to a **substantial lessening of competition** will be investigated by a country's competition authorities.

A detailed investigation often takes six months to complete and may result in a block to the bid or a requirement that the acquiring company disposes of parts of the acquired business.

In the UK the **Competition and Markets Authority** may intervene to prevent mergers that cause the creation of a company with a market share of above 25%, if it feels that there will be a substantial lessening of competition.

Mergers fall within the exclusive jurisdiction of the **European Commission (Competition)** where, following the merger, the following two tests are met.

(a) **Worldwide revenue** of more than **€5 billion p.a.**

(b) **European Union** revenue of more than **€250 million p.a.**

The European Commission will assess the merger in a similar way as the Competition and Markets Authority in the UK, by considering the effect on competition in the market.

The merger will be blocked if the merged company results in such a dominant position in the market that consumer choice and prices will be affected.

Essential reading

See Chapter 9 Sections 2 and 3 of the Essential reading for further discussion of regulation.

The Essential reading is available as an Appendix of the digital edition of the Workbook.

6 Defence against a takeover

6.1 Post-bid defences

Where a bid is not welcomed by the board of the target company, then the bid becomes a **hostile bid**. Where the board feels that the takeover is not in the **best interest of their shareholders**, they can consider launching a defensive strategy.

This will normally involve attacking the value created for shareholders by the bid and sometimes this will extend to attacking the track record of the bidder.

A defence could also involve the following tactics:

Tactic	Explanation
White knights	This would involve inviting a firm that would rescue the target from the unwanted bidder.
	The white knight would act as a friendly counter-bidder.
Crown jewels	Valuable assets owned by the firm may be the main reason that the firm became a takeover target. By selling these the firm is making itself less attractive as a target. Care must be taken to ensure that this is not damaging the company.
	If the funds raised are used to grow the core business and therefore enhancing value, then the shareholders would see this positively and the value of the corporation will probably increase.
	Alternatively, if there are no profitable alternatives, the funds could be returned to the shareholders through **special dividends or share buybacks**. In these circumstances, disposing of assets may be a feasible defence tactic.
	This will require shareholder approval.
Litigation or regulatory defence	The target company can challenge the acquisition by inviting an investigation by the regulatory authorities or through the courts. The target may be able to sue for a temporary order to stop the bidder from buying any more of its shares.

6.2 Pre-bid defences

In order to deter takeover bids in the first place, the best defence is to have an efficiently run company with no underutilised assets. This will contribute to excellent relationships with shareholders and will help to maximise a company's share price, which will help to deter takeover bids.

However, subject to local regulations, schemes can also be designed to make any takeover difficult, for example:

(a) **Poison pills**

If a hostile bid is made, or the stake held by single shareholder rises above a certain key level (eg 15% in the case of Yahoo) then a 'poison pill' within the target's capital structure is triggered: eg new shares are issued to existing shareholders at a discount, or convertibles can be exchanged into ordinary shares on favourable terms.

Poison pills are controversial because they hinder an active market for corporate control and by giving directors the power to deter takeovers. They also put directors in a position to enrich themselves, as they may ask to be compensated for consenting to a takeover.

(b) **Golden parachutes**

These are significant payments made to board members when they leave. In many countries these schemes are illegal/non-compliant with local codes (eg the City Code in the UK).

Essential reading

See Chapter 9 Section 4 of the Essential reading for a summary of defensive tactics.

The Essential reading is available as an Appendix of the digital edition of the Workbook.

Chapter summary

Acquisitions: strategic issues and regulation

Growth strategies

Advantages and disadvantages of acquisitions vs internal development
- **Advantages:** speed, synergies, acquisition of intangible assets
- **Disadvantages:** acquisition premium, lack of control, integration problems

Advantages and disadvantages of acquisitions vs joint ventures
- **Advantages:** reliability, autonomy
- **Disadvantages:** cost and risk, access to overseas markets

Acquisition targets

Types of synergy
- Sales synergy (eg share sales outlets)
- Cost synergy (eg share R&D)
- Financial synergy (eg lower risk, lower tax bill)

Working relationship
- Culture, strategy
- Due diligence (legal/financial, commercial)

Reasons for failure of acquisitions

- Clash of cultures
- Uncertainty among staff
- Customer uncertainty – fear of problems leads to a fall in sales
- Assets or staff prove to be lower quality than expected
- Paying too high a price for the target – empire building
- Risk can be managed by a clear integration strategy and by due diligence

Reverse takeovers

Advantages and disadvantages of reverse takeover vs an IPO
- A smaller quoted company (S Co) takes over a larger unquoted company (L Co) by a share for share exchange
- A reverse takeover is a route **to a stock market listing**
- An IPO has a number of **advantages** compared to an IPO:
  - **Speed** – a reverse takeover can be completed in a few months
  - **Cost** – a reverse takeover will have significantly lower issue costs
  - **Availability** – it may be difficult attract investors to an IPO
- In addition a reverse takeover results in two companies combining together, with the possibility of **synergies**
- As a route to obtaining a stock market listing, **drawbacks** include:
  - **Risk** (the listed company being used may have some hidden liabilities),
  - **Lack of expertise** – running a listed company requires an understanding of compliance procedures

Regulation of takeovers

Defence against a takeover

UK regulation – the City Code

- **A bid announcement is required** if the offeree company is the subject of speculation due to the bidding company's actions
- The bidding company will be forced to state whether an offer is being considered, within 28 days, if a firm bid is **not made** then the bidding company will have to **wait six months before it can make another bid**
  - Where a bid involves an element of cash, the **bidding company must obtain confirmation by a third party that it can obtain these resources.**
  - An offer must be made for all other shares if the % shareholding rises above 30%, at **not less than the highest price paid by the bidding company in last year.**
  - After a formal offer there is a 14 day deadline for the defence document to be published, a 46 day deadline for the offer to be improved and finalised, and a 81 day deadline for shareholder votes to be assessed and the result announced. **Offers are normally conditional on more than 50% of the shares being secured.**
  - If a bid fails, the bidder cannot make another bid for another 12 months.

EU Takeovers Directive

- **The mandatory-bid rule** – aims to protect minority shareholders by providing them with the opportunity to exit the company at a fair price once the bidder has accumulated a certain percentage of the shares
  - In the UK, this threshold is specified by the City Code for Takeovers and Mergers and is at 30%
  - Once the bidder obtains control they may exploit their position at the expense of minority shareholders
  - This is why the mandatory-bid rule normally also specifies the price that is to be paid for the shares.
- **The principle of equal treatment** – requires the bidder to offer to minority shareholders the same terms as those offered to earlier shareholders from whom the controlling block was acquired
- **Squeeze-out rights** – give the bidder who has acquired a specific percentage of the equity (usually 90%) the right to force minority shareholders to sell their shares
  - Enables the bidder to acquire 100% of the equity once the threshold percentage has been reached and eliminates potential problems that could be caused by minority shareholders

Regulation of large takeovers

Regulated by national (eg CMA) or supranational authorities (eg EU)

Post-bid defences

- Where the board feels that a takeover is not in its shareholders' best interest it may decide to launch a **defence** against the bid
- This can include:
  - White knights
  - Crown jewels
  - Litigation/regulation

Pre-bid defences

- Poison pills and golden parachutes
- May not be permitted by local takeover panel rules

Knowledge diagnostic

1. Alternative growth strategies other than acquisition

Joint venture and internal development (organic growth).

2. Types of synergy

Three types: revenue, cost, financial.

3. Reverse takeover

The takeover of a small listed company by a larger unlisted company using a share for share exchange.

4. EU Takeovers Directive

Key points include the mandatory bid rule, the principle of equal treatment and squeeze-out rights.

5. Pre-bid defences

These deter a bid in the first place.

6. Post-bid defences

These are used after a bid has been received.

Further study guidance

Question practice

Now try the following from the Further question practice bank (available in the digital edition of the workbook):

Q15 *Saturn Systems*

Q16 *Gasco*

Further reading

There is a Technical Article available on ACCA's website, called 'Reverse Takeovers'.

We recommend you read this article as part of your preparation for the AFM exam.

Activity answers

Activity 1: Homework exercise

Other points could be made in addition to the points made below.

(1) Prevents the offeree company from being constantly distracted from their core business by rumours. The so-called 'put up or shut up rule' was changed in 2011 by the Takeover Panel, the body which polices mergers and acquisitions, so that from the day a company announces it has received an approach, the business making the offer has 28 days to put forward a firm bid.

   This also means a company has 28 days to prepare a defence before a business returns with a firm offer.

(2) To prevent unrealistic bids.

(3) Encourages the offeree company **not** to reject bids that are in the best interests of their own shareholders.

(4) Prevents the bidder from exercising control without giving other shareholders the chance to sell out.

(5) Bid timetable aims to get bids out of the way quickly. Conditional offers mean that extra shares only have to be bought by the bidding company if they have achieved more than 50% control.

(6) See (1).

Skills checkpoint 3

Communication

Chapter overview

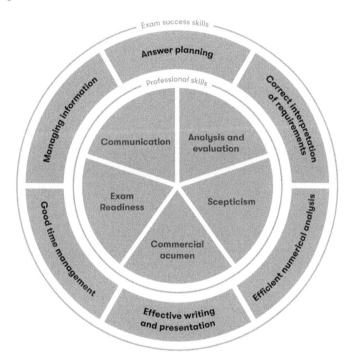

Introduction

Communication is one of the four professional skills that have been introduced to the AFM exam.

This skill will be examined in Section A of the exam, a compulsory 50 mark question, which tests all of the four professional skills for 10 marks in total. This skill will **not be examined in section B.**

AFM Professional Skill: Communication

Approximately 4-5 marks will be available in the 50-mark Section A question for this professional skill.

You can score marks in this area by demonstrating **a number of features** of good communication in your answer:

Appropriate answer format and structure

Here is an example of an extract from an answer exhibiting good practice for answer format and structure:

Report

To: Board of Directors, Avem Co
From: AN Consultant
Subject: Proposed acquisition of Fugae Co
Date: XX/XX/XX

Introduction

This report considers whether Avem Co should acquire Fugae Co. In order to assess the additional value created from bringing the two companies together the value of the two companies is determined separately and then as a combined entity. The report concludes by considering whether or not the acquisition will be beneficial to Avem Co and to Nahara Co.

(i) **Additional value created for Avem without considering the luxury transport project**

xxxxxxx

(ii) **Additional value created for Avem including the luxury transport project**

xxxxxxx

(iii) **Assumptions**

xxxxxxx

Concluding comments

Although Nahara Co would gain more than Avem Co from the acquisition both in percentage terms and in monetary terms, **both companies benefit from the acquisition.** *As long as all the parties are satisfied that the value is reasonable despite the assumptions highlighted above, it would appear that the acquisition should proceed.*

Answer format and structure marks can be obtained by:

(a) Providing a suitable, simple, heading to the answer (eg a **simple report format**)

(b) Providing a **short introduction** paragraph outlining the structure of the report

(c) Use of subheadings within the report

(d) Providing a concise conclusion to complete the report

Review the example given above to make sure you can see each of these features.

Only 1-2 marks are likely to be available for format so do not spend too long on formatting issues.

Clarity and effectiveness of message

Where possible, your answer should aim to **simplify complex issues**. By doing so, you will be conveying information in a way that is easily understood by, and reflects the requirements of, the intended audience.

Effective communication means that your answer is specifically relevant to the company in the question, rather than making a general point. For example, a discussion of synergy would be expected to address the possible synergies in a scenario rather than being a general discussion of different types of synergy.

1-2 marks are likely to be available for clarity and style (see quality of argument section later).

Use of appropriate technology

Make sure that your spreadsheet calculations are clear to the marker with clear signposting to the logic of the approach being followed. Calculations should also be headed up as a numbered Appendix.

Your key spreadsheet calculations should also be referenced in the main body of the report (eg see Appendix 1 in accompanying spreadsheet).

Here is an example of an extract from an answer exhibiting these features:

Report

To: *Board of Directors, Avem Co*
From: *AN Consultant*
Subject: *Proposed acquisition of Fugae Co*
Date: *XX/XX/XX*

Introduction

xxxxxx

(i)   ***Additional value created for Avem without considering the luxury transport project***
Appendix 1 shows that the additional value created from combining the two companies is approximately $451.5 million. $276.8 million of this will go to Nahara Co, which represents a premium of about 30% which is the minimum acceptable to Nahara Co. The balance of the additional value will go to Avem Co which is about $174.7 million. This represents an increase in value of 1.46% [$174.7 million /$12,000 million].

Extract from spreadsheet

| F15 | ▼ | : | × | ✓ | f_x | =76.5*(1+F11)/(F15-F11) | | | | |

◢	A	B	C	D	E	F	G	H	I	J
1										
2		**Appendix 1: Additional value created from combining Avem Co and Fugae Co**								
3										
4		Avem Co, current value			7.5	x	12,000	=	90,000	
5					per share		no.shares (million)			
6										
7		To estimate Fugae's current value we need to estimate the growth rate.								
8										
9		b				0.267				
10		re				0.11				
11		Fugae Co, estimate of growth rate = b x re				0.025				
12										
13		Fugae Co, current value estimate using dividend growth model								
14										
15		Fugae Co, current value estimate ($m)				922.5				
16										

1 mark is likely to be available for use of tools to provide effective communication.

Quality of argument

Ideally your writing will be persuasive. One way of achieving this is by linking together your ideas in a logical way and by counter-arguing to display an awareness of alternative views (where relevant).

Possible pitfalls

- **Excessive attention to creating an elaborate report format**

There are no marks for a visually attractive report – so don't waste time on this!

- **Copying the requirements of a question directly into a report**

The sub-headings in a report should reflect the requirements of the report but **should not be an exact copy** of the requirement's wording since this will not be appropriate as a report heading (for example the requirement's wording would include a mark allocation!).

- **Unclear calculations**

Your calculations are not expected to be perfect, but you are more likely to benefit from the own answer principle (ie may being given credit for correct method or discussion based on your calculations even if these calculations are not perfect) if the marker can follow the logic of your workings.

Avoid too much writing in the spreadsheet as this is often difficult for the marker to read. You can comment on the spreadsheet calculations in the main body of the report (as illustrated in the example given earlier).

Applying this professional skill

Communication marks should be easy to achieve with practice of 50-mark Section A questions.

Throughout your studies, whenever you are tackling questions, you will need to practice:

- Using the ACCA software to create clear reports with accompanying marks in a spreadsheet.
- Using a simple clear report format with an introduction, sub-headings and a conclusion.
- Presenting your numerical analysis clearly. There is guidance on the general exam success skill of **'efficient numerical analysis'** in the introduction section at the start of this workbook (exam success skill 4).
- Using a simple concise style of argument, without resorting to short single-sentence bullet points. There is guidance on the general exam success skill of **'effective writing and presentation'** in the introduction section at the start of this workbook (exam success skill 5).
- Ensuring that your answer accurately addresses instructions given in the scenario ie ensuring that your report is **complete** (answers all of the requirements) and **provides the information required** (and does not stray into areas that are not relevant).

Question practice

From the further study guidance practice bank, the solution to question 17 (Pursuit), which is set as homework at the end of the next chapter, gives an illustration of how points can be scored for 'communication' in the context of a scenario-based question.

10

Financing acquisitions
and mergers

Learning objectives

On completion of this chapter, you should be able to:

	Syllabus reference no.
Compare the various **sources of financing** available for a proposed cash-based acquisition	C4(a)
Evaluate the advantages and disadvantages of a financial offer for a given acquisition proposal using pure or mixed mode financing and recommend the most appropriate offer to be made	C4(b)
Assess the **impact of a given financial offer** on the reported financial position and performance of the acquirer	C4(c)

Exam context

This chapter completes Section C of the syllabus 'acquisitions and mergers'.

The chapter starts by discussing how a bidding firm can finance an acquisition, either by cash or by a share offer or a combination of the two, and the funding of cash offers.

The next theme is how to evaluate a financial offer in terms of the impact on the acquiring company's shareholders and the criteria for acceptance or rejection. Finally, we discuss ways of estimating the possible impact of an offer on the performance and the financial position of the acquiring firm.

The topics covered in this chapter are likely to be discussed in conjunction with the valuation techniques covered in Chapter 8.

Chapter overview

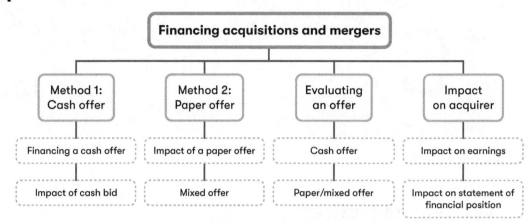

BPP
LEARNING
MEDIA

1 Method 1: Cash offer

The most common ways of paying for a target company's shares are by offering **cash** or **paper** (normally shares).

1.1 Financing a cash offer

How to obtain the cash required to finance a **cash offer** is a **gearing decision** and has been covered in earlier chapters – note that a cash offer/bid does not **necessarily** mean that any extra borrowing takes place, although this will often be the case.

1.2 Impact of a cash offer

Impact	Explanation
Value	Cash has a **definite** value, this will often be attractive to shareholders in the target company and may enhance the chances of a bid succeeding.
Control	**Less impact** on the control exercised by the owners of the bidding company, although any new debt used may carry restrictive covenants.
Gearing	**Gearing may rise** *if* cash is raised by borrowing, this may bring benefits in terms of tax savings on debt finance (see APV in Chapter 8) or may cause problems if it affects a company's credit rating.
Tax	Exposes a shareholder in the target company to **capital gains tax** (CGT), although this is not an issue for some investors (eg pension funds do not pay CGT).
Risk	**The risk of problems post-acquisition is borne by the acquirer** – if the share price falls post-acquisition then this only affects the acquirer as the target company shareholders have received their definite cash payment.

2 Method 2: Paper offer

2.1 Impact of a paper offer

The impact of paper (ie shares) being used to finance an acquisition can be assessed using the same factors considered above.

Impact	
Value	Shares have an **uncertain value**, often a higher price will have to be offered if the bid is a paper bid than if it was a cash bid to compensate the target's shareholders for this.
Control	The percentage of the shares owned by the bidding company's shareholders will be reduced as more shares are issued, so their **control will be diluted.**
Gearing	**Gearing will fall** as more equity is issued.
Tax	Gain is not realised for tax purposes until shares are sold – the timing of share sales can be staggered across different years to maximise the use of CGT allowances.
Risk	Post-acquisition **risk is shared between the bidding company and the target** – if the share price falls post-acquisition this affects both are affected.

2.2 Mixed offer

Because cash might be preferred by some shareholders (eg due to certainty) and paper by others (eg wanting to share in anticipated gains from a takeover), it is not uncommon for an acquisition to be financed by a **mixture** of cash and shares.

Vodafone

In 2014 the acquisition of Vodafone's American subsidiary by Verizon was financed by approximately 30% cash and 70% shares.

Essential reading

See Chapter 10 Sections 1–2 of the Essential reading for further discussion of financing bids.

The Essential reading is available as an Appendix of the digital edition of the Workbook.

3 Evaluating an offer

In the exam, you may be asked to evaluate a given offer and/or to suggest an offer.

3.1 Cash offer

A cash bid can simply be compared against the current market value of the target company or against an estimated value of an acquisition using **the techniques covered in Chapter 8** (these techniques will help to form the basis for a suggested cash offer).

While a significant premium above the market price is often expected (20%–30% is not uncommon), it is important (to the buyer) that the amount paid is **not greater than the value** that will be generated from the target company **under new ownership**.

3.2 Paper/mixed offer

How much a paper bid, or a bid that is partly financed by the issue of paper, is worth can be **assessed quickly** by looking at the value of the shares of the bidding company before acquisition.

However, a more accurate valuation would be based on the **value of the shares post-acquisition**.

The value of shares **post-acquisition** will be a matter of concern for the both the bidding company and the target company:

*   The **bidding company** will not want to issue so many shares that its share price falls post acquisition, and there may also be concerns about the effect of a paper bid on diluting the control of existing shareholders.
*   The **target company** will want to estimate the likely post-acquisition value of the shares to assess the attractiveness of the takeover bid.

Having evaluated a paper bid, you may choose to suggest an increase or a decrease in the number of shares offered.

The techniques for valuing a company post-acquisition have been covered in Chapter 8.

Note that post-acquisition values may also be required to evaluate a cash bid, but this is especially likely to be tested in the context of paper bids which forms the context for the recap of post-valuation techniques given here.

3.2.1 Post-acquisition value using earnings

Post-acquisition earnings valuation	
1	Estimate the group's **post-acquisition earnings** including synergies
2	Use **an appropriate P/E ratio to value these earnings** (this will be given)

Having obtained a post-acquisition valuation you may need to take one of the following steps:

Step 1 Deduct the cash element of the bid (if any) and then divide by the new number of shares in issue to calculate a **post-acquisition share price.**

(To allow the **bidding company** to assess whether its share price will rise or fall, and to allow the **target company** to estimate the likely post-acquisition value of the shares to assess the attractiveness of the takeover bid.)

Step 2 Deduct the value of whole bid to see **if value is created for the bidding company's shareholders.**

Step 3 Split up the post-acquisition value between the bidder and the target to calculate the number of shares each will own and therefore to **estimate the terms of a paper bid.**

Activity 1: Technique demonstration

Minprice Co is considering making a bid for the entire share capital of Savealot Co. Both companies operate in the **same industry**. It is anticipated that Minprice Co's P/E ratio will remain unchanged after the takeover.

You are given the following information:

	Minprice	Savealot
Revenue	$284m	$154m
Current share price ($1 ordinary shares)	$3.00	$5.00
EPS	$0.191	$0.465
No shares in issue	155m	21m
Gearing (D:E)	40:60	20:80

The acquisition will be financed by issuing ordinary shares in Minprice to replace those in Savealot. A 2-for-1 offer is proposed in order to deliver a significant bid premium to Savealot's shareholders.

Required

1 Estimate the likely impact on both groups of shareholders; would they approve of the proposal?

2 Calculate the maximum number of shares that Minprice could justify in terms of a paper bid.

3 Estimate the required terms of a paper bid if Savealot required a 30% bid premium before accepting the bid.

Solution

3.2.2 Post-acquisition value using cash flows

Post-acquisition cash flow valuation
(a) Estimate the group's **post-acquisition cash flows** including synergies.
(b) Calculate an appropriate **cost of capital** and complete a **cash flow valuation**.

As before, having obtained a post-acquisition valuation you may need to take one of the following steps:

Step 1 Deduct the cash element of the bid (if any) and then divide by the new number of shares in issue to calculate a **post-acquisition share price**.

Step 2 Deduct the value of whole bid to see **if value is created for the bidding company's shareholders**.

Step 3 Split up the post-acquisition value between the bidder and the target to calculate the number of shares each will own and therefore to estimate the terms of a paper bid.

4 Impact of a given offer on the financial performance and position of the acquiring firm

4.1 Impact on earnings

You may also be asked to evaluate the impact of a given offer on earnings (profits after tax and preference dividends) and key ratios such as EPS.

Activity 2: Continuation of Activity 1

	Minprice	Savealot
Revenue	$284m	$154m
Current share price ($1 ordinary shares)	$3.00	$5.00
EPS	$0.191	$0.465
Number of shares in issue	155m	21m
Gearing (D:E)	40:60	20:80

The acquisition will be financed by issuing ordinary shares in Minprice to replace those in Minprice to replace those in Savealot.

A 2-for-1 offer is proposed in order to deliver a significant bid premium to Savealot's shareholders.

Required

Evaluate the likely impact on the EPS of Minprice.

Solution

4.2 Impact on statement of financial position

The consolidated statement of financial position may need to be analysed using ratio analysis. Basic ratios have been covered earlier in the Workbook and will be returned to in Chapter 14.

The main issue to be aware of here is that the difference between the value of a take-over bid and the net assets of the company being acquired is accounted for as **goodwill** in the consolidated statement of financial position.

 ### Essential reading

See Chapter 10 Section 3 of the Essential reading for further discussion on forecasting the impact of a given financial offer on the acquiring firm.

The Essential reading is available as an Appendix of the digital edition of the Workbook.

 ### PER alert

You will be expected to demonstrate competence in the analysis of various finance options when fulfilling the performance objective 'evaluate potential investment and financing decisions'. This chapter has focused on the various ways in which mergers could be financed and assesses the costs and benefits of each option – knowledge which you can put into practice if your organisation is involved in merger and acquisition activity.

Chapter summary

Financing acquisitions and mergers

Method 1: Cash offer

Financing a cash offer

This is a **gearing decision** and has been covered in earlier chapters – note that a cash offer/bid does not **necessarily** mean that any extra borrowing takes place.

Impact of cash bid

- Definite value
- Few control issues
- Gearing may increase
- Tax issue for target
- Risk borne by bidder

Method 2: Paper offer

Impact of a paper offer

- Uncertain value
- Control issues
- Gearing reduced
- Risk shared

Mixed offer

It is not uncommon for an acquisition to be financed by a mixture of cash and shares

Evaluating an offer

Cash offer

A cash bid can simply be compared against the current market value of the target company or against an estimated value of an acquisition using the **techniques** covered in Chapter 8

Paper/mixed offer

This may require a post-acquisition valuation (using earnings or cash flow) following which you may need to:

1 Deduct the cash element of the bid (if any) and then divide by the new number of shares in issue to calculate a **post-acquisition share price**

2 Deduct the value of whole bid to see **if value is created for the bidding company's shareholders**

3 Split up the post-acquisition value between bidder and target to calculate the number of shares each will own and therefore the terms of a paper bid

Impact on acquirer

Impact on earnings

You may also be asked to evaluate the impact of a given offer on earnings and key ratios such as EPS

Impact on statement of financial position

This may need to be analysed using ratio analysis

Knowledge diagnostic

1. Cash offer

Often cheaper because more attractive to target shareholders.

2. Paper offer

Impacts on control of bidding company.

3. Mixed offer

May combine the advantages of cash (certainty) and paper (cash flow).

4. Post-acquisition valuation

Especially important if evaluating a paper offer.

5. Impact of higher P/E of bidder

If this is higher than the implied P/E of the offer, EPS will rise and shareholder wealth may also rise.

6. Goodwill

This will result from an acquisition at above the value of the net assets of the target.

Further study guidance

Question practice

Now try the following from the Further question practice bank (available in the digital edition of the workbook):

Q17 *Pursuit*

Q18 *Truffle*

Activity answers

Activity 1: Technique demonstration

1 Estimate the group's post-acquisition earnings including synergies

	Minprice	*Savealot*
EPS	$0.191	$0.465
Number of shares in issue	155m	21m
Total earnings	$29.605m	$9.765m

Combined earnings = 29.605 + 9.765 = $39.37m

Use an appropriate P/E ratio to value these earnings

	Minprice	*Savealot*
P/E	300/19.1 = **15.71**	500/46.5 = **10.75**

Valuation at Minprice's P/E of 15.71

39.37 × 15.71 = $618.5m

Divide by the new number of shares in issue to get the estimated post-acquisition share price

	Minprice	*Savealot*
No shares in issue	155m +	42m (21 × 2) new shares = **197m**

$618.5m/197m shares = post-acquisition share price of **$3.1396**

Deduct the value of whole bid to see if value is created for the bidding company's shareholders

Value of offer to Savealot = $3.1396 × 21m shares × 2 = $131.9m

Post-acquisition value $618.5m – amount paid in shares of $131.9 = $486.6m

This is the value belonging to the existing shareholders post acquisition and is higher than the existing market value of Minprice before the bid of $3 × 155m = $465m. So Minprices's shareholders will gain by $486.6m - $465m = **$21.6m**.

Evaluation of result

	Minprice	*Savealot*
Wealth before bid	$3 × 155 = **$465m**	$5 × 21m = **$105m**
Wealth after bid	$3.1396 × 155= **$486.6m**	$3.1396 × 42m = **$131.9m**
Gain*	**$21.6m**	**$26.9m**

* (so shareholders would approve)

Percentage of shares owned by Minprice shareholders = 155m/197m = **79%**

2 The maximum bid will leave Minprice Co's share price unchanged at $3.00

The post-acquisition value of $618.5m divided by the new number of shares in issue = $3.00

So $618.5m/$3 = total number of shares post acquisition = 206.2 million

There are currently 155 million Minprice shares, so this is an increase of 51.2 million.

51.2 million Minprice shares for 21 million Savaealot shares is approximately a **2.4-for-1 paper bid**.

3 Savealot's current value is $105m, so the required bid value is 105 × 1.3 = $136.5m

The post-acquisition value of the combined group has been estimated as $618.5m.

So Savealot requires ownership of 22.07% (136.5/618.5) of the combined group, which means that Minprice's 155m shares will account for 1−0.2207 = 0.7793 or 77.93% of the combined group.

The total number of shares will therefore be 155 / 0.7793 = 198.9m shares so this means that 43.9m (198.9−155) new shares will have to be issued to acquire the 21m shares in Savealot.

This implies a paper bid of 2.09 (43.9/21) shares per share in Savealot.

Activity 2: Continuation of Activity 1

	Minprice	Savealot
EPS	$0.191	$0.465
No shares in issue	155m	21m
Total earnings	$29.605m	$9.765m

Combined earnings = 29.605 + 9.765 = $39.37m

New number of shares in issue = 155m + (2 × 21m) = 197m

EPS = $39.37m ÷ 197m = $0.199

The P/E implied by the original bid is 2 shares × $3 = $6 ÷ 0.465 = **12.90**

Minprice's current P/E ratio is $3/0.191 = **15.71**.

EPS has improved (from $0.191 to $0.199) because the P/E ratio of the acquiring company exceeds the P/E ratio implied by the amount paid for the target.

The role of the treasury function

Learning objectives

On completion of this chapter, you should be able to:

	Syllabus reference no.
Discuss the role of the treasury management function within:	E1(a)
• The short-term management of an organisation's financial resources	
• The longer-term maximisation of corporate value	
• The management of risk exposure	
Discuss the operations of the derivatives market, including risks such as delta, gamma, and theta, and how these can be managed	E1(b) (iv)
Advise on the use of bilateral and multilateral **netting** and matching as tools for minimising FOREX transactions costs and the management of market barriers to the free movement of capital and other remittances (covered in Chapter 16)	E2(c)

Exam context

This chapter moves into **Section E** of the syllabus: '**Treasury and advanced risk management techniques**'; this syllabus section is covered in **Chapters 11–13**.

Following the introduction of the new exam structure in September 2018 **every exam will have a question that has a focus on syllabus Section E**.

This chapter briefly outlines the role of the treasury function before moving on to consider currency and interest rate risk management techniques in the following two chapters.

There is a significant overlap between this chapter and Chapter 2 where the principles behind risk management have already been discussed.

Chapter overview

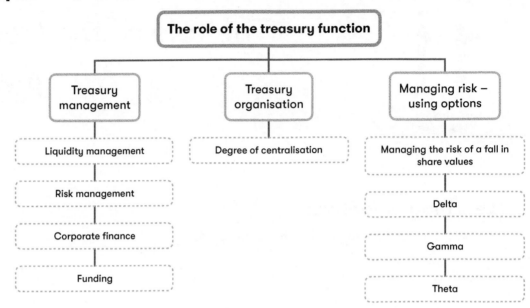

1 Treasury management

The Association of Corporate Treasurers' definition of treasury management is given below:

> **Treasury management:** Primarily involves the management of liquidity and risk, and also helps a company to develop its long term financial strategy.

A treasury department is likely to focus on four key areas:

1.1 Liquidity management

This is the management of short-term funds to ensure that a company has access to the cash that it needs in a **cost-efficient manner** (ie ensuring that a company is not holding unnecessarily high levels of cash, or incurring high costs from needing to organise unforeseen short-term borrowing). This is a key function of treasury management.

1.1.1 Netting

Netting involves identifying amounts owed between subsidiaries of a company in different foreign currencies. All foreign currency transactions are converted to a single common currency and netted-off. This reduces transaction fees and the time and cost of hedging inter-company transactions.

Activity 1: Technique demonstration

ZA group consists of a French company, a US company and a UK company. ZA has the following inter-company transactions for the first half of the year.

		Paying subsidiary		
		UK	US	French
Receiving subsidiary	UK	—	£2m	£1m
	US	$1.8m	—	$0.6m
	French	€3.3m	€4.84m	—

ZA has decided to implement a system of multilateral netting using £s as the settlement currency.

Exchange rates on 31 March are: €1.1 per £ and US$1.2 per £.

Required

Complete the following table, to illustrate multilateral netting and discuss its impact.

Solution

		Paying subsidiary					
		UK	US	French	Total receipts	Total payments	Net
Receiving subsidiary	UK	–	£2m	£1m			
	US		–				
	French			–			

1.2 Risk management

This involves understanding and quantifying the risks faced by a company and deciding whether or not to manage the risk. This is an **important area** and has been covered in **Section 3 of Chapter 2**.

For firms that are facing **significant levels of interest rate risk or currency risk**, risk management is likely to be appropriate. Specific techniques of currency and interest rate risk management are covered in the next two chapters.

However, some general risk measurement and management techniques relating to the Black-Scholes options pricing model are introduced in Section 3 of this chapter.

1.3 Corporate finance

This is the examination of a company's investment strategies. For example, how are investments appraised, and how are potential acquisitions valued? These areas have all been covered in earlier chapters and are central to the maximisation of shareholder wealth.

1.4 Funding

This involves deciding on suitable forms of finance (and by implication the level of dividend paid), and has been covered in earlier chapters.

PER alert

One way in which you can demonstrate competence in the performance objective 'manage cash using active cash management and treasury systems' is to manage cash on a centralised basis to both maximise returns and minimise charges. This section introduces the treasury management function and how it can be used to pool cash from various sources which can be placed on deposit

2 Treasury organisation

It is the responsibility of the board of directors to ensure that a treasury department is organised appropriately to meet the organisation's needs. This will involve making decisions about the degree of centralisation of the treasury department, and whether it should be organised as a profit centre or a cost centre.

2.1 Degree of centralisation

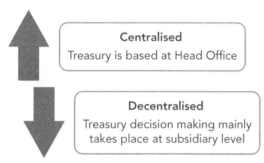

Centralised
Treasury is based at Head Office

Decentralised
Treasury decision making mainly takes place at subsidiary level

2.1.1 Advantages of centralisation

Within a **centralised** treasury department, the treasury department effectively acts as an **in-house** bank serving the interests of the group. This has a number of advantages:

Advantage	Explanation
Economies of scale	Borrowing required for a number of subsidiaries can be arranged **in bulk** (meaning lower administration costs and possibly a better loan rate), also combined cash surpluses can be invested **in bulk**.
Matching	Cash surpluses in one area can be used to **match** to the cash needs in another, resulting in an overall saving in finance costs. It is also possible to **match** receipts and payments in a given currency across all the subsidiaries. The time and cost of currency hedging is therefore minimised.
Control	Better control through the use of standardised procedures.
Expertise	Experts can be employed with knowledge of the latest developments in treasury management.
Netting	Netting of inter-company balances can be applied to save on transaction costs (as discussed).

Other approaches

It is also possible to have a mixture of the two approaches, this might involve **regional** treasury departments with each department being responsible for the activities of a number of different countries.

This approach will also allow some of the benefits of decentralisation (see next activity).

Activity 2: Decentralised treasury

What advantages could there be to having an element of decentralisation in treasury operations?

Solution

Essential reading

See Chapter 11 Section 1 of the Essential reading for further discussion of the organisation of the treasury function.

The Essential reading is available as an Appendix of the digital edition of the Workbook.

---

3 Managing risk – using options

One technique for **managing risk** involves the use of options. These will be applied to currency and interest rate risk in later chapters but are introduced here in the context of shares.

3.1 Managing the risk of a fall in share values

A treasury department may be responsible for managing a company's portfolio of investments. The company will be faced with **the risk that the value of these assets** (eg shares) **decreases**.

3.1.1 Use of put options

Put options entitle the holder to **sell** the shares at a fixed price. Put options result in compensation being received if **share prices fall** which allows investors to protect themselves against a drop in the share price (note that this makes put options unsuitable as an incentive scheme for senior management because it would be a reward for a falling share price).

When an **investor** buys an option they are setting up a **long position**.

Hez Co

Hez Co currently owns 100,000 shares in Zeta Co. Zeta Co's shares are currently trading at $10, but Hez Co is concerned about the risk of a fall in Zeta's share price.

Hez is considering the purchase of put options on Zeta shares which entitle the holder to sell Zeta shares at an exercise price of $10 per share. Remember, the purchaser of an option is said to have a **long** position.

Currently the put option is at-the-money (it is not worth anything now but will be in-the-money if the share price falls even slightly). However, if Zeta's share price fell to $9, the put option would be in-the-money and $1 (per share) of compensation would be received by the holder of the put option.

3.1.2 Black-Scholes (BSOP) model

In Chapter 4 we introduced the Black–Scholes option pricing (BSOP) model which shows how the price for call and put options is set and in Chapter 8 we saw the application of this model to business valuation and default risk.

The BSOP model is built around a number of variables, often referred to as **'the greeks'**, which each have **implications for risk management**.

3.2 Delta

Delta is $N(-d_1)$ for a put option (and $N(d_1)$ for a call option).

Delta measures **how much an option's value changes as the underlying asset value changes**.

Hez Co 2: continuation of previous example

If the delta of put options on Zeta shares is −0.5 this means that a $1 fall in the share price causes a rise in the value of a put option of $0.5.

If there is an equal chance of a rise or a fall in Zeta's share price from its current value of $10 of say $1.00, then the expected value of a put option at $10 is made of a 50% chance of a value of $1.00 (if the share price falls, the option will be in-the-money by $1) and a 50% chance 0 (if the share prices rises, the option will be out-of-the-money).

This means the value of the option, ie the amount it will cost to buy a put option, is

(0.5 × $1) + (0.5 × 0) = **$0.50.**

However, suppose the share price has now fallen to $9. From a price of $9, if the share price may rise or fall with equal probability by $1.00, then the expected value of a put option (with a strike price of $10) is made of a 50% chance of a value of $2.00 (if the share price falls, the option will be in-the-money) and a 50% chance of $0 (if the share prices rises, the option will have no value).

This means the new value of the option ie the amount you will need to pay to own a put option is

(0.5 × $2) + (0.5 × 0) = **$1.**

So, the value of the put option has risen by $0.50 due to a fall in the share price of $1.

This is a delta of −0.50.

3.2.1 Values of delta

−1	0	+1
Deltas can be near −1 for a long put option which is deep **in-the-money**; the price of the option and the value of the underlying asset move in line with each other.	Deltas can be near zero for a long put (or call) option which is deep **out-of-the-money**, where the price of the option will be insensitive to changes in the price of the underlying asset.	Deltas can also be near +1 for a long call option which is deep **in-the-money**; the price of the option and the value of the underlying asset move in line with each other.

3.2.2 Hedge ratio

Delta also defines the hedge ratio, ie the number of option contracts required to manage the risk of the underlying assets.

> **Delta hedge:** Defines the number of options required.

For example, the number of share options required = number of shares ÷ delta

Hez Co 3: continuation of previous example

If the price of Zeta shares is $10 and the put option has a delta of −0.5, Hez Co would need to buy put options on 100,000 shares ÷ 0.5 = 200,000 put options to maintain their wealth in the event of a fall in Zeta's share price.

If the number of put options had been 100,000, this would not have given sufficient compensation because put options will cost a premium of $0.50 per share (see Illustration 2).

The impact of 200,000 put options is demonstrated below:

Before buying options and with share price at $10:

Hez's wealth = $10 × 100,000 shares = $1,000,000

After buying 200,000 options and if the share price is $9, Hez's wealth would become:

($9 × 100,000) + ($1 value of put option × 200,000 put options) − ($0.50 cost of options × 200,000 put options) = $1,000,000

If put options on only 100,000 shares are bought wealth would have fallen because the put options will not provide adequate compensation, after taking into account the premium for buying the option.

Activity 3: Delta hedging

Cautious Co owns 1,000 shares in For4Fore plc which are currently trading at 444p.

Required

There are European style put options to sell shares in For4Fore at 430p per share in exactly four months' time. The delta value of this option has been correctly calculated as 0.3483.

How many put options should Cautious Co purchase to hedge this risk?

Solution

3.3 Gamma

Gamma measures **how much delta changes with the underlying asset value**.

This indicates by how much the delta hedge needs to be adjusted as the underlying asset value changes.

Gamma

For example, if the gamma is 0.01 this means that for a 1% rise in the underlying asset value the delta should change by a factor of 0.01%.

3.3.1 When the value of gamma is low (ie delta change is small as the asset value changes)

As we have seen, deltas can be near zero for a long put or call option which is deep **out-of-the-money**, where the price of the option will be insensitive to changes in the price of the underlying asset because a small change in the value of the asset will still mean that the option is deep out-of-the-money.

Deltas can also be near –1 for a long put option which is **deep in-the-money** (or +1 for a long call option which is deep in-the-money), where the price of the option and the value of the underlying asset move mostly in line with each other and this will still be the case even if there is a small move in the asset value.

3.3.2 When the value of gamma is high (ie delta change is high as the asset value changes)

When a long put option is **at-the-money** (which occurs when the exercise price is the same as the market price) the delta is –0.5 (+0.5 for a call option) but also changes rapidly as the asset price changes.

Therefore, the highest gamma values are when a call or put option is at-the-money.

3.4 Theta

> **Theta:** The change in an option's price (specifically its time premium) over time.

An option's price has two components, its **intrinsic value** and its **time premium**. When it expires, an option has no time premium.

Thus, the time premium of an option diminishes over time towards zero and theta measures **how much value is lost over time**, and therefore how much the option holder will lose through retaining their options.

Theta is generally expressed in terms of the value lost per day.

Chapter summary

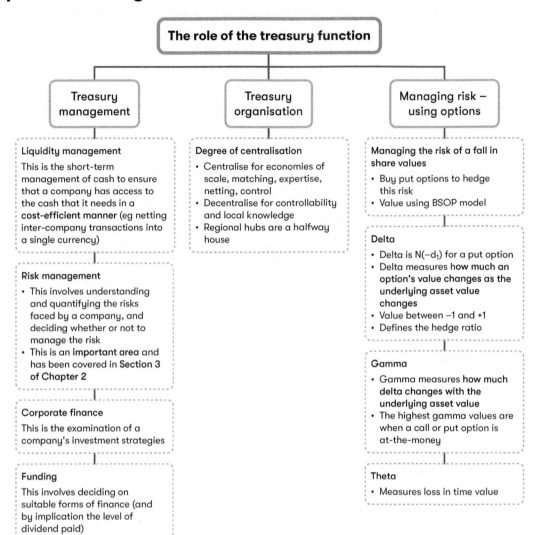

The role of the treasury function

Treasury management

Liquidity management

This is the short-term management of cash to ensure that a company has access to the cash that it needs in a **cost-efficient manner** (eg netting inter-company transactions into a single currency)

Risk management

- This involves understanding and quantifying the risks faced by a company, and deciding whether or not to manage the risk
- This is an **important area** and has been covered in **Section 3 of Chapter 2**

Corporate finance

This is the examination of a company's investment strategies

Funding

This involves deciding on suitable forms of finance (and by implication the level of dividend paid)

Treasury organisation

Degree of centralisation

- Centralise for economies of scale, matching, expertise, netting, control
- Decentralise for controllability and local knowledge
- Regional hubs are a halfway house

Managing risk – using options

Managing the risk of a fall in share values

- Buy put options to hedge this risk
- Value using BSOP model

Delta

- Delta is $N(-d_1)$ for a put option
- Delta measures how much an option's value changes as the underlying asset value changes
- Value between –1 and +1
- Defines the hedge ratio

Gamma

- Gamma measures how much delta changes with the underlying asset value
- The highest gamma values are when a call or put option is at-the-money

Theta

- Measures loss in time value

Knowledge diagnostic

1. Treasury management

Involves the management of liquidity, risk, funding and corporate finance.

2. Netting

Netting involves identifying amounts owed between subsidiaries of a company in different foreign currencies. All foreign currency transactions are converted to a single common currency and netted-off; reduces transaction fees and the time and cost of hedging inter-company transactions.

3. Centralisation

This allows development of expertise, and for techniques such as matching and netting to be applied.

4. Delta hedge

A delta hedge defines the number of options required.

For example the number of share options required = number of shares ÷ delta.

5. Gamma

Measure the impact of a change in delta of the underlying asset value.

6. Theta

Theta measures how much of the time value of an option is lost over time.

Further study guidance

Question practice

Now try the following from the Further question practice bank (available in the digital edition of the Workbook):

Q19 *Treasury management*

Q20 *For4fore*

Further reading

In Chapter 3 we recommended a useful Technical Article available on ACCA's website is called 'Risk Management'. This article examines the potential for risk management to 'add value' and is written by a member of the AFM examining team.

If you have not yet read this, we recommend you read it as part of your preparation for the AFM exam.

Own research

Use an internet search engine to identify treasury practices by searching for a company's annual report and searching for treasury management within this. For example, Britvic's annual report is interesting, but choose any company you are familiar with or are interested in.

There is no solution to this exercise.

Activity answers

Activity 1: Technique demonstration

		Paying subsidiary			Total receipts	Total payments	Net
		UK	US	French			
Receiving subsidiary	UK	–	£2m	£1m	**£3m**	**£4.5m**	**(£1.5m)**
	US	£1.5m	–	£0.5m	**£2m**	**£6.4m**	**(£4.4m)**
	French	£3m	£4.4m	–	**£7.4m**	**£1.5m**	**£5.9m**

Discussion:

This minimises transaction costs for inter-company payments.

Only three transactions will take place, two payments to central treasury by the UK and US operations and a receipt from central treasury by the French subsidiary. Don't forget to state this in your answer to an exam question (this is a common error).

It is possible that government regulations will prevent multilateral netting, in order to protect the income that local banks derive from transaction fees associated with currency transactions.

Another potential issue is that delaying the settlement of transactions (everything is settled in six months) may create cash flow problems for the affected subsidiaries.

Activity 2: Decentralised treasury

Advantages of decentralisation include:

- If subsidiaries have control over treasury operations, such as hedging, then they have greater control over their financial performance. Enhancing controllability can make performance appraisal easier, and also increase the motivation of local management.

- Local managers may have greater knowledge of local financing opportunities which centralised treasury would not be aware of.

Activity 3: Delta hedging

Options needed = Number of shares held divided by delta

Options needed = 1,000/0.3483 = 2,871

(Although this is a positive number, by convention the delta of a put option is referred to as a negative because the put option will fall in value as the share price rises and vice versa).

BPP
LEARNING
MEDIA

12

Managing currency risk

Learning objectives

On completion of this chapter, you should be able to:

	Syllabus reference no.
Discuss the operations of the derivatives market, including: • The relative advantages and disadvantages of exchange-traded vs OTC agreements • Key features, such as standard contracts, tick sizes, margin requirements and margin trading • The source of basis risk and how it can be minimised	E1(b) (i), (ii) and (iii)
Assess the impact on an organisation's to exposure in translation, transaction and economic risks and how these can be managed (translation and economic risk are covered in Chapter 5)	E2(a)
Evaluate, for a given hedging requirement, which of the following is the most appropriate strategy, given the nature of the underlying position and the risk exposure: • The use of the forward exchange market and the creation of a money market hedge • Synthetic foreign exchange agreements (SAFEs) • Exchange-traded currency futures contracts • Currency swaps (covered in the next chapter) • FOREX swaps (covered in the next chapter) • Currency options	E2(b)

Exam context

This chapter continues **Section E** of the syllabus: **'Treasury and advanced risk management techniques'**.

Every exam will have a question that has a focus on syllabus Section E, which is most likely to focus mainly on Chapter 12 and/or Chapter 13.

This chapter focuses on currency risk management.

Chapter overview

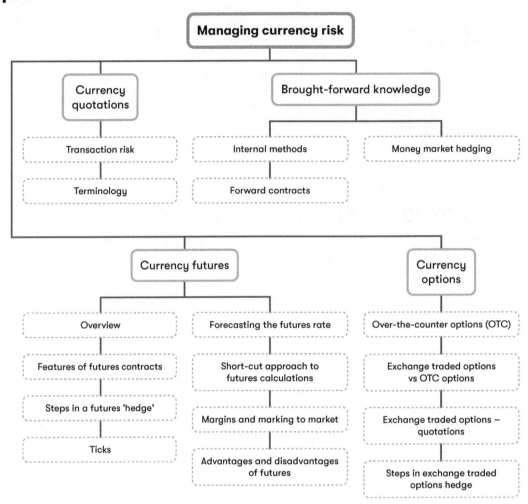

BPP
LEARNING
MEDIA

1 Currency quotations

1.1 Transaction risk

The **main focus of this chapter is transaction risk** (the risk that changes in the exchange rate adversely affect the value of foreign exchange transactions) and how this risk can be managed or 'hedged'.

The management of other currency-related risks (political, translation, economic) is also important but these have already been covered in Chapter 5 (which also considered reasons why exchange rates change).

In this chapter we mainly deal with the £ (UK sterling) as the local or domestic currency and the A$ (dollars) as the foreign currency. Many countries use the $ as a currency (for example USA, Australia, Canada) and the A$ is intended to be a generic reference to a $ based currency.

In exam questions the domestic and foreign currency could involve any combination of currencies.

1.1.1 Impact on exporters if local currency strengthens (foreign currency weakens)

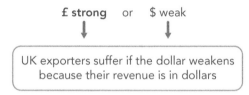

£ strong   or $ weak

UK exporters suffer if the dollar weakens because their revenue is in dollars

1.1.2 Impact on importers if local currency weakens (foreign currency strengthens)

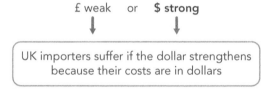

£ weak   or $ strong

UK importers suffer if the dollar strengthens because their costs are in dollars

Activity 1: Introduction to transaction risk

The value of the pound sterling has decreased from 1.8 A$ to the £ to 1.5 A$ to the £.

Required

Calculate the impact of this on:

1   A UK exporter due to receive A$360,000 from a foreign customer

2   A UK importer due to pay A$360,000 to a foreign supplier

Solution

1.2 Terminology

1.2.1 Spot rate and spreads

A **spot rate** is the rate available if **buying** or **selling** a currency **immediately**.

By offering a **different exchange rate** to exporters and importers, a bank can make a profit on the spread (ie the difference). Exchange rates are therefore often quoted as a spread.

Tutorial Note

It is vital that you can identify which part of a spread will be offered to a company in an exam question.

Spread

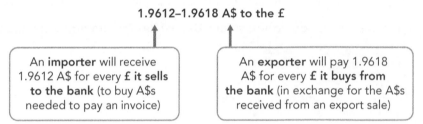

1.9612–1.9618 A$ to the £

An **importer** will receive 1.9612 A$ for every **£ it sells to the bank** (to buy A$s needed to pay an invoice)

An **exporter** will pay 1.9618 A$ for every **£ it buys from the bank** (in exchange for the A$s received from an export sale)

If you are unsure which part of a spread to use, remember that a company will always be offered the **worst rate by the bank**.

1.2.2 Direct and indirect rates

In some countries, such as the UK, exchange rates are normally shown **per unit of the domestic currency,** ie per £ (as above). This is called an indirect quote because it does not immediately tell you the value of a foreign currency.

In other countries it is more common for exchange rates to be quoted **per unit of the foreign currency**. This is called a direct quote.

An exam question will normally make it clear which approach is being used but be aware that if an exchange rate is quoted as a currency pair, eg 1.5 A$/£, then it is describing the value of the currency on the right-hand side, ie the value of one £ in this example.

Exchange rates

In the previous example the exchange rates were quoted to the £, ie an indirect quote.

These rates **can** be converted so that they are per $ (ie direct quote) as follows: 1 ÷ 1.9612 = 0.5099, and 1 ÷ 1.9618 = 0.5097.

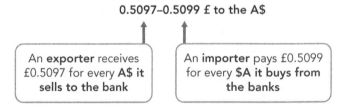

0.5097–0.5099 £ to the A$

An **exporter** receives £0.5097 for every **A$ it sells to the bank**

An **importer** pays £0.5099 for every **$A it buys from the banks**

The interpretation of the spread is based on the same logic but the importer now uses the right-hand side **and** the exporter the left-hand side.

Again, if you are unsure which part of a spread to use, remember that a company will always be **offered** the **worst rate for a specific transaction by the bank**.

Activity 2: Interpreting spreads

Spot exchange rates are as follows:

1.9612–1.9618 A$ per £

0.8500–0.9000 £ per €

Required

1   Calculate the receipts in £s for a UK company from a receipt of A$200,000.

2   Calculate the cost in £s for a UK company paying an invoice of €400,000.

Solution

2 Brought-forward knowledge

2.1 Internal methods

Simple techniques can be used within a company to eliminate some of the transaction risk it faces.

Wherever possible, a company that expects to have receipts in a foreign currency will net this off against payments in the same currency before looking to lock into hedging arrangements. This is called **matching**.

Matching payments against receipts will result in a single, smaller amount of currency to be hedged. This will be cheaper than hedging each transaction separately.

Netting has already been considered in the previous chapters.

Essential reading

See Chapter 12 Section 1 of the Essential reading for a general discussion of these basic approaches.

The Essential reading is available as an Appendix of the digital edition of the Workbook.

2.2 Forward contracts

A **contract** with a bank covering a **specific** amount of foreign currency (FX) for delivery on a specific future date **at an exchange rate agreed now**.

As with spot rates, a bank will quote a forward exchange rate as a (larger) **spread**, eg:

Forward rate: 1.9600–1.9612 ($ per £)

Again, a company will always be offered the **worst rate**.

Activity 3: Forward contracts

The spot exchange rate on 30 January 20X7 is 1.9612–1.9618 A$ per £ and the three-month forward rate is 1.9600–1.9615 A$ per £.

Required

1   Calculate the receipts from a $2 million sale, due to be received in three months' time, if forward rates are used.

2   Calculate the cost of paying an invoice of $2 million in three months' time, if forward rates are used.

Solution

Advantages of forward contracts	Disadvantages of forward contracts
Simple, no up-front transaction cost	Fixed date agreements (only apply on a specific date)

Advantages of forward contracts	Disadvantages of forward contracts
Available for many currencies, normally for more than one year ahead	Rate quoted may be unattractive

2.3 Money market hedging

2.3.1 For exporters

Borrowing in the foreign currency allows an exporter to take their foreign currency revenue now, at **today's spot rate** and thereby avoiding exchange rate risk. The foreign currency revenue will be used to repay the loan when it is received.

2.3.2 For importers

Transferring an amount of money into an overseas bank account, at **today's spot rate**, that is sufficient to repay the amount owed to the supplier in future allows an importer to avoid exchange rate risk.

Essential reading

See Chapter 12 Sections 2 and 3 of the Essential reading for further discussion of forward contracts and money market hedges. It is especially **important** that you carefully review the section on **money market hedging**.

The Essential reading is available as an Appendix of the digital edition of the Workbook.

3 Currency futures

3.1 Overview

Like a forward, a futures contract is intended to **fix the outcome of a transaction**.

However, unlike forwards, this is achieved by entering into a futures contract that is **separate** from the actual transaction and operates in such a way that if you make a loss in the spot market, you will expect to make a profit in the futures market (and vice-versa).

The gain or loss on a futures contract derives from future exchange rate movements – so futures are a **derivative**.

3.2 Features of futures contracts

Currency futures are mainly available from the US markets such as the New York Board of Trade (NYBOT) futures and options exchange.

- Each contract fixes the exchange rate on a large, standard amount of currency.
- Contracts normally expire at the end of each quarter (March, June, September and December) but can be used on any date up to the expiry date.
- A smaller range of currencies are traded on the futures market compared to those available on the forward market.

They fix the exchange rate for a set amount of currency for a specified time period.

Futures have **less credit risk** than forward contracts, as organised exchanges have clearing houses that guarantee that all traders in the market will honour their obligations.

3.3 Steps in a futures 'hedge'

Step 1   Now

Contracts should be set in terms of **buying or selling the futures contract currency** – choosing the closest standardised futures date **after** the transaction date.

Step 2   In the future

Complete the **actual** transaction on the **spot market**.

Step 3   At the same time as Step 2

Close out the futures contract by doing the opposite of what you did in Step 1.

Calculate net outcome.

3.4 Ticks

> **Tick:** The smallest movement in the exchange rate, which is normally quoted on the futures market to four decimal places.

If a futures contract (on a US market) is for £125,000 every 0.0001 movement will give a company £125,000 × 0.0001 = $12.5 **profit or loss**. This is called the **tick size: note** this profit or loss is in **dollars**.

If the futures exchange rate has moved in your favour by 0.0030 then this will be

30 ticks × $12.5 = $375 per contract.

Illustration 1: Futures hedging

Today is 31 December. Collai Co (based in France) anticipates that in two months' time it will need to pay for purchases of $11 million. The exchange rates on 31 December are:

Spot rate: 1.9615 $ per Euro (€)

Futures rates:

	March	June
$ per € – contract size €125,000	1.9556	1.9502

Required

Calculate the outcome of using a futures hedge in two months' time if the spot rate is 1.9900 $ per € and the futures rate is 1.9880 $ per €.

Solution

Steps as follows:

Step 1   Now (31 December)

(1) Type of contract:

The contract currency is €s and Collai will need to sell €s (to obtain the $s needed), so **contracts to sell** are needed.

(2) Date of contract:

The earliest futures expiry date after the transaction is **March** so this will be chosen.

(3) Number of contracts:

The standard contract size is €125,000. At the March futures rate of 1.9556, the number of contracts needed is $11m ÷ 1.9556 = €5,624,872. So the number of contracts needed is

5,624,872/€125,000 = **45 contracts** (rounding to the nearest whole contract)

So Collai will need to enter into **45 March contracts to sell @ 1.9556**

Step 2   End February

Complete the actual transaction on the spot market. So $11m invoice will cost @ Feb spot rate 1.9900 = €5,527,638

This cost is lower because the Euro has strengthened. This means that a loss is likely to be made on the futures contract.

Step 3   At the same time as Step 2

Close out the futures contract by **buying** €s back from the futures market.

31 Dec: contracts to sell €s at	1.9556
End Feb: contracts to buy €s at	1.9880
Difference	0.0324

A **loss** has been made as the buying price is above the selling price.

The loss can be quantified in one of two ways (either can be used):

(1)   0.0324 × 125,000 × 45 contracts = $182,250, or

(2) $12.50 × 324 ticks × 45 contracts = $182,250

Converting $182,250 into €s at February's spot rate = $182,250/1.9900 = €91,583 loss

So the net outcome from the futures hedge =

€5,527,638 cost (Step 2) + €91,583 (Step 3) loss = €5,619,221.

Activity 4: Futures demonstration

Today is 31 December. Spandau plc anticipates that in four months' time it will have receipts of A$5.1 million; it has a policy of hedging 100% of its transaction risk in the month the transaction arises.

The exchange rates on 31 December are:

Spot rate: 1.9615 A$ per £.

Futures rates:

	March	June
A$ per £ – contract size £125,000	1.9556	1.9502

Required

Calculate the outcome of the futures hedge in four months' time if the spot rate is 2.0000 A$ per £ and the futures rate is 1.9962 A$ per £.

Solution

3.5 Forecasting the futures rate

In the previous example the closing futures price (needed for Step 2) was given but **in the exam you may have to calculate it** on the assumption that the difference between the spot price and futures price (known as the '**basis**') falls evenly over time.

Typical movement of futures price vs spot price through time:

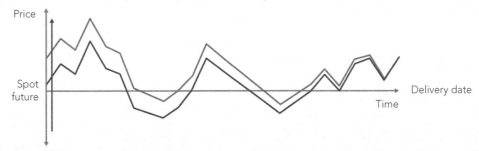

We can use the assumption of a gradual reduction in the difference between the spot rate and the futures rate over time to make a sensible estimated of the closing futures price.

Illustration 2: (continuation of previous illustration)

Today is 31 December. Collai Co anticipates that in two months' time it will need to pay for purchases of $11 million. The exchange rates on 31 December are:

Spot rate: 1.9615 $ per €

Futures rates:

	March	June
$ per € – contract size €125,000	1.9556	1.9502

Required

Calculate the estimated March futures price in two months' time, assuming the spot rate at that point is 1.9900 $ per €.

Solution

	Now (31 Dec)
March futures contract	1.9556
Spot rate	1.9615
Difference (basis)	
Future – spot	**(0.0059)**
Time difference	3 months (to expiry of March contract)

In two months' time (end of February) there will only be one month to the expiry of the March future so only one month of the basis should remain which is (0.0059) × 1/3 = (0.0020) rounding to four decimal places.

We can forecast the March future in two months' time as being the spot rate of 1.9900 $ per € less 0.0020 = 1.9880.

This was the closing futures price given in the previous example, and shows how it could be calculated.

If the forecast future spot rate is not given by a question, you can make a sensible assumption eg, assume that it will be the same as the forward rate.

3.5.1 Basis risk

There is risk that basis will not decrease in this predictable way. This is known as **basis risk**.

The futures price will change constantly as the market reacts to changes in expectations of exchange rate movements. Generally, the spot rate and the futures price will move by a similar amount but not in exactly the same way, and will tend to move in a similar direction. So, unlike a forward contract, where the exchange rate is fixed, one does not know the precise end result when entering into a futures contract – although any variations in the outcome are likely to be minor.

To **manage basis risk** it is important that the futures contract chosen is the one with the closest maturity date after the actual transaction.

Activity 5: Technique demonstration (Activity 4 continued)

Today is 31 December. The exchange rates on 31 December are:

Spot rate: A$ per £ 1.9615

Futures rates:

	March	June
A$ per £ – contract size £125,000	1.9556	1.9502

Required

Calculate the June futures rate in four months' time if the spot rate is 2.0000 A$ per £.

Solution

3.6 Short-cut approach to futures calculations

The approach demonstrated helps you to understand the mechanics of the futures hedge and is important **if** you are asked to show the full mechanics of the future calculation, ie what happens in the spot market and what happens in the futures market.

However, **many exam questions do not require this level of detailed analysis** and simply ask for an assessment of the overall outcome of using a futures hedge.

A **quicker** method is available which will deliver full marks if all that is required is to show the overall outcome of a future's hedge.

Effective futures rate = opening future's rate – closing basis

Short-cut approach

From Illustration 2, the closing basis was calculated as:

	Today 31 Dec	28 Feb
March future	1.9556	1.9880
Spot	1.9615	1.9900
Basis	−0.0059	−0.0020

The closing basis was then used to calculate the closing rate on the future's contract and an overall net outcome of €5.619 million from a payment of $11 million.

This can be thought of as an **effective exchange rate** of $11m/5.619m = **1.9576**.

Using the quicker method, we could calculate the outcome from the futures hedge with two pieces of information: opening futures rate and closing basis.

Here the opening futures rate is 1.9556 and the closing basis is (0.0020).

So using the quick method we would forecast the effective futures rate as:

1.9556 − −0.0020 = **1.9576**

This is the same answer as we had using the longer method but is **much quicker** because it removes the need for any detailed analysis of the outcome of the futures hedge.

This is a better method to use in most exam questions.

Activity 6: Quicker method

The previous activity produced a net revenue of **£2,610,375** from receipts of A$5.1 million, ie an effective exchange rate of A$5.1m/£2.61m = 1.9540.

Required

Recalculate this outcome using the quick method.

Solution

3.7 Margins and marking to market

The futures exchange will demand an **initial margin** (a deposit) which is put into a client's 'margin account'. Each day any profit or loss on the client's position (**variation margin**) is debited or credited to this account so losses are not allowed to build up.

The process of settling the gains and losses on future contracts at the end of each trading day is referred to as **'marking to market'**. If losses are made that reduce the account below the **maintenance margin** (the minimum balance) the investor will be required to restore the margin account to its maintenance margin level.

Real life example

If, for example, a company has entered into a futures contract to buy €62,500 at a rate of USD/EUR 1.6246 (equivalent to $101,538) with an initial margin of $2,000 and a maintenance margin of $1,500, then marking to market could work as shown in the following table:

	Closing futures price	Sell €62,500	Profit/(loss)	Pay in	Account balance
	$	$	$	$	$
				2,000	2,000
Day 1	1.6350	102,188	650	–	2,650
Day 2	1.6200	101,250	(938)	–	1,712
Day 3	1.6150	100,938	(312)	100	1,500

Profit on Day 1 is because if the contract were closed out it would be worth $102,188 compared to its value of $101,538 at the start of the day ie a profit of $650. On the other days the value falls and so losses are made.

On Day 3, because the account balance fell to $1,400, a further $100 had to be paid in to meet the requirement for a maintenance margin of $1,500.

In fact, in most futures exchanges if the balance falls below the variation margin action needs to be taken to increases the account balance back to its **initial margin** level. For example, in this case a further $600 would need to be paid to take the balance back to the $2,000 value of the initial margin.

Either approach is acceptable in the exam, the key point is that **if the balance falls below the variation margin then action has to be taken to top up the funds in the futures account.**

Marking to market, and the requirement for an initial margin, has **liquidity implications** for companies and this is often given as the reason why other derivatives are preferable to the use of futures contracts for hedging.

3.8 Advantages and disadvantages of futures

Advantage of futures	Disadvantages of futures
• Flexible dates, ie a September futures can be used on any day up to the end of September	• Only available in large contract sizes and a limited range of currencies • Margin payments • Basis may not fall in a linear way over time (basis risk)

Essential reading

See Chapter 12 Section 4 of the Essential reading for further discussion of currency futures.

The Essential reading is available as an Appendix of the digital edition of the Workbook.

4 Currency options

We have already looked at options in earlier chapters.

Unlike forwards and futures, currency options protect against adverse exchange rate movements but still **allow a company to take advantage of favourable exchange rate movements**.

> **Currency options:** Contracts giving the holder the right, but not the obligation, to buy (call) or sell (put) a fixed amount of currency at a fixed rate in return for an upfront fee or premium.

Options are another **derivative** product.

4.1 Over-the-counter options (OTC)

Currency options can be purchased directly (over the counter) from a merchant bank; these options are normally **fixed date** options (**European options**) which means that they can only be exercised on a specific date.

Activity 7: Technique demonstration

It is 1 October. Z Co, a company based in the Eurozone, wishes to hedge the **possible** receipt of A$2 million from the sale of a foreign subsidiary that it expects to be completed in December. The current spot rate is 1.4615 A$ per €.

A$2 million of December dollar OTC put options with an exercise price of A$1.47 can be bought for a premium of €50,000.

Required

What will the outcome of the hedge be in each of the following scenarios?

1 The spot exchange rate on 31 December is 1.50 A$ per €.

2 The spot exchange rate on 31 December is 1.30 A$ per €.

3 The sale of the subsidiary does not happen.

Solution

4.2 Exchange-traded options vs OTC options

Currency options are also available from the US exchanges markets such as the Philadelphia Stock Exchange (PHLX).

Advantages vs OTC options	Disadvantages vs OTC options
Exchange-traded options cover a period of time (American options); OTC options are fixed date (European options).	Exchange-traded options are normally offered up to two years ahead; OTC options can be agreed for longer periods.
Exchange-traded options are tradable – so if they are not needed they can be sold on.	Exchange-traded options are in standard contract sizes.

4.3 Exchange-traded options – quotations

Call option – a right to buy (the option contract currency).

Put option – a right to sell (the option contract currency).

The prices of exchange traded options are normally quoted as a price per unit of the contract currency as shown in the table below.

Exchange traded US$ per £ Options £31,250 (cents per £1)

Call = right to buy £s (contract currency)

Size of the contract

Strike price	Calls				Puts		
	Apr	May	June		Apr	May	June
1.2500	2.20	2.75	3.10		0.65	1.20	1.60
1.2750	0.88	1.45	1.85		1.70	2.40	2.85
1.3000	0.25	0.70	1.05		3.65	4.10	4.50

Premium in cents per £1

Activity 8: Understanding of option pricing

1   Why is the cost of an April call at 1.2500 more expensive than an April call at 1.3000?

2   Why is a May call option more expensive than an April call option?

Solution

4.4 Steps in an exchange-traded options hedge

Step 1   **Now**

Contracts should be selected in terms of **buying or selling the option contract currency** – choosing the closest standardised options date **after** the transaction date and a logical exercise price (eg cheapest or closest to current spot rate).

Assess any shortfall or surplus if option exercised (this can be covered with a forward contract).

Calculate the **premium** this must be paid immediately.

Step 2   **In the future**

Calculate the outcome if the option is exercised (or whether the spot rate is better). If unsure **assume the option is exercised** (this gives a worst case scenario since if the option is **not** exercised it means that the **spot rate is better**).

Step 3   **In the future**

Calculate the net position, taking into account the premium (Step 1), and the outcome (Step 2, including any surplus or shortage if the option is exercised).

 ## Illustration 3: Exchange-traded options

Vinnick, a US company, purchases goods from Santos, a Spanish company, on 15 May on three months' credit for €600,000.

Vinnick is unsure in which direction exchange rates will move so has decided to buy options to hedge the transaction at a rate of €0.7700 = $1.

The details for €10,000 options at 0.7700 are as follows.

Calls			Puts		
July	August	September	July	August	September
2.55	3.57	4.01	1.25	2.31	2.90

The current spot rate is 0.7800.

Required

Calculate the dollar cost of the transaction, assuming that the option is exercised.

Solution

Steps as follows:

Step 1   **Set up the hedge**

(1)   Which contract date? August

(2)   Put or call? Call – we need to buy euros (the contract currency)

(3)   Which strike price? 0.7700 (given)

(4)   How many contracts?

$$\frac{600,000}{10,000} = 60 \text{ (no shortage or surplus)}$$

Use August call figure of 3.57. Remember it has to be multiplied by 0.01 because it is in cents.

Premium = (3.57 × 0.01) × contract size × number of contracts

Premium = 0.0357 × 10,000 × 60 = $21,420

Step 2 Outcome

Options market outcome

60 contracts × €10,000	
Outcome of options position	€600,000 No surplus or shortfall

Step 3 Net outcome

	$
Options position (600,000/0.77)	(779,221)
Premium	(21,420)
	(800,641)

Activity 9: Exchange-traded options

Today is 31 December, the spot rate is 1.2653 US$ per £. XP plc anticipates that in four months' time it will need to make purchases of $5 million and in six months' time it will have receipts of $2 million.

Options prices are quoted in Section 4.3 – assume that XP plc will take out an option at a rate closest to the spot rate, ie 1.2750 US$ per £.

Required

1   Calculate the outcome of the four-month hedge (import).

2   Calculate the outcome of the six-month hedge (export).

Illustrate the outcome if the option is exercised in both cases.

Assume the forward rate for four months is $1.25 per £, and for six months is $1.3 per £.

Solution

Activity 10: Further practice

It is now 28 February and the treasury department of Smart Co, a quoted European company (in a country where the Euro is the domestic currency), faces a problem. At the end of May the treasury department may need to advance to Smart Co's US subsidiary the amount of $12,750,000. This depends on whether the subsidiary is successful in winning a franchise. The department's view is that the US dollar will strengthen over the next few months, and it believes that a currency hedge would be sensible.

The following data is relevant.

Exchange rates US$/ €

28 Feb **spot**: 1.2311–1.2318

Three months **forward**: 1.2164–1.2198

Futures market contract prices

Euro €62,500 contracts:

March contract: 1.2274

June contract: 1.2143

Currency **options**:

Euro €31,250 contracts (US cents per €)

	Calls	Puts
Exercise price	*June*	*June*
$1.190/€	3.40	0.38
$1.211/€	1.20	0.68
$1.233/€	0.40	2.38

Required

1 Explain the relative merits of forward currency contracts, currency futures contracts and currency options as instruments for hedging in the given situation.

2 Assuming the franchise is won, illustrate the results of using forward, future and option currency hedges if the US$/€ spot exchange rate at the end of May is 1.1509.

Solution

PER alert

One of the optional performance objectives in your PER is to advise on managing or using instruments or techniques to manage financial risk. This chapter has focused on a range of techniques for managing exchange rate risk, which is an aspect of financial risk.

Chapter summary

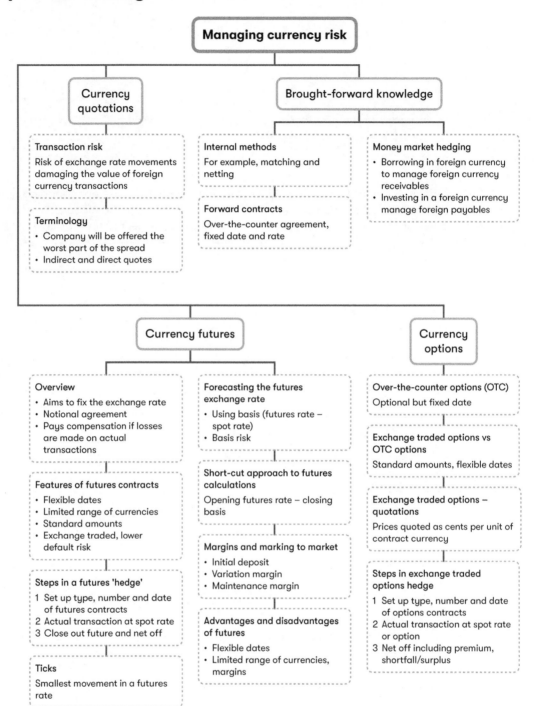

Managing currency risk

Currency quotations

Transaction risk

Risk of exchange rate movements damaging the value of foreign currency transactions

Terminology

- Company will be offered the worst part of the spread
- Indirect and direct quotes

Brought-forward knowledge

Internal methods

For example, matching and netting

Forward contracts

Over-the-counter agreement, fixed date and rate

Money market hedging

- Borrowing in foreign currency to manage foreign currency receivables
- Investing in a foreign currency manage foreign payables

Currency futures

Overview

- Aims to fix the exchange rate
- Notional agreement
- Pays compensation if losses are made on actual transactions

Features of futures contracts

- Flexible dates
- Limited range of currencies
- Standard amounts
- Exchange traded, lower default risk

Steps in a futures 'hedge'

1 Set up type, number and date of futures contracts
2 Actual transaction at spot rate
3 Close out future and net off

Ticks

Smallest movement in a futures rate

Forecasting the futures exchange rate

- Using basis (futures rate – spot rate)
- Basis risk

Short-cut approach to futures calculations

Opening futures rate – closing basis

Margins and marking to market

- Initial deposit
- Variation margin
- Maintenance margin

Advantages and disadvantages of futures

- Flexible dates
- Limited range of currencies, margins

Currency options

Over-the-counter options (OTC)

Optional but fixed date

Exchange traded options vs OTC options

Standard amounts, flexible dates

Exchange traded options – quotations

Prices quoted as cents per unit of contract currency

Steps in exchange traded options hedge

1 Set up type, number and date of options contracts
2 Actual transaction at spot rate or option
3 Net off including premium, shortfall/surplus

Knowledge diagnostic

1. Direct quote

This means that an exchange rate is quoted to one unit of the foreign currency.

2. Indirect quote

This means that an exchange rate is quoted to one unit of the domestic currency.

3. Basis

The difference between the future and the spot rate. This is used to forecast the closing futures rate on the assumption that basis decreases in a linear way over time.

4. Basis risk

This is the risk that basis does not decrease in a linear way over time.

5. OTC options

Fixed-date options offered by banks.

6. Exchange-traded options

Flexible dates, offered by exchanges.

Further study guidance

Question practice

Now try the following from the Further question practice bank (available in the digital edition of the workbook):

Q21 *Fidden plc*

Q22 *Curropt plc*

Activity answers

Activity 1: Introduction to transaction risk

1   A$360,000/1.8 = £200,000 revenue expected

   A$360,000/1.5 = £240,000 received

   Profits = £40,000

   UK exporters gain when the £ gets weaker

2   A$360,000/1.8 = £200,000 cost expected

   A$360,000/1.5 = £240,000 paid

   Losses = £40,000

   UK importers lose when the £ gets weaker

Activity 2: Interpreting spreads

1   The worst rate for buying £s is 1.9618, so this is the rate that will be offered by a bank.
   A$200,000 ÷ 1.9618 = £101,947

2   The worst rate for buying €s is 0.9000, so this is the rate that will be offered by a bank.

   €400,000 × 0.9000 = £360,000

Activity 3: Forward contracts

1   The worst rate for selling A$s and buying £s is 1.9615, so this is the rate that will be offered by a bank.

   A$2m ÷ 1.9615 = £1,019,628.

2   The worst rate for selling £s and buying A$s is 1.9600, so this is the rate that will be offered by a bank

   A$2m/1.9600 = £1,020,408

Activity 4: Futures demonstration

Steps as follows:

Step 1   Now (31 December)

   Type of contract:

   Contract currency is £s and Spandau will need to buy £s (with $ receipts), so contracts to buy are needed.

   Date of contract:

   The earliest futures expiry date after the transaction is June, so this will be chosen.

   Number of contracts:

   The standard contract size is £125,000. At the June futures rate of 1.9502, the number of contracts needed is A$5.1m ÷ 1.9502 = £2,615,116. So, the number of contracts needed is £2,615,116/£125,000 = 21 contracts (to the nearest contract).

   Therefore, Spandau will need to enter into 21 June contracts to buy @ 1.9502.

Step 2   End April

   Complete the actual transaction on the spot market. So, A$5.1m revenue will be worth @ April spot rate 2.0000 = £2,550,000

Step 3   At the same time as Step 2

   Close out the futures contract by selling £s back to the futures market.

BPP
LEARNING
MEDIA

31 Dec: contracts to buy £s at	1.9502
End April contracts to sell £s at	1.9962
Difference	0.0460

A profit has been made as the selling price is above the buying price.

The profit can be quantified in one of two ways (either can be used):

(1) 0.0460 × 125,000 × 21 contracts = A\$120,750; or

(2) \$12.50 × 460 ticks × 21 contracts = \$120,750.

Converting A\$120,750 into £s at April's spot rate = A\$120,750/2.0000 = £60,375 profit

The net outcome from the futures hedge is £2,550,000 (Step 2) + £60,375 (Step 3) profit = £2,610,375

Activity 5: Technique demonstration (Activity 4 continued)

	Now (31 Dec)
June futures contract	1.9502
Spot rate	1.9615
Difference (basis) **Future – spot**	**(0.0113)**
Time difference	Six months (to expiry of June contract)

In four months' time (end of April) there will only be two months to the expiry of the June future so only two months of the basis should remain which is (0.0113) × 2/6 = (0.0038) rounding to four decimal places.

We can forecast the June future in four months' time as being the spot rate of 2.0000 A\$ per £ less 0.0038 = **1.9962**.

This was the rate given in Activity 4.

Activity 6: Quicker method

Quick method:

Opening futures rate – closing basis = effective exchange rate

1.9502 − −0.0038 = 1.9540

Footnote – comparison of the two methods

Longer method

The longer method adjusts the impact of the spot rate changing by noting the counteracting influence of the futures contract (if the spot rate gets worse the future contract provides compensation, and if the spot rate gets better the future contract incurs a loss).

Opening future 1.9502 = a	Closing future 1.9962 = b	Change 0.0460 = c
	Closing spot 2.0000 = d	
Effective rate = e	Closing spot – change in future 2.0000 − 0.046 = **1.9540** Or e = d - c where c is (b-a) so this becomes e = d - (b-a) which is e = d - b + a	

Quick method

This will be expected to give the same outcome.

Opening future 1.9502 = a	
	Closing basis −0.0038 Closing basis is calculated as closing future (b from the long method) minus closing spot (d from the long method).
Effective rate = e	Opening future rate – closing basis 1.9502 – – 0.0038 = **1.9540** In mathematical terms this is $e = a - (b-d)$ or $e = a - b + d$ this is the same as the expression used in the long method of $e = d - b + a$ (this mathematical proof is intended to be helpful but is not examinable and can be ignored if you prefer!)

Activity 7: Technique demonstration

1   The option rate is better than the spot so the option is used giving a value of A$2m/1.47 = €1.36m, which becomes €1.31 million after the premium (which is paid up front).

2   The option rate is worse than the spot, so the spot is used giving a value of €1.54 million or €1.49 million after the premium (calculated as €1.54m – €0.05m premium).

3   If the option is worthless it will be abandoned (eg in (b)) or the company can exercise the option and make a profit (buy A$2 million at spot for €1.33 million and then sell the A$2 million for €1.36 million). In either case the premium still has to be paid.

Activity 8: Understanding of option pricing

1   1.25 is a better intrinsic value for a call option to buy £s than 1.3, ie an option to buy something for 1.25 is better than an option to buy it at 1.30

2   A May call gives cover in April and May, so it will be more expensive; it has a higher time value

Activity 9: Exchange-traded options

1   Steps as follows:

Step 1   Set-up today – 31 December

Calculate the £ required = $5m/1.275 = £ 3,921,569

Number of contracts = £3,921,569/£31,250 = **125 contracts**

Note that 125 × 31,250 = £3,906,250 × 1.275 = $4,980,469

There is a **shortfall of $19,531** if the option is exercised

(This could be hedged with a forward, or left unhedged; do whichever is easier because the amount is not material)

Date and type: 125 April put options at $1.275

Calculate premium: $0.0170 × 125 × 31,250 = **$66,406**

Paid at **today's spot** of 1.2653 = **£52,482**

Step 2   Outcome – end of April

Option exercised @ option rate (1.275)

125 × £31,250 = £3,906,250

Shortfall of $19,531 @ April forward 1.25 = £15,625

Step 3   Net outcome

£3,906,250 cost of exercising option + premium for option £52,482 + shortfall £15,625 = **£3,974,357**. This is the worst case outcome; if the spot rate is better than the option rate then the outcome could be better.

2   Steps as follows:

Step 1   Set-up today – 31 December

Calculate the £ required $2m/1.275 = £1,568,627

Number of contracts   £1,568,627/£31,250 = 50 contracts

Note that 50 × 31250 × 1.275 = $1,992,188

There is an unhedged amount of $7,812 to be received

(This could be hedged with a forward)

So 50 June call options at $1.275 are needed

Premium = $0.0185 × 50 × 31250 = $28,906

Paid at today's spot of 1.2653 = £22,845

Step 2   Outcome – end of June

Option exercised @ option rate (1.275)

50 × £31,250 = £1,562,500

Shortfall of $7,812 @ June forward 1.3 = £6,009 to be received

Step 3   Net outcome

£ 1,562,500 revenue + £6,009 – premium £22,845 = £1,545,644

Activity 10: Further practice

1   The company needs to buy dollars in May.

Forward contract

A forward currency contract will fix the exchange rate for the date required near the end of May. This will remove currency risk **provided that the franchise is won**. If the **franchise is not won** and the group has no use for US dollars, it will still have to buy the dollars at the forward rate. It will then have to sell them back for euros at the spot rate, which might result in an exchange loss.

Futures contract

A currency hedge using futures contracts will attempt to create a **compensating gain** on the futures market which will **offset** the **increase** in the **euro cost** if the dollar strengthens. The hedge works by entering into futures contracts to sell **euros** now and closing out by entering into futures contracts to buy **euros at the end of May** at a lower dollar price if the dollar has strengthened. Like a forward contract, the exchange rate in May is effectively fixed because, if the dollar weakens, the futures hedge will produce a loss which counterbalances the cheaper euro cost. However, because of inefficiencies in future market hedges, the exchange rate is not fixed to the same level of accuracy as a forward hedge.

A futures market hedge has the same weakness as a forward currency contract – if the franchise is not won, an **exchange loss** may result.

Currency option

A currency option is an ideal hedge in the franchise situation. It gives the company the **right but not the obligation** to sell euros for dollars in May (or in theory up to the end of June). It is only exercised if it is to the company's advantage; that is, if the dollar has strengthened. If the **dollar strengthens** and the franchise is won, the exchange rate has been **protected**. If the dollar strengthens and the **franchise is not won**, a **windfall gain** will result by **selling euros** at the exercise price and buying them more cheaply at spot with a stronger dollar. The only downside is the premium.

2 **Results of using currency hedges if the franchise is won**

Forward market

Using the forward market, the rate for **buying dollars** at the end of May is 1.2164 US$/€. The cost in euros is $12.75m/1.2164 = €10,481,749. This is a cost.

Futures

Date of contract

June future

Type of contract

Sell euro futures

Number of contracts

$12.75m / 1.2143 (futures rate) = 10,499,877 euros

10,499,877 / 62,500 euro contract size = 167.998 ie 168 contracts (to the nearest whole number)

Tick size

0.0001 × 62,500 = $6.25

Closing futures price

This can be estimated by assuming that the difference between the futures rate and the spot rate (ie basis) decreases constantly over time. On 31 May there will be one month left of this June contract, so the basis should have fallen to zero.

	28 Feb	31 May
Futures price	1.2143	
Spot rate now	1.2311	
		−0.0042
Basis (future − spot)	−0.0168	(0.0168 × 1/4)
Timing	4 months to expiry of future	1 month to expiry of future

Assuming basis = −0.0042 then the futures price will 0.0042 lower than the spot price.

Hedge outcome

Spot price	1.1509
	$
Opening futures price	1.2143
Closing futures price (1.1509 − 0.0042)	1.1467
Movement in ticks	676
Futures profits/(losses)	
168 contracts × tick movement × $6.25	709,800

Net outcome

	$
Spot market payment	(12,750,000)
Futures market profits/(losses)	709,800
	(12,040,200)

Translated at closing rate (1.1509) €10,461,552

This gives an effective rate of $12.75m/€10.461,552m = 1.2187

A **shortcut** that will deliver **approximately** the same answer is:

Opening futures price – closing basis = effective futures rate

Here this gives: 1.2143 – –0.0042 = 1.2185

Applying this rate gives an outcome in €s of $12.75m/1.2185 = €10,463,685

This is preferred approach for tackling futures questions because it is so much quicker.

The slight difference arises because this shortcut does not account for the fact that the futures hedge is for 168 contracts, not 167.998.

Options

Date of contract

June

Option type

Buy $, sell €, therefore a Euro put

Exercise price

Assume the option closest to the current spot (1.233) is used (other assumptions are justifiable)

Number of contracts

$12.75m / 1.233 (option rate) = 10,340,633 euros

10,340,633 / 31,250 euro contract size = 330.9 ie 331 contracts (to the nearest whole number)

This means that there is cover for selling euros for 331 × 31,250 × 1.233 = 12,753,844 dollars so there is a surplus of $3,844 which could be hedged at the forward rate (using the right-hand side of the spread as this is revenue) or left unhedged. At the forward rate $3,844 / 1.2198 = €3,151.

Premium

0.0238 × 31,250 × 331 = $246,181 at 1.2311

= €199,968

Outcome

	1.1509
	$
Option market	
Strike price	1.233
Closing price	1.1509
Exercise?	Yes
Outcome of option 331 × 31,250 × 1.233 = Surplus in $s vs $12.75m needed	$12,753,844 $3,844
At forward rate of 1.2198 (or spot rate of 1.1509 could be used)	€3,151

Net outcome

		1.1509
		€
Option exercised (331 × 31,250)	costing	10,343,750
Surplus (revenue)		(3,151)
Premium (cost)		199,968
		10,540,567

Summary

The company will either choose to purchase a **future** (which is cheaper than a forward) or an **option**. Although futures are slightly more advantageous at lower exchange rates, the net benefits of using an option are significant if the exchange rate moves in Smart's favour. Also, given that the transaction is not certain to be required, an option will be more suitable because it can be sold on if it is not needed.

On this basis an option is recommended.

Other conclusions are possible.

Managing interest rate risk

Learning objectives

On completion of this chapter, you should be able to:

	Syllabus reference no.
Evaluate, for a given hedging requirement, which of the following is most appropriate given the nature of the underlying position and the risk exposure: • Forward rate agreements (FRAs) • Interest rate futures • Interest rate swaps (and currency swaps from E2(b)) • Interest rate options	E3(a)

Exam context

This chapter completes **Section E** of the syllabus: '**Treasury and advanced risk management techniques.**'

Every exam will have a question that has a focus on syllabus Section E, which is most likely to focus mainly on Chapter 12 and/or Chapter 13.

This chapter focuses on interest rate risk management.

Chapter overview

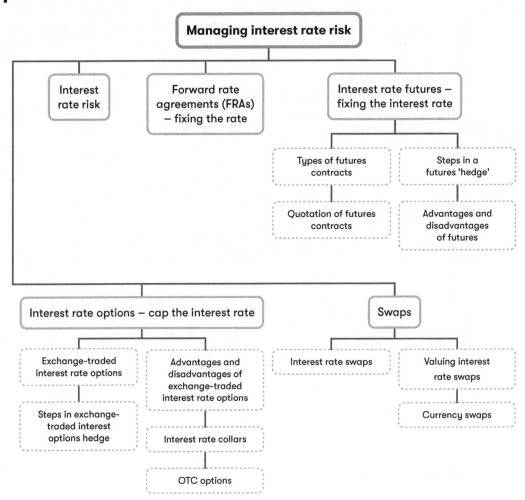

BPP
LEARNING
MEDIA

1 Interest rate risk

Interest rate risk is faced by both borrowers and lenders. It is the risk that the interest rate will move in such a way so as to cost a company, or an individual, money.

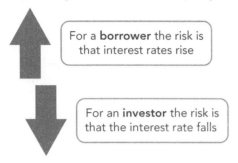

For a **borrower** the risk is that interest rates rise

For an **investor** the risk is that the interest rate falls

Note that a borrower will benefit from an interest rate fall and an investor (or lender) will benefit from an interest rate increase.

From the perspective of a company **borrowing** money, interest rate risk can be managed by **'smoothing'**, ie using a prudent mix of fixed and floating rate finance. If the company is risk averse or expects interest rates to rise, then the emphasis will be on using fixed rate finance.

If, however, a major loan (or investment) is being planned in the **future**, then the risk is harder to manage; this is shown below:

Now	3 months' time

Plan to take out a $5 million loan **in three months' time**

Take out $5 million loan; by this time **rates (even fixed rates) may have risen**

This risk (for a borrower or an investor) can be managed by a variety of interest rate derivatives; these techniques can achieve one of two outcomes.

Fix the rate of interest
Forward rate agreements, futures

Cap the rate of interest
Options

Finally, swaps can be used to **adjust the mix** of fixed and variable rate and the currency of the finance.

Essential reading

See Chapter 13 Section 1 of the Essential reading for a general introduction to interest rate risk.

The Essential reading is available as an Appendix of the digital edition of the Workbook.

2 Forward rate agreements (FRAs) – fixing the rate

KEY TERM

Forward rate agreement: A contract with a bank to receive or pay interest at a pre-determined interest rate on a notional amount over a fixed period in the future.

Like a currency forward, an FRA effectively **fixes** the rate. **Unlike** a currency forward, the FRA is a separate transaction, and is structured to create a fixed outcome by counterbalancing the impact that interest rate movements have on the actual transaction (ie a loan or an investment).

Quotation of forward rates

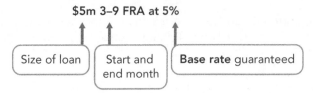

$5m 3–9 FRA at 5%

Size of loan | Start and end month | **Base rate** guaranteed

An FRA is over-the-counter agreement with an investment bank, it is separate from actual transaction allows a company to borrow (or invest) at a future date at the best rate available at that time.

Advantages of forward rates	Disadvantages of forward rates
Simpler than other derivative agreements	Fixed date agreements (the term of a 3–9 FRA is fixed in the FRA contract)
Normally free, always cheap (in terms of arrangement fees)	Rate quoted may be unattractive
Tailored to the company's precise requirements (in terms of amount of cover needed)	Higher default risk than an exchange-based derivative

Illustration 1: Altrak Co

Altrak Co is planning to take out a six-month fixed rate loan of $5 million in three months' time. It is concerned about the base rate rising above its current level of 5.25% per year. Altrak has been offered a 3–9 FRA at 5.5%.

Altrak can borrow at about 1% above the base rate.

Required

Advise Altrak of the likely outcome if in three months' time the base rate rises to 5.75%.

Solution

FRA outcome

Bank pays compensation because interest rates have risen compared to the 5.5% that is fixed in the FRA.

The bank will therefore pay 5.75% – 5.5% = 0.25% to Altrak

In $s this is:

0.25 ÷ 100 × $5m × 6 months (term of loan) ÷ 12 months (interest rate is annual) = $6,250

Actual loan

Altrak borrows at the best rate available, eg 5.75 + 1 = 6.75%

In $s this is 6.75 ÷ 100 × $5m × 6 months ÷ 12 months = $168,750

Net outcome

Net costs = 6.75% – 0.25% = 6.5%

In $s this is $168,750 – $6,250 = $162,500

Activity 1: Technique demonstration

Altrak Co is planning to take out a six-month fixed rate loan of $5 million in three months' time. It is concerned about the base rate rising above its current level of 5.25% per year. Altrak has been offered a 3–9 FRA at 5.5%.

Altrak can borrow at about 1% above the base rate.

Required

Advise Altrak of the likely outcome if in three months' time the base rate falls to 4.5%.

Solution

Prominent Note

The base rate may also be referred to by using the precise name given to the benchmark rate at which banks lend to each other in different countries, such as:

*   SONIA (the Sterling overnight index average) in the UK (this used to be known as LIBOR)
*   ESTR (the Euro short-term rate) in Europe
*   TONAR (Tokyo overnight average rate) in Japan
*   SARON (Swiss overnight rate) in Switzerland
*   SOFR (the secured overnight financing rate) in the US

3 Interest rate futures – fixing the interest rate

Futures contracts were used in the previous chapter to hedge currency. The points made in that chapter about the general features of futures including standardised dates and amounts, margins and marking to market all apply to interest rate futures.

A key **difference** from currency futures is that interest rate futures have a **standardised period** of three months. This means that a company that is intending to borrow for, say, a six-month term and is worried about interest rates rising will only receive compensation from an interest rate future as if it has borrowed for three months (the standard term of the future). As a result, two three-month contracts will be needed to cover a six-month loan.

Like FRAs, interest rate futures allow the **'fixing' of an interest rate.**

| Losses on actual transaction | Profits from futures | | Profits from actual transaction | Losses on futures |

KEY TERM

> **Interest rate future:** An agreement with an exchange to pay or receive interest at a pre-determined rate on a notional amount over a fixed **standard period** (usually **three months**) in the future.

3.1 Types of futures contract

A company with a **cash surplus** over a period of time in the future will be worried about interest rates falling; a futures contract to **receive interest** is needed, this is a **contract to buy** (so called because buying assets results in interest being received).

A company needing to **borrow money** in future will be worried about interest rates rising; this requires a futures contract to **pay interest**, this is a **contract to sell** (borrowers would sell bonds, which creates an obligation to pay interest).

KEY TERM

> **Contracts to buy:** Companies that will have a cash flow surplus require **contracts to buy**.
>
> **Contracts to sell:** Companies that will borrow require **contracts to sell**.

3.2 Quotation of futures contracts

Futures prices are quoted as follows:

December	94.75
March	94.65
June	94.55

The dates refer to the date at which the future expires eg a December future can be used at any time during the year until it expires at the end of December.

The price is in fact an **interest rate if it is subtracted from 100**, as follows:

December	100 − 94.75 = 5.25%
March	100 − 94.65 = 5.35%
June	100 − 94.55 = 5.45%

The easiest way of interpreting interest rate futures is to **convert them into percentages** and this is the method adopted in this chapter.

3.3 Steps in a futures 'hedge'

Step 1   **Now**

Contracts should be set in terms of **buying or selling interest** – choosing the closest standardised futures date **after** the loan begins, and **adjusting for the term of the loan compared to the three-month standard term of an interest rate future.**

Step 2   **In the future**

Complete the **actual** transaction on the **spot market**.

Step 3   **At the same time as Step 2**

Close out the futures contract by doing the opposite of what you did in Step 1.

Calculate net outcome.

BPP LEARNING MEDIA

Illustration 2: Altrak Co (cont.)

Altrak (see Illustration 1) is considering using the futures market.

It is 1 December, and an exchange is quoting the following prices for a standard $500,000 three-month contract. Contracts expire at the end of the relevant month. Base rate is 5.25%.

Prices are as follows:

December 94.75 = 5.25%	March 94.65 = 5.35%	June 94.55 = 5.45%

Required

Illustrate the outcome of a futures hedge, assuming that a loan is taken out at base rate +1% fixed at the start of the loan and that the base rate is 5.75% on 1 March.

It is quicker to leave your answer in %, and to convert into $s as a final step.

Solution

Step 1   On 1 December

Contracts **to sell** are required as Altrak is borrowing.

Number of contracts:

$$= \$5m \text{ loan} \div \$0.5m \text{ contract size} \times \frac{6 \text{ (term of loan)}}{3 \text{ (standard term of future)}}$$

$$= 20 \text{ contracts}$$

Contract date: Cover is required until the loan begins because it is the interest rate at this point that determines the risk (assuming the loan taken out is at a fixed rate, interest rate changes after the loan is taken out do not have any effect on loan repayments). Therefore, a March future at 5.35% (which covers the start of the loan on 1 March) is required.

Altrak should enter into 20 March futures (to sell) at 5.35%.

Step 2   1 March

Take out the actual loan: Altrak will borrow at base rate + 1% so this is 5.75 + 1 = 6.75%

Step 3   1 March

	Forecasting the futures price on 1 March (as for currency futures)	
	Now to 1 Dec	1 March
March future	5.35	
Base rate	5.25	
Basis	0.10	× 1/4 = 0.03
	4 months of time until the end of future	1 month remaining

The March future rate is forecast to be 0.03% (or 3 basis points, where 0.01% = 1 basis point) above the base rate on 1 March, so if the base rate is 5.75% the future price should be 5.75 + 0.03 = **5.78**%

Close out the futures contract by doing the opposite of what you did in Step 1.

1 Dec contract to pay interest at	5.35%
1 March contract to buy receive interest at	5.78%
Difference	0.43%

This is profit as interest is received at a higher rate than it is paid; this net amount acts as compensation for interest rates rising.

Calculate net outcome

As a percentage this is 6.75% (Step 2) minus 0.43% (Step 3) = 6.32%

In $s this is 0.0632 × $5m × 6 months (term of loan) ÷ 12 months (interest rates are in annual terms) = $158,000

This is a better outcome than the FRA in Illustration 1.

Activity 2: Technique demonstration

Altrak (see Activity 1) is considering using the futures market. It is 1 December, and an exchange is quoting the following prices for a standard $500,000 three-month contract. Contracts expire at the end of the relevant month. The base rate is 5.25%. Prices are quoted **at (100 − annual yield)** in basis points, as follows:

December	94.75	March	94.65	June	94.55

Required

Illustrate the outcome of a futures hedge, assuming that a loan is taken out at base rate +1% fixed at the start of the loan and that the base rate is 4.50% on 1 March.

It is quicker to leave your answer in %, and to convert into $s as a final step.

Solution

3.4 Advantages and disadvantage of futures

Advantage of futures	Disadvantages of futures
Flexible dates, ie a September future can be used on any day until the end of September	Only available in large contract sizes
Lower credit risk because exchange-traded	Margin may need to be topped up on a daily basis to cover expected losses
	Basis may not fall in a linear way over time (basis risk)

4 Interest rate options – cap the interest rate

4.1 Exchange-traded interest rate options

The mechanics of exchange-traded interest options are **not** similar to exchange-traded currency options that were covered in the previous chapter.

In fact exchange-traded interest rate options are the same as interest rate futures contracts except that they only ever pay compensation, they never incur losses.

For this reason, exchange-traded interest rate options are often called **'options on futures'**.

A key **difference** from interest rate futures is that exchange-traded interest options involve the payment of a **premium**.

Exchange-traded interest rate option: An agreement with an exchange to pay or receive interest at a pre-determined rate on a **standard** notional amount over a fixed standard period (usually **three months**) in the future.

There are two types of option contract, calls and puts.

Put option: An option to **pay interest** at a pre-determined rate on a standard notional amount over a fixed period in the future.

Call option: An option to **receive interest** at a pre-determined rate on a standard notional amount over a fixed period in the future.

- **Call option** – a right to buy (receive interest)
- **Put option** – a right to sell (pay interest)

4.2 Steps in an exchange-traded options hedge

The steps are almost identical to the futures hedge, **the differences are in bold**.

Step 1   **Now**

Contracts should be set in terms of **call or put options** – choosing the closest standardised **option** date after the loan begins, and adjusting for the term of the loan compared to the three-month standard term of an interest rate future.

Pay a premium for the option.

Step 2   **In the future**

Complete the actual transaction on the spot market.

Step 3   **At the same time as Step 2**

Close out the options contract on the futures market by doing the opposite of what you did in Step 1 but **only if the option makes a profit.**

Calculate net outcome.

 Illustration 3: Altrak Co (cont.)

Altrak is considering using the options market. It is 1 December, and the exchange is quoting the following prices for a standard $500,000 three-month contract. Contracts expire at the end of the relevant month. The base rate is 5.25%.

Strike price	Calls		Puts	
	March	June	March	June
94.35	0.018	0.025	0.125	0.140
94.55	0.010	0.012	0.245	0.248

This the interest rate when subtracted from 100

This the premium as a %

Required

Illustrate an option hedge at 5.45% (the rate closest to the current spot rate implying a strike price of 100 – 5.45 = 94.55), assuming a loan is taken out at base rate +1% and the base rate on 1 March is 5.75%.

It is quicker to leave your answer in %, and to convert into $s as a final step.

Solution

Steps as follows:

Step 1   **On 1 December**

Put options are required as Altrak is borrowing.

Number of contracts:

$$= \$5m \text{ loan} \div \$0.5m \text{ contract size} \times \frac{6 \text{ (term of loan)}}{3 \text{ (standard term of future)}}$$

= 20 contracts

Date: As for futures, cover is required until the loan begins.

Altrak should enter into 20 March put options (to sell) at 5.45%.

A premium of 0.245% is paid.

Step 2   1 March

Complete the actual loan: Altrak will borrow at base rate + 1% so this is 5.75 + 1 = 6.75%

Step 3   1 March

Forecasting the futures price on 1 March (as for interest rate futures)

	Now to 1 Dec	1 March
March future	5.35	
Base rate	5.25	
Basis	0.10	× 1/4 = 0.03
	4 months of time until end of future	1 month remaining

The March future rate is forecast to be 0.03% above the base rate on 1 March, so if the base rate is 5.75% the future price should be 5.75 + 0.03 = **5.78%**

Close out the options by doing the opposite of what you did in Step 1 (if a profit is made).

1 Dec contract to pay interest at	5.45%
1 March contract to buy receive interest at	5.78%
Difference	0.33%

Opting to pay interest at 5.45% and receive interest at 5.78% gives a profit of 0.33%. This is paid to Altrak by the exchange as compensation for interest rates rising.

Calculate net outcome

As a percentage this is 0.245% (Step 1) + 6.75% (Step 2) minus 0.33% (Step 3) = 6.665%

In $s this is 0.0665 × $5m × 6 months (term of loan) ÷ 12 months (interest rates are in annual terms) = $166,250.

This is a worse outcome than the FRA or the future as shown in Illustrations 1 and 2. This is due to the cost of the options (the premium), but if interest rates fall then the result of the options hedge will improve (but the forward and futures hedge both result in a fixed outcome and will not improve if interest rates fall).

Activity 3: Technique demonstration

Altrak is considering using the options market. It is 1 December, and the exchange is quoting the following prices for a standard $500,000 three-month contract. Contracts expire at the end of the relevant month. The base rate is 5.25%.

Strike price	Calls		Puts	
	March	June	March	June
94.35	0.018	0.025	0.125	0.140
94.55	0.010	0.012	0.245	0.248

Required

Illustrate an option hedge at 5.45%, again assuming a loan is taken out at base rate +1% and the base rate on 1 March is 4.50%.

Solution

4.3 Advantages and disadvantages of exchange traded interest rate options

Advantages of options	Disadvantages of options
Flexible dates (like a future)	Only available in large contract sizes
Allow a company to take advantage of favourable movements in interest rates	Can be expensive due to the requirement to pay an up-front premium
Useful for uncertain transactions, can be sold if not needed	

4.4 Interest rate collars

A company can write and sell options to raise revenue to reduce the expense of an exchange traded interest rate options.

A combined strategy of buying and selling options is called a **collar**.

For a borrower a collar will involve buying a put option to cap the cost of borrowing and selling a call option at a lower rate to establish a floor (the borrower will not benefit if interest rates fall below this level).

If interest rates rise the borrower is protected by the cap.

If interest rates fall the borrower will benefit until the interest rate falls to the level of the floor. If interest rates fall below this then the borrower will have to pay compensation to the purchaser of the call option.

This is illustrated below.

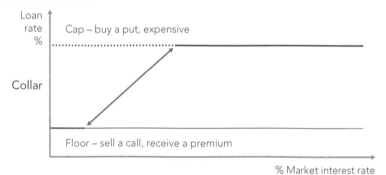

For an investor a collar will involve **buying a call option** to establish a floor for the interest rate and **selling a put option** at a higher rate to establish a cap (the investor will not benefit if interest rates rise above this level).

If interest rates fall the investor is protected by the floor.

If interest rates rise the investor will benefit until the interest rate rises to the level of the cap. If interest rates rise above this then the investor will have to pay compensation to the purchaser of the put option.

Illustration 4: Altrak Co (cont.)

Altrak is considering using the options market. It is 1 December, and the exchange is quoting the following prices for a standard $500,000 three-month contract. Contracts expire at the end of the relevant month. The base rate is 5.25%.

Strike	Calls		Puts	
Price	March	June	March	June
94.35	0.018	0.025	0.125	0.140
94.55	0.010	0.012	0.245	0.248
94.75	0.008	0.010	0.490	0.492

Required

Illustrate the outcome of a collar with a put at 5.45% and the call at 5.25% if the base rate in three months is 5.75%.

It is quicker to leave your answer in %, and to convert into $s as a final step.

Solution

Steps as follows:

Step 1 On 1 December

Put options are required as Altrak is borrowing.

Number of contracts: as before = **20 contracts**

   Date: as before, March.

Altrak should enter into 20 March put options (to sell) at 5.45% **and sell 20 March call options at 5.25%.**

A net premium of 0.245% – **0.008%** = 0.237% is paid.

Step 2 1 March

Complete the actual loan: Altrak will borrow at base rate + 1% so this is 5.75 + 1 = 6.75%

Step 3 1 March

As before, the March future rate is forecast to be 0.03% above base rate on 1 March, so if base rate is 5.75% the future price should be 5.75 + 0.03 = **5.78%**

Close out the options by doing the opposite of what you did in Step 1 (if a profit is made).

1 Dec contract to pay interest at	5.45%
1 March contract to buy receive interest at	5.78%
Difference	0.33%

Call options will not be exercised by the holder as interest rates have risen.

Calculate net outcome

As a percentage this is 0.237% (Step 1) + 6.75% (Step 2) minus 0.33% (Step 3) = 6.657%

This is cheaper than simply buying put options if interest rates rise.

Activity 4: Technique demonstration

Activity 3 continued – Altrak's FD considers the options market to be too expensive.

Required

Illustrate the outcome of a collar with a put at 5.45% and the call at 5.25% if the base rate in three months is 4.50%.

Solution

4.5 Over-the-counter options

Options are also available directly from a bank. These are tailored to the precise loan size and timing required by a company, but will be more expensive and cannot be sold on if not needed.

5 Swaps

A swap is where two counterparties agree to pay each other's interest payments. This may be in the same currency (an interest rate swap) or in different currencies (a currency swap).

5.1 Interest rate swaps

Swaps enable a company to:

(a) **Manage interest rate risk** – for example, by swapping some of its **existing** variable rate finance into fixed rate finance a company can protect itself against interest rate rises; this may be cheaper than refinancing the original debt (which may involve redemption fees for early repayment and issues costs on new debt).

(b) **Reduce borrowing costs** – by taking out a loan in a market where they have a comparative interest rate advantage.

Usually **a bank will organise the swap** to remove the need for counterparties to find each other and to remove default risk.

Tutorial Note

A useful approach to adopt in an exam for a swap organised by a bank is to assume – unless told otherwise – that the variable interest rate payment is at the base rate (eg SONIA). This is what normally happens in reality

Illustration 5: Altrak Co (cont.)

Altrak is interested in the idea of using a swap arrangement to create a fixed rate for a long-term loan of $20 million that is also being arranged. The swap will be organised and underwritten by a bank which has found another company (Company A) willing to participate in a swap arrangement; the merchant bank will charge a fee of 0.20% to both companies.

Company A is a retailer with low levels of gearing; it has reviewed its balance of existing fixed and variable rate finance and wants to increase its exposure to variable rate finance.

The borrowing rates available to Altrak and to Company A are:

	Altrak	Company A
Fixed	6.50%	5.55%
Variable	Base rate + 1.00%	Base rate + 0.75%

Required

1   Explain why Altrak wants a fixed rate loan at the same time as Company A wants a variable rate.

2   Identify whether a swap could be organised to the benefit of both companies.

3   If so, identify the reason(s) for this.

Solution

1   Altrak could have:

• Different expectations about the future direction of interest rates.

• A different attitude to risk – Altrak's business risk or financial risk could be higher.

2 Could a swap be beneficial to both companies:

Step 1 **Assess potential for gain from swap**

	Altrak	**Company A**	**Difference**
Fixed	6.50%	5.55%	0.95% Company A cheaper
Variable	Base rate + 1.00%	Base rate + 0.75%	0.25% Company A cheaper
			Difference of differences = 0.95% − 0.25% = 0.70%

If a swap uses company A's comparative advantage in fixed rate finance, as is suggested here, then a gain of 0.70% (before fees) is available. This falls to 0.70 − (2 × 0.20%) = 0.30% after fees. If this is split evenly it gives a gain of 0.15% to each party.

Step 2 **Swap, variable rate at base rate, designed to splitting gain 50:50, ie 0.15% each**

Position if no swap	6.50%	Base rate + 0.75%
	Altrak	**Company A**
Actual loan	Base rate + 1 %	5.55%
Fees	0.20%	0.20%
Swap: variable	(Base rate)	Base rate
Swap: fixed*	5.15%	(5.15%)
	6.35%	Base rate + 0.60%
	0.15% gain vs no swap	0.15% gain

* The fixed rate is a balancing figure designed to give the required gain to each party.

3 The swap has worked by using Company A's access to cheap fixed rate finance to drive down finance costs. In addition it will have saved Company A the costs of redeeming fixed rate finance and organising new variable rate finance.

Activity 5: Swap example

Company A is investigating the possibility of an interest rate swap.

A bank would charge 0.1% fees to both parties for organising the swap.

	Company A	**Company B**
Fixed	8.00%	7.00%
Variable	Base rate + 1.00%	Base rate − 1.00%

Required

Show how a swap could benefit both companies.

Solution

5.1.1 Swaps as a spread

Where a bank is operating as a middle-man in an interest rate swap, it will set up the swap by identifying the swap partners and will set up the two legs of the swap (ie fixed and variable) so that the companies involved are entering into contracts with the bank and not directly with each other.

This helps to minimise default risk.

Using the two companies from Illustration 5, the role of the bank can be illustrated as:

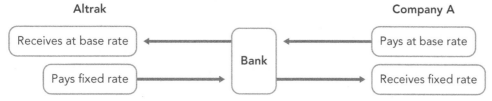

Because the variable rate of a swap can be assumed to be at the base rate (unless otherwise stated in a question) then all the bank has to establish is the rate to apply to the fixed rate leg of the deal.

The fixed rate can then be quoted by the bank as a **spread**, for example:

The bank makes its profit from the swap from the difference between these rates. Here the profit is 5.35 – 4.95 = 0.40%. This is another way of showing the fee of 0.2% to each company (0.40% in total) that is mentioned in Illustration 5.

If bid and ask prices are quoted like this then interest rate swap questions become simpler.

 ## Illustration 6: Interest rate swap

This example draws from the scenario set up in Illustration 5 but presents the information relating to the swap in a different way.

Altrak is interested in using a swap to create a **fixed rate** for a loan of $20 million. The swap will be organised and underwritten by a merchant bank.

The rate being quoted by the bank is 4.95%–5.35%.

The borrowing rates available to Altrak are:

Altrak	
Fixed	6.50%
Variable	Base rate + 1.00%

Required

Calculate the net gain to Altrak from the swap.

Solution

Altrak	
Borrows at a variable rate	Base rate + 1%

Impact of the swap

Altrak	
Receives variable %	(Base rate)

Altrak	
Pays fixed %	5.35%*

Total costs = 6.35%

Potential gain (vs 6.5%) = 0.15%

* This is rate **received** by the bank, and is the higher of the two rates offered in the spread.

This is the same outcome as Illustration 5.

The other company involved in the swap will receive 4.95% on their fixed leg of the swap (the bank pays the lower of the two rates offered in the spread).

5.2 Valuing interest rate swaps

An interest rate swap can also be valued as the NPV of the net cash flows under the swap.

At the start of the swap the swap contract is designed to give an NPV of zero based on the current FRA rates (remember a zero NPV means that a project is delivering exactly the return required).

Steiner Co

Annual spot rates (from the yield curve) available to Steiner Co for the next three years are as follows:

One year	Two years	Three years
3.00%	4.10%	4.90%

This means that if Steiner wants to borrow for two years (for example) it will able to borrow at annualised rate of 4.1% per year for the two-year period.

Forward rates can be calculated from this data, as follows:

If Steiner wanted to have a FRA for one year this would be 3.0% (as above).

If Steiner wanted to have a FRA starting at the end of Year 1 and ending a year later this would be calculated by comparing the borrowing costs for two years to the borrowing costs for one year, ie:

$$\frac{1.041^2}{1.03} - 1 = 0.0521 = 5.21\%$$

If Steiner wanted to have a FRA starting at the end of Year 2 and ending a year later this would be calculated by comparing borrowing costs for three years to the borrowing costs for two years, ie:

$$\frac{1.049^3}{1.041^2} - 1 = 0.0652 = 6.52\%$$

Activity 6: Interest rate swap

Annual spot rates (from the yield curve) available to Steiner Co for the next three years are as follows:

One year	Two years	Three years
3.00%	4.10%	4.90%

This means that if Steiner wants to borrow for two years (for example) it will able to borrow at annualised rate of 4.1% per year for the two-year period.

Forward rates have been calculated from this data (as shown in the previous illustration), as follows:

FRA for year two:	3.00%
FRA for year two:	5.21%
FRA for year three:	6.52%

Steiner Co has $100 million of variable rate borrowings repayable in three years' time and is concerned about interest rates rising.

A variable – fixed swap deal is being negotiated with a bank. This will be based on paying the bank a fixed rate over the three-year period in exchange for a variable rate less 0.50%.

Required

Estimate the fixed rate that will be paid as part of the swap.

Solution

5.3 Currency swaps

Currency swaps enable a company to:

(a) **Manage currency risk** – by swapping some of its **existing or new** domestic debt into foreign currency debt a company can match foreign currency cash inflows and assets to costs/liabilities in the same currency.

(b) **Reduce borrowing costs** – by taking out a loan in a (domestic) market where they have a comparative interest rate advantage.

Currency swaps are similar to interest rate swaps but normally involve the **actual transfer of the funds that have been borrowed** (the initial capital is swapped at the start and then back at the end to repay the original loans).

Illustration 7: Currency swap

Altrak Co intends to purchase a European company for €90 million with euro debt finance. Franco is a European company that is setting up operations in the US and wants to use $ debt finance. A bank has indicated that it can organise a swap for a fee of 0.2% to each party.

The principal amount will be exchanged and re-exchanged at the start and end of the swap. The exchange of principal will be at the rate of €0.90 to the $.

Variable rates	Altrak	Franco
$ %	6.25%	7.25%
€ %	4.50%	5.00%

Required

Estimate the gain or loss in % to both Altrak and Franco from entering into this swap.

Solution

Steps as follows:

Step 1   Assess potential for gain from swap

	Altrak	Franco	Difference
$ %	6.25%	7.25%	1.00% Altrak 1% cheaper
€ %	4.50%	5.00%	0.50% Altrak 0.5% cheaper
			Difference of differences = 1.00% − 0.50% = 0.50%

If a swap uses Altrak's comparative advantage in $ finance, as is suggested here, then a gain of 0.50% (before fees) is available. This falls to 0.5 − (2 × 0.20%) = 0.1% after fees. If this is split evenly it gives a gain of 0.05% to each party.

Step 2   Swap, variable rate at the base rate, designed to split gain 50:50, ie 0.05% each

Position if no swap	4.50% in euros	7.25% in dollars
	Altrak	**Franco**
Actual loan	6.25%	5.00%
Fees	0.20%	0.20%
Swap: in dollars	(6.25)%	6.25%
Swap: in euros	4.25%	(4.25%)
	4.45%	7.20%
	0.05% gain vs no swap	0.05% gain

5.3.1 Valuing a currency swap

A currency swap can be valued as the NPV of the net cash flows under the swap.

Activity 7: Technique demonstration

Steiner Co has a ten-year fixed rate loan of €8.8 million, which pays 5% p.a. interest at the end of each six-month period. The company is concerned about the risk of the euro strengthening against the pound over the next **two years** and is considering whether to use a currency swap or forward rates.

The available forward rates are (in terms of euros to the pound):

6 months	12 months	18 months	24 months
€1.201 to the £	€1.203 to the £	€1.205 to the £	€1.206 to the £

UK base rate is as follows:

6 months	12 months	18 months	24 months
3.25%	3.45%	3.50%	3.52%

The swap currently being proposed is €1.2032 to the £.

Required

1   Estimate the present value of the gain or loss (in £m) from entering into the swap compared to using forward rates.

2   Estimate the swap rate that would make it competitive with the use of forward rates.

Solution

5.3.2 Swaptions

A 'swaption' is an option to enter into a swap in return for an up-front premium. For example, if there was any uncertainty over the proposed acquisition in the previous Activity, then a swaption could be used.

5.3.3 FOREX swaps

> **FOREX swap:** A short-term swap made up of a spot transaction and a forward transaction which allows a company to obtain foreign currency for a short time period (usually within a week) and then to swap back into the domestic currency a short time later at a known (forward) rate.

A FOREX swap is useful for hedging because it allows companies to shift temporarily into or out of one currency in exchange for a second currency without incurring the exchange rate risk of holding an open position in the currency they temporarily hold.

FOREX swap

An example of a FOREX swap is where an American company has a surplus cash balance in euros which is not required for any transactions in the next week.

If this company knows that they need to pay their manufacturers in US dollars in one week's time they could:

(a) Sell some euros **at the spot rate** and buy US dollars to cover this expense

(b) Then in one week buy euros and sell dollars to replenish their cash balance in euros

However, this exposes the company to transaction risk.

This can be avoided by:

(a) Sell some euros **at the spot rate** and buy US dollars to cover this expense

(b) **At the same time arrange a forward contract** to sell dollars for euros in one week

This combination of a simultaneous forward and spot transaction is called a FOREX swap.

> ## PER alert
>
> One of the optional performance objectives in your PER is to advise on using instruments or techniques to manage financial risk. This chapter has looked at interest rate risk, which is an aspect of financial risk.

Chapter summary

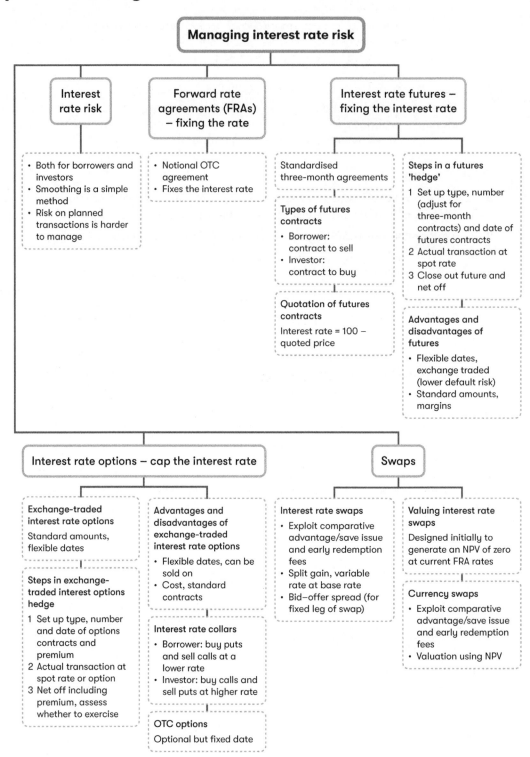

Managing interest rate risk

Interest rate risk

- Both for borrowers and investors
- Smoothing is a simple method
- Risk on planned transactions is harder to manage

Forward rate agreements (FRAs) – fixing the rate

- Notional OTC agreement
- Fixes the interest rate

Interest rate futures – fixing the interest rate

Standardised three-month agreements

Types of futures contracts

- Borrower: contract to sell
- Investor: contract to buy

Quotation of futures contracts

Interest rate = 100 – quoted price

Steps in a futures 'hedge'

1. Set up type, number (adjust for three-month contracts) and date of futures contracts
2. Actual transaction at spot rate
3. Close out future and net off

Advantages and disadvantages of futures

- Flexible dates, exchange traded (lower default risk)
- Standard amounts, margins

Interest rate options – cap the interest rate

Exchange-traded interest rate options

Standard amounts, flexible dates

Steps in exchange-traded interest options hedge

1. Set up type, number and date of options contracts and premium
2. Actual transaction at spot rate or option
3. Net off including premium, assess whether to exercise

Advantages and disadvantages of exchange-traded interest rate options

- Flexible dates, can be sold on
- Cost, standard contracts

Interest rate collars

- Borrower: buy puts and sell calls at a lower rate
- Investor: buy calls and sell puts at higher rate

OTC options

Optional but fixed date

Swaps

Interest rate swaps

- Exploit comparative advantage/save issue and early redemption fees
- Split gain, variable rate at base rate
- Bid–offer spread (for fixed leg of swap)

Valuing interest rate swaps

Designed initially to generate an NPV of zero at current FRA rates

Currency swaps

- Exploit comparative advantage/save issue and early redemption fees
- Valuation using NPV

Knowledge diagnostic

1. Forward rate agreements

Unlike currency forwards, interest rate FRAs are 'notional' derivative-style agreements.

2. Interest rate futures

Unlike currency futures these are based on a standardised time period of three months; this influence the number of interest rate futures contracts that are needed.

3. Interest rate options (exchange traded)

Unlike exchange traded currency options, these are closed out on the futures market.

4. Interest rate swaps

Variable rate leg of the swap is at the base rate.

5. Bid–offer quotes for swaps

If given, this is the rate at which the fixed rate is being offered. As ever the company gets the worst part of the spread.

6. Swap valuation

Uses FRA which can be derived from the yield curve.

Further study guidance

Question practice

Now try the following from the Further question practice bank (available in the digital edition of the workbook):

Q23 *Shawter*

Q24 *Carrick plc*

Q25 *Theta Inc*

Further reading

There are two Technical Articles available on ACCA's website, one called 'Currency swaps', and the other 'Determining interest rate forwards and their application to swap valuation'.

We recommend you read these articles as part of your preparation for the AFM exam. Both are written by a member of the ACCA AFM examining team.

Activity answers

Activity 1: Technique demonstration

FRA outcome

Altrak pays compensation to the bank because interest rates have fallen compared to the 5.5% that is fixed in the FRA.

Altrak will therefore pay 5.5% − 4.5% = 1.00% to the bank

In $s this is:

1.00 ÷ 100 × $5m × 6 months (term of loan) ÷ 12 months (interest rate is annual) = $25,000

Actual loan

Altrak borrows at the best rate available, eg 4.5 + 1 = 5.5%

In $s this is 5.5 ÷ 100 × $5m × 6 months ÷ 12 months = $137,500

Net outcome

Net costs = 5.5% + 1% = 6.5%

In $s this is $137,500 + $25,000 = $162,500

This is the same outcome whether interest rates rise or fall; an FRA **fixes** the company's borrowing costs.

Activity 2: Technique demonstration

Steps as follows:

Step 1 On 1 December

Contracts **to sell** are required as Altrak is borrowing.

Number of contracts:

$$= \$5m \text{ loan} \div \$0.5m \text{ contract size} \times \frac{6 \text{ (term of loan)}}{3 \text{ (standard term of future)}}$$

= 20 contracts

Date – Cover is required until the loan begins because it is the interest rate at this point that determines the risk (assuming the loan taken out is at a fixed rate, interest rate changes after the loan is taken out do not have any effect on loan repayments). Therefore, a March future at 5.35% (which covers the start of the loan on 1 March) is required.

Altrak should enter into 20 March futures (to sell) at 5.35%.

Step 2 1 March

Complete the actual loan: Altrak will borrow at base rate + 1% so this is 4.5 + 1 = 5.5%

Step 3 1 March

	Forecasting the futures price on 1 March (as for currency futures)	
	Now to 1 Dec	*1 March*
March future	5.35	
Base rate	5.25	
Basis	0.10	× 1/4 = 0.03
	4 months of time until end of future	1 month remaining

The March future rate is forecast to be 0.03% above the base rate on 1 March, so if the base rate is 4.5% the future price should be 4.5 + 0.03 = **4.53%**

Close out the futures contract by doing the opposite of what you did in Step 1.

1 Dec contract to pay interest at	5.35%
1 March contract to buy receive interest at	4.53%
Difference	(0.82)%

Interest rate have fallen. Since the rate of interest received is below the rate of interest paid, a **loss** is made; this is paid by Altrak to the exchange.

Calculate net outcome

As a percentage this is 5.5% (Step 2) plus 0.82% (Step 3) = 6.32%.

In $s this is 0.0632 × $5m × 6 months (term of loan) ÷ 12 months (interest rates are in annual terms) = $158,000.

This is the same outcome as the illustration, showing that futures fix the outcome.

Activity 3: Technique demonstration

Step 1 **On 1 December**

Put options are required as Altrak is borrowing.

Number of contracts:

$$= \text{\$5m loan} \div \text{\$0.5m contract size} \times \frac{6 \text{ (term of loan)}}{3 \text{ (standard term of future)}}$$

= 20 contracts

Date: as for futures, cover is required until the loan begins.

Altrak should enter into 20 March put options (to sell) at 5.45%.

A premium of 0.245% is paid.

Step 2 **1 March**

Complete the actual loan: Altrak will borrow at base rate + 1% so this is 4.5 + 1 = 5.5%

Step 3 **1 March**

Forecasting the futures price on 1 March (as for currency futures)

	Now to 1 Dec		1 March
March future	5.35		
Base rate	5.25		
		× 1/4	
Basis	0.10	=	0.03
	4 months of time until end of future		1 month remaining

The March future rate is forecast to be 0.03% above the base rate on 1 March, so if the base rate is 4.5% the future price should be 4.5 + 0.03 = **4.53%**

Close out the options by doing the opposite of what you did in Step 1 (if a profit is made).

1 Dec put options to pay interest at	5.45%
1 March contract to buy receive interest at	4.53%

Difference would generate a loss so the option is NOT exercised.

Calculate net outcome

As a percentage this is 0.245% (Step 1) + 5.5% (Step 2) = 5.745%

In $s this is 0.05745 × $5m × 6 months (term of loan) ÷ 12 months (interest rates are in annual terms) = $143,625.

This is a better outcome than the FRA or the future in Illustrations 1 and 2, showing that the worst case scenario is that the option is exercised but if it is not then there will be a better outcome because interest rates have moved in a company's favour.

Activity 4: Technique demonstration

Steps as follows:

Step 1   On 1 December

Put options are required as Altrak is borrowing.

Number of contracts: as before = **20 contracts**

Date: as before, March.

Altrak should enter into 20 March put options (to sell) at 5.45% **and sell 20 March call options at 5.25%.**

A net premium of 0.245% **– 0.008%** = 0.237% is paid.

Step 2   1 March

Complete the actual loan: Altrak will borrow at base rate + 1% so this is 4.5 + 1 = 5.5%

Step 3   1 March

As before, the March future rate is forecast to be 0.03% above base rate on 1 March, so if base rate is 4.5% the future price should be 4.5 + 0.03 = **4.53%**

Close out the options by doing the opposite of what you did in Step 1 (if a profit is made).

Put options are not valuable because interest rates have fallen.

The holder of call option will make profits if interest rates fall and Altrak will have to pay this to the holder of the call option.

1 Dec call options to receive interest at	5.25%
1 March contract to pay interest at	4.53%
Difference	0.72%

Calculate net outcome.

As a percentage this is 0.237% (Step 1) + 5.5% (Step 2) + 0.72% (Step 3) = 6.457%

Activity 5: Swap example

Step 1   Assess potential for gain from swap

	Company A	Company B	Difference
Fixed	8%	7%	1% Company B cheaper
Variable	Base rate + 1.00%	Base rate – 1%	2% Company B cheaper
			Difference of differences = 2% – 1% = 1%

Here no swap has been suggested.

If a swap uses company B's comparative advantage in variable rate finance then a gain of 1.0% (before fees) is available.

This means company B will need to borrow at a variable rate and swap to fixed.

Company A will therefore swap from fixed to variable.

0.1% fees are charged to both companies so this gain will be 0.8% after fees, split 50:50 ie 0.8% × 0.5 = 0.40% each.

Step 2   Swap, variable rate at the base rate, designed to splitting gain 50:50

Position if no swap	Base rate + 1%	7%
	Company A	**Company B**
Actual loan	8%	Base rate – 1%
Fees	0.1%	0.1%
Swap: variable	Base rate	(Base rate)
Swap: fixed*	(7.5%)	7.5%
	Base rate + 0.6%	6.6%
	0.4% gain vs no swap	0.4% gain

* the fixed rate is a balancing figure designed to give the required gain to each party.

Activity 6: Interest rate swap

The swap will be designed so that the bank makes a reasonable return; the bank will expect to at least make an NPV of 0 from the deal.

The bank's expected payments (receipts to the company) at a variable rate are estimated, using the FRA rates as:

	One year	Two years	Three years
FRA	3.00%	5.21%	6.52%
FRA – 0.5%	2.50%	4.71%	6.02%
In $m	$2.50m	$4.71m	$6.02m

The bank's expected receipts (payments by the company) at a fixed rate = R

The bank's net cash flows will be:

	One year	Two years	Three years
In $m	R – $2.5m	R – $4.71m	R – $6.02m

These are discounted at the spot yield rates of 3% for one year, 4.1% for two years and 4.9% for three years:

Time	1	2	3	Total NPV
Net cash flows	R – 2.5	R – 4.71	R – 6.02	
Df 3%	0.971			
Df 4.1%		0.923		
Df 4.9%			0.866	
Total	0.971R – 2.428	0.923R – 4.347	0.866R – 5.213	2.76R – 11.988

For the NPV to be zero then 2.76R = 11.988 so R = $4.343m per year.

As a percentage this is 4.343/100 = 4.343%.

Although at the start of the swap the present value of the swap is zero, the value of the swap will change as rates fluctuate.

Activity 7: Technique demonstration

1   Steiner has a loan in Euro which pays interest every 6 months at an ANNUAL rate of 5%; this means they must pay = 5% x €8m x 6/12 = €220,000, every 6 months.

Steiner is worried that if the € strengthens it will end up having to pay more interest in £s.

To deal with this risk Steiner can either enter into a swap contract with a fixed exchange rate over the entire period of €1.2032, or enter into a forward contract for each payment all the way out to the end of the two years of the loan.

These choices can be assessed separately, by calculating the present value of each approach, or together by looking at the differences in the cash flows from using the two approaches (this is the approach shown below).

Whichever approach is used a discount rate will be required. Since the time periods are 6 monthly, the discount rate should be the 6 monthly base rates given in the question.

Working

Discount rate

Time (in six-month periods)	1	2	3	4
Annual base interest rate	3.25%	3.45%	3.50%	3.52%
In terms of six-month periods	1.625%	1.725%	1.750%	1.760%

Time (in six-month periods)	1	2	3	4
Cash flow in €'000 (2.5% every six months)	220	220	220	220
Proposed swap rate	1.2032	1.2032	1.2032	1.2032
£ cash paid (cash outflow)	182.846	182.846	182.846	182.846
Forward rate	1.201	1.203	1.205	1.206
£ equivalent of euro receipts (cash inflow)	183.181	182.876	182.573	182.421
Net gain/loss	0.335	0.030	−0.273	−0.425
Discount rate **(see workings above)**	0.984	0.966	0.949	0.933
Present value	0.330	0.029	−0.259	−0.396

Total **−0.296** in £000s

The swap is not acceptable on these terms (ie the forward is cheaper).

2   This requires you to understand the total present value of the cost of the forward contracts in £000s and then convert these to an amount paid **per year** in £000s. The swap rate is calculated by comparing the payment in Euros of €220,000 to the rate paid under the forward contract per year in £000s.

Working

Swap in £'000

Time (in six-month periods)	1	2	3	4
Cash flow in €'000 (2.5% every six months)	220	220	220	220
Forward rate	1.201	1.203	1.205	1.206
£ equivalent	183.181	182.876	182.573	182.421
Discount rate	0.984	0.966	0.949	0.933
Present value	180.252	176.726	173.313	170.125
Total	700.416	in £000s		
Cumulative discount factor	3.832	(addition of the discount factors given)		
Annuity	182.768	in £000s		

Swap proposed

Time (in six-month periods)	1	2	3	4
Cash flow in €'000	220	220	220	220
Cash flow in £'000	182.768	182.768	182.768	182.768
ie swap rate =	**1.2037**	(220/182.768)		

14

Financial reconstruction

Learning objectives

On completion of this chapter, you should be able to:

	Syllabus reference no.
Assess an organisational situation and **determine whether a financial reconstruction is an appropriate strategy** for a given business situation	D1 (a)
Assess the likely response of the capital market and/or individual suppliers of capital to any reconstruction scheme and the impact their response is likely to have upon the value of the organisation	D1 (b)

Exam context

Chapters 14 and 15 cover Section D of the syllabus 'Corporate reconstruction and re-organisation'.

The chapter starts by discussing how to approach an evaluation of a reconstruction scheme designed to avoid business failure.

The chapter then moves on to consider other types of reconstruction schemes which are designed to increase value.

In either case debt covenants may be relevant, and the chapter ends by discussing the importance of forecasting in assessing whether debt covenants are likely to be breached; this relates to financial ratio analysis, which has been introduced in Chapter 2 and Chapter 10.

Exam questions in this area are also likely to link to business reorganisation (covered in the next chapter) because companies that are in financial difficulties often need to consider **both** financial reconstruction **and** business reorganisation.

Chapter overview

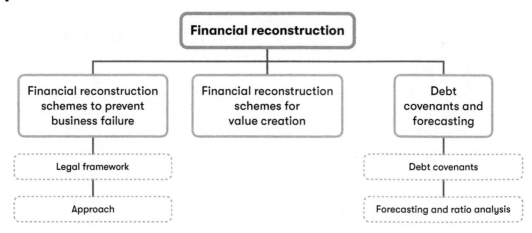

BPP
LEARNING
MEDIA

1 Financial reconstruction schemes to prevent business failure

A company might be on the brink of becoming insolvent due to a high interest burden or severe cash flow problems in the short term, but may have plans that it believes hold out a good promise of profits in the future.

In such a situation, the company might be able to attract fresh capital and to persuade its creditors to accept some shares (or new debt) in the company as 'payment', and achieve a reconstruction which allows the company to carry on in business.

Existing shareholders are likely to see a large dilution of their holding as reconstructions often involve issuing many new shares to creditors.

1.1 Legal framework

In insolvency proceedings the proceeds from selling the assets are shared out to repay creditors and investors in a predetermined rank:

(a) Creditors with a fixed charge on a specific asset

(b) Creditors with a floating charge on the company's assets in general or a class of assets

(c) Unsecured creditors

(d) Preference shareholders

(e) Ordinary shareholders

In addition there may be amounts due to other parties, such as tax authorities and employees. The rank of these parties, in terms of order of repayment, will be specified in an exam question.

The proposed reconstruction must be agreed by all parties – classes of creditors should meet separately, every class must vote in favour for the scheme to succeed.

1.2 Approach

1 Estimate the position if insolvency proceedings go ahead
- Restate assets at realisable value
- Repay according to legal framework
- If insufficient funds for a class of creditors, a % of the amount owed will be paid

2 Apply the reconstruction
- This will be given in the exam question
- Is each group better off as a result of the reconstruction?

3 Check if the company is now financially viable
- May involve a brief comment, forecasting and/or ratio analysis may sometimes be required

Activity 1: Evaluating a reconstruction

Nomore Ltd, a private company that has for many years been making mechanical tools, is faced with rapidly falling sales. Its bank overdraft (with M A Bank) is at its limit of $1,200,000.

The company has just lost another two major customers.

STATEMENT OF FINANCIAL POSITION (EXTRACT)

	31.3.X2 Projected $'000
Non-current assets	
Freehold property	5,660
Plant and machinery	3,100
Motor vehicles	320
Current assets	1,160
Total assets	10,240
Ordinary shares of $1	5,600
Accumulated reserves/(deficit)	(6,060)
Total equity	(460)
Non-current liabilities	
10% loan 20X8 (secured on freehold property)	1,600
Other loans (VC bank, floating charges)	4,800
	6,400
Current liabilities	
Trade payables	3,100
Bank overdraft (MA bank, unsecured)	1,200
Total equity and liabilities	10,240

Other Information:

- The freehold property has a market value of about $5,750,000.
- It is estimated that the break-up value of the plant at 31 March 20X2 will be $2,000,000.
- The motor vehicles owned at 31 March 20X2 could be sold for $200,000.
- In insolvency, the current assets at 31 March 20X2 would realise $1,000,000.
- Insolvency proceeding costs would be approximately $500,000, this will rank first for repayment.

The company believes that it has good prospects due to the launch next year of its new Pink Lady range of tools and has designed the following scheme of reconstruction:

- The existing ordinary shares to be cancelled and ordinary shareholders to be issued with $2,000,000 new $1 ordinary shares for $1.00 cash.
- The secured loan to be cancelled and replaced by a $1,250,000 10% secured bond with a six-year term and $600,000 of new $1 ordinary shares.
- VC Bank to receive $3,200,000 13% loan secured by a fixed charge and 1,100,000 $1 new ordinary shares.
- MA bank to be repaid the existing overdraft and to keep the overdraft limit at $1,200,000 secured by a floating charge.

If this plan is implemented, the company estimates that its profits before interest and tax will rise to $1.441 million and its share price will rise to $1.50. If this plan is implemented, the company estimates that its profits before interest and tax will rise to $1.441 million and its share price will rise to $1.50.

Required

Evaluate whether the suggested scheme of reconstruction is likely to succeed.

Solution

2 Financial reconstruction schemes for value creation

Reconstruction schemes may also be undertaken by companies which are not in difficulties as part of a strategy to create value for the owners of the company.

The management of a company can try to improve operations and increase the value of the company, by:

(a) Returning cash to shareholders using a share repurchase scheme.

(b) A significant injection of further capital, either debt or equity, to fund investments or acquisitions.

(c) A leveraged buy-out: where a publicly quoted company is acquired by a specially established private company which funds the acquisition by substantial borrowing.

This is a mechanism for taking a company private which is sometimes seen as being desirable because it avoid the costs of a listing and potentially allows a company to **concentrate** on the **long-term needs** of the business rather than the short-term expectations of shareholders.

Essential reading

See Chapter 14 Section 1 of the Essential reading for further discussion of taking a company private.

The Essential reading is available as an Appendix of the digital edition of the Workbook.

3 Debt covenants and forecasting

3.1 Debt covenants

Debt finance often involves 'covenants' – these are conditions that the borrower must comply with and, if they do not, the loan can be considered to be in default and the bank can demand repayment.

Positive covenants: These involve taking positive action to achieve an objective.

This could involve achieving certain levels for particular financial ratios, eg gearing, interest cover. In addition, it may also include the need to provide the bank with regular financial statements/forecasts, to maintain assets used as security and to insure key assets and staff.

Negative covenants: These place restrictions on the borrower's behaviour.

These place restrictions on the borrower's behaviour.

For example, they may prevent borrowing from another lender, disposal of key assets, paying dividends above a certain level, or making major investments.

3.2 Forecasting and ratio analysis

In any type of financial reconstruction care will need to be taken that debt covenants are not breached. In order to assess whether a positive covenant relating to financing ratios has been broken, you may be required to forecast a company's profits and statement of financial position.

Ratio analysis has been covered in earlier chapters.

3.2.1 Forecast profit statement

It makes sense to start with the profit forecast. This will allow the following to be identified:

Measure	Explanation of possible use
Profits before interest and tax	Required for interest cover calculations
Interest	Required for interest cover calculation
Profits after interest and tax	Required for earnings per share calculation
Retained earnings	Affects the book value of equity

3.2.2 Forecast statement of financial position (SOFP)

Next, the SOFP can be forecast (which will be impacted by the profit forecast which will have forecast the level of retained earnings).

The format of the SOFP is likely to be given in the exam question, and in any case a precise proforma will not be required.

Measure	Explanation of possible use
Book value of equity (Share capital plus retained earnings)	Required for gearing calculation
Non-current liabilities	Required for gearing calculation
Current assets and liabilities	Required for liquidity ratios (eg current ratio)

There is a numerical exercise on forecasting in the next chapter.

Chapter summary

```
                    ┌─────────────────────────────┐
                    │   Financial reconstruction   │
                    └─────────────────────────────┘
```

```
┌─────────────────────┐   ┌─────────────────────┐   ┌─────────────────┐
│ Financial           │   │ Financial           │   │ Debt            │
│ reconstruction      │   │ reconstruction      │   │ covenants and   │
│ schemes to prevent  │   │ schemes for         │   │ forecasting     │
│ business failure    │   │ value creation      │   │                 │
└─────────────────────┘   └─────────────────────┘   └─────────────────┘
```

Legal framework

1 Creditors with a fixed charge on a specific asset
2 Creditors with a floating charge on the company's assets
3 Unsecured creditors
4 Preference shareholders
5 Ordinary shareholders

The deal must be agreed by all parties – classes of creditors should meet separately, every class must vote in favour for the scheme to succeed

Approach

1 Estimate the position if insolvency occurs
2 Apply reconstruction scheme and check position of each party
3 Assess if the company is viable

(a) Returning cash to shareholders using a share repurchase scheme
(b) A significant injection of capital (debt or equity)
(c) A leveraged buy-out. A mechanism for taking a company private (avoiding the costs of a listing and allowing a company to **concentrate** on the **long-term needs** of the business).

Debt covenants

• Positive covenants
  – Involve taking positive action to achieve an objective eg gearing, interest cover
• Negative covenants
  – These place restrictions on the borrower's behaviour

Forecasting and ratio analysis

1 Forecast profit
2 Forecast SOFP

Use ratio analysis to evaluate (see earlier chapters)

Knowledge diagnostic

1. Order of repayment

In insolvency proceedings, ordinary shareholders rank behind all other claims.

2. Schemes to increase value

These include share repurchase schemes, and issues of new capital.

3. Taking a firm private

Can be viewed as a means of reducing listing expenses and increasing the ability of a firm to take a long-term view.

4. Positive debt covenants

These require positive action, eg to attain an objective.

5. Negative debt covenants

These place restrictions on management behaviour.

Further study guidance

Question practice

Now try the following from the Further question practice bank (available in the digital edition of the workbook):

Q26 Brive Inc

Activity answers

Activity 1: Evaluating a reconstruction

Steps as follows:

Step 1 Estimate the position if insolvency proceedings go ahead

Break-up values of assets at 31 March 20X2

	$'000
Freehold	5,750
Insolvency costs	(500)
10% loan (fixed charge)	(1,600)
	3,650
Plant and machinery	2,000
Motor vehicles	200
Current assets	1,000
	6,850
Secured creditors (floating charges)	(4,800)
	2,050
Trade payables and overdraft	4,300

If the company was forced into insolvency, the secured loan and other loans would be met in full but, after allowing for the expenses of insolvency proceedings, the bank and trade creditors would receive a dividend of 48c per $. The ordinary shareholders would receive nothing.

Step 2 Apply the reconstruction and evaluate the impact on affected parties

(1) **Secured loan**

Under the scheme they will receive securities with a total nominal value of $2,150,000 ($1.25m bond + $0.9m shares being 600,000 shares at $1.5); this is a significant increase. The new bonds issued can be secured on the freehold property. So, this may well be acceptable but it depends on whether they agree with the share valuation and whether the increase in wealth compensates for the greater risk (less security).

(2) **VC**

VC's existing loan of $4.8 million will, under the proposed scheme, be changed into a $3.2 million secured loan and $1.65 million of ordinary shares (1.1 million shares at $1.50). In total this gives total loans of $4,450,000 (including the bond) secured on property with a net disposal value of $5,750,000 (so the security given by the property comfortably covers the full value of the debt that is secured on the property). The scheme will give an improvement in security for VC on the first $3,200,000 to compensate for the risk involved in holding ordinary shares. This is a marginal gain for a position that exposes the bank to high levels of risk.

(3) **MA bank**

This should be acceptable because of the security of a floating charge.

(4) **Ordinary shareholders**

In insolvency proceedings, the ordinary shareholders would also receive nothing. Under the scheme, they will lose a degree of control of the company because 3.7 million shares will be in issue (2m for existing shareholders + 0.6m for secured loan holder + 1.1m for VC bank) and they will only own 2 million of these, ie 54% of the total. However, in exchange for their additional investment, equity in a company which will have sufficient funds to finance the expected future capital requirements and which will offer a capital gain compared to their initial investment of $1.

Step 3 **Check if the company is now financially viable**

Cash flow forecast, on reconstruction

	$'000
Cash for new shares from equity shareholders	2,000
Repayment of overdraft	1,200
Cash available	800

A cash flow forecast will be required to establish whether this is a sufficient cash base for the company post-reconstruction.

Conclusion

This scheme of reconstruction might not be acceptable to all parties, if the future profits of the company seem unattractive. In particular, VC might be reluctant to agree to the scheme.

In such an event, an alternative scheme of reconstruction must be designed, perhaps involving another provider of funds (such as another venture capitalist). Otherwise, the company will be forced into insolvency.

15

Business reorganisation

Learning objectives

On completion of this chapter, you should be able to:

	Syllabus reference no.
Recommend, with reasons, strategies for unbundling parts of a quoted company	D2(a)
Evaluate the likely financial and other benefits of unbundling	D2(b)
Advise on the financial issues relating to a management buy-out and buy-in	D2(c)

Exam context

Chapters 14 and 15 cover Section D of the syllabus 'Corporate reconstruction and re-organisation'.

In this chapter we discuss methods of business reorganisations, concentrating primarily on methods of unbundling companies.

Exam questions in this area are also likely to link to **financial reconstructions** (covered in the previous chapter) because companies that are in financial difficulties often need to consider **both** financial reconstruction **and** business reorganisation.

There is also a strong link between this chapter and business valuations (Chapter 8) because:

(a) there may be a need to value a part of a business that is being 'unbundled'

(b) business re-organisation can be viewed as an aspect of **portfolio restructuring** ie the **acquisition** of companies, or **disposals** via divestments, demergers, spin-offs, MBOs and MBIs.

Chapter overview

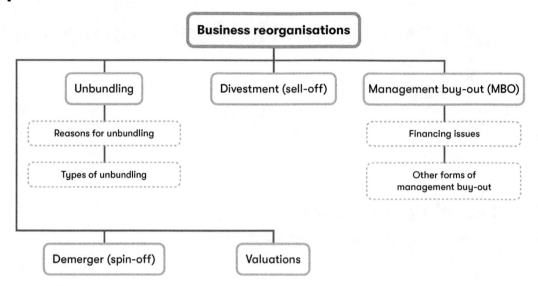

BPP
LEARNING
MEDIA

1 Unbundling

To improve the performance (and therefore the value) of a business, management may consider one of two forms of business reorganisation:

- Organisational reconstruction
- Portfolio reconstruction

Organisational restructuring involves changing the way a company's current operations are organised, which may involve:

- Changing its corporate governance (discussed in Chapter 1)
- Altering the degree of centralisation within an organisation (eg Treasury, Chapter 11)
- Amending the terms of licensing or joint venture agreements (discussed in Chapter 5)

Portfolio restructuring involves improving value by changing the portfolio of businesses operations being managed by a company. This may involve:

- The **acquisition** of companies (the potential for acquisitions to add value has been considered in Chapters 8 and 9).
- The possibility of improving value by restructuring the organisation's portfolio using divestments, demergers, spin-offs, MBOs and MBIs. These approaches are sometimes called unbundling and are the main focus of this chapter.

KEY TERM

> **Unbundling:** Involves restructuring a business by reorganising it into a number of separate parts.

1.1 Reasons for unbundling

Unbundling may be considered for financial and strategic reasons.

Motives	Explanation
Financial	Selling off a division may allow cash to be raised to: • Ease the group's **liquidity problems**; • Reduce the group's **gearing**; or • Reinvest elsewhere in the business to earn a **higher return**.
Strategic	There may be divisions within of a business where the current organisation structure is not adding value. For example, a division may have been neglected because it is **not** seen as being **core** to the group's strategy. If this division existed outside the group it may have a more efficient management structure and take quicker, more effective decisions. If the stock market believes that the organisation structure is not adding value, then it is possible that the market value of the company will be lower than the sum of the value of its individual divisions; this is called a **conglomerate discount**. Finally, to **protect the rest of the business from takeover**, it may choose to split off a part of the business which is particularly attractive to a buyer.

1.2 Types of unbundling

There are a number of different types of unbundling.

Types	Definition
Divestment (sell-off)	Sale of a part of a company to a third party (ie another company).
Management buy-out (MBO)	A form of divestment involving selling a part of the business to its management team (different forms of MBO are discussed in Section 3).
Demerger (spin-off)	A demerger is the opposite of a merger. It is the splitting up of a corporate body into two or more separate and independent bodies.

The type of unbundling that is appropriate will depend on the motive(s) for the strategy.

If the motive is financial then a demerger would not be considered as it **does not** directly raise cash.

2 Divestment (sell-off)

The sale of a division to a third party will add value if the estimated sale price exceeds the present value of lost cash flows (including economies of scale lost as a result of the sell-off).

A **buyer** may be prepared to pay an amount that is greater than the present value of the cash flows of the division because under **their ownership** the division is **worth more** eg due to synergies with the buyer's other business operations.

To value a division, a **cost of capital** that reflects the risk of the division will be required. This is discussed in Section 5.

3 Management buy-out (MBO)

This is **another form of sell-off** but may be preferred to a divestment because:

- It allows a division to be sold with the co-operation of divisional management, and a lower risk of redundancies
- It will be less likely to attract the attention of the competition authorities than a sale to another company

As with a divestment, an MBO will add value if the estimated sale price exceeds the existing present value of lost cash flows (including economies of scale lost as a result of the sell-off).

The management team may be prepared to pay an amount that is greater than the present value of the cash flows of the division because under **their ownership** the division will be **worth more** eg the division achieves better performance because of **greater personal motivation, quicker decision making and savings in overheads** (eg head office costs).

To value a division, a **cost of capital** that reflects the risk of the division will be required. This is discussed in Section 5.

3.1 Financing issues

Typically, an MBO will be **mainly financed** by a **mixture** of equity (referred to as private equity as the MBO will be unlisted), debt and mezzanine finance.

If an MBO is mainly financed (80%+) by debt, this may be referred to as a leveraged buy-out (LBO) and has been discussed in the **previous chapter** (note that this term is also used to describe any highly leveraged takeover, whether linked to an MBO or not).

The **equity and mezzanine finance element** will be mainly provided by **a venture capital/private equity firm,** although venture capital investors will usually want to see that managers are financially committed to the venture as well, so an element of the equity will be provided by managers.

3.1.1 Venture capital/private equity finance

The type of finance offered by the private equity company will normally **be in the form of an injection of equity and mezzanine finance**.

KEY
TERM

> **Mezzanine finance:** Finance that had some of the characteristics of both debt and equity.

Convertible debt and convertible preference shares are forms of **mezzanine finance** as they have characteristics of both debt (eg a fixed return is expected) and also equity (the investor can convert into ordinary shares if the venture is successful).

A private equity company that is concerned about the risk of an MBO will **increase the proportion of their investment provided as mezzanine finance** (ie loans/convertibles etc).

3.1.2 Venture capital/private equity – other issues

In addition to providing finance, venture capitalists can also be a source of **strategic advice** and **business contacts**.

Private equity/venture capital groups will normally expect to exit their investment either by a flotation or sale to another firm. Much of the gain expected by the venture capitalist will be through selling their interests and making a substantial capital gain.

In order to make sure that an MBO is on track to deliver this, the venture capitalist will set demanding financial targets. Failure to hit targets set by the private equity provider/venture capitalist can lead to extra shares being transferred to their ownership at no additional cost (an **equity ratchet**), or the venture capitalist having the right to make new appointments to the board.

Activity 1: Financing issues

Lomax Co has decided to sell one of its subsidiaries (free of debt). The managers of the subsidiary are attempting to purchase it through a leveraged MBO to form a new company, Retro. The cost of $52.5 million would come from $7.5 million of equity invested equally by the venture capitalist, VC, and the management team and $15 million of mezzanine finance, provided by VC, and a $30 million bank loan.

The mezzanine finance is unsecured convertible debt, redeemable at nominal value in five years' time and paying a fixed interest rate of 18% per year. The conversion rights would allow VC to convert $100 of debt into 10 Retro shares at any time after three years from the date the loan is agreed.

The bank loan is at a fixed rate of 8%, for a period of three years. Interest is payable annually on the amount outstanding at the start of the year and the loan will be repaid in three equal annual instalments (see the Appendix below). The loan will be secured against Retro's land and buildings.

A condition of the loan is that gearing, measured by the book value of total loans to equity, is no more than 200% by the end of Year 2. If this condition is not met the bank has the right to call in its loan at one month's notice. Another condition is that no dividends can be paid in the first two years.

Most recent statement of profit or loss for the subsidiary

	$'000
Revenue	33,899
Operating costs	(18,749)
Central overhead payable to Lomax	(6,000)
Interest paid	(3,750)
Taxable profit	5,400
Taxation (20%)	(1,080)
Retained earnings	4,320

Lomax will continue to provide central accounting, personnel and marketing services to Retro for a fee of $4.5 million per year, with the first fee payable in year one. All revenues and cost (excluding interest) are expected to increase by approximately 5% per year.

Appendix

To calculate the loan repayment each year we need the annuity factor for 8% over three years; this is 2.577. The annual repayments (in $'000s) are therefore $30,000/2.577 = **$11,641**.

The element of this repayment that represents interest is therefore:

	Year 1	Year 2	Year 3
Loan brought forward	30,000	20,759	10,779
Interest due (8% × b/f)	2,400	1,661	862
Repayment	(11,641)	(11,641)	(11,641)
Loan carried forward			
(b/f + interest due – repayment)	20,759	10,779	0

Required

Evaluate whether the bank's gearing restriction in two years' time is likely to be a problem.

Solution

(1) Forecast statements of profit or loss

	Year 1	Year 2
	$'000	$'000
Revenue		
Operating costs		
Direct operating profit		
Central services from Lomax		
VC loan interest at 18% on $15m		
Bank loan at 8% (interest only)		
Year 1		
Year 2		

	Year 1 $'000	Year 2 $'000
Profit before tax		
Tax at 20%		
Profit after tax		
Retained earnings		

(2) Forecast levels of debt and equity

	Year 1 $'000	Year 2 $'000
Reserves b/f		
Reserves c/f		
Share capital + closing reserves		
Total debt at end of year (see working)		
Gearing: debt/equity		

3.2 Other forms of management buy-out

3.2.1 Management buy-in

A management buy-in is when a team of **outside managers**, as opposed to managers who are already running the business, mount a takeover bid and then run the business themselves.

An MBI might occur when a business venture is running into trouble, and a group of outside managers see an opportunity to take over the business and restore it to profitability.

Alternatively, research suggests that buy-ins often occur when the major shareholder of a small family company wishes to retire.

Many features are common to MBOs and MBIs, including **financing**.

Buy-ins work best for companies where the existing managers are being replaced by managers of **much better quality**. However, managers who come in from outside may take **time** to get used to the company and may encounter **opposition** from employees if they seek to introduce significant changes.

3.2.2 Buy-in management buy-out

Sometimes the management team will be a combination of an MBO (ie existing management) and new managers (with specialist skills that the existing management team do not have, eg finance).

This is sometimes referred to as a buy-in management buy-out (**BIMBO**).

4 Demerger (spin-off)

A demerger is the opposite of a merger. It is the splitting up of a corporate body into two or more separate and independent bodies, it does not raise finance.

The motives for a demerger are likely to be strategic. For example, the removal of a conglomerate discount/possible takeover defence.

The aims of a demerger are to create a **clearer management structure** and to allow **faster decision making**. A spin-off may facilitate a **future merger or takeover**.

A demerger risks **losing synergies** between different parts of the group. It is also an expensive and time-consuming process. Assets and liabilities will have to be clearly segregated between the demerged units.

To value a demerged operation, a cost of capital that reflects the risk of the division will be required, this is discussed in the next section.

Essential reading

See Chapter 15 Section 1 of the Essential reading for further discussion of demergers.

The Essential reading is available as an Appendix of the digital edition of the Workbook.

5 Valuations

To value a divestment, a MBO, or a demerged operation, a cost of capital that reflects the risk of the division will be required. This means that a project-specific cost of capital will need to be calculated.

This topic has already been covered in Chapter 6 where we looked at investments that change business risk and also in Chapter 8 where business valuations have been considered.

We have seen that when a company is moving into a new business area it can use the beta of a company in that sector (a comparable quoted company, or CQC) and ungear the equity beta to establish the asset beta which measures the risk of the new business area. This approach can also be applied in valuing a specific business unit that a company is planning to unbundle.

Alternatively, you may be given the asset beta, or you may be told that a division represents a given percentage of a company's value in which case you can calculate the asset beta of a division from the asset beta of a company.

Illustration 1: Asset beta

Company X has an asset beta of 0.94.

Company X has two divisions, Division A and Division B; it is planning to unbundle Division B.

The asset beta of Division A has been estimated as 1.06 and Division A represents 70% of the value of Company X.

Required

Estimate the asset beta of Division B.

Solution

Division B's asset beta can be estimated by laying out the workings for Company X's overall asset beta:

Division A asset beta × 70% + Division B asset beta × 30% = 0.94

So

1.06 × 0.70 + Division B asset beta × 0.30 = 0.94

So

0.742 + Division B asset beta × 30% = 0.94

So

Division B asset beta × 0.30 = 0.94 − 0.742 = 0.198

So

Division B asset beta = 0.198 ÷ 0.30 = 0.66

Once an asset beta of the specific business has been calculated then a cash flow valuation of the unbundled entity can be made as follows (recap of Chapter 8).

Step 1   Calculate the asset beta of the division being demerged

Step 2   Regear the beta to reflect the gearing of the division being unbundled

Step 3   Calculate the division's new WACC

Step 4   Discount the division's post-acquisition free cash flows at this WACC

Step 5   Calculate the revised NPV of the division and subtract debt to calculate the value of the equity

Chapter summary

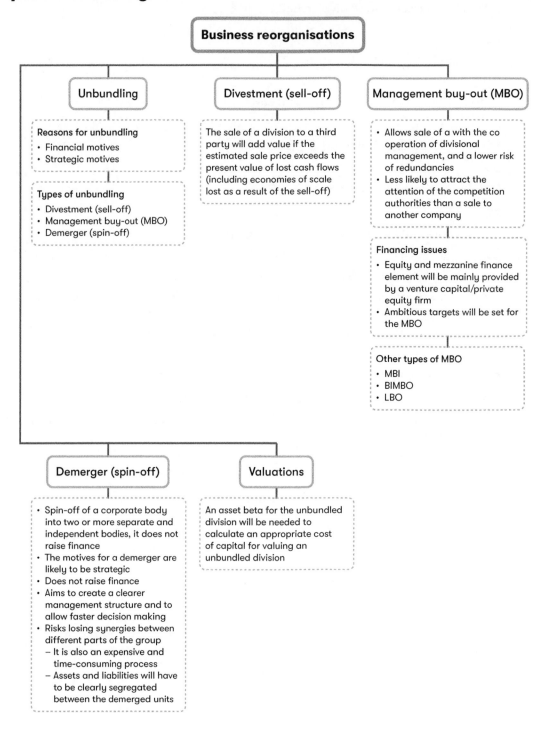

Business reorganisations

Unbundling

Reasons for unbundling
- Financial motives
- Strategic motives

Types of unbundling
- Divestment (sell-off)
- Management buy-out (MBO)
- Demerger (spin-off)

Divestment (sell-off)

The sale of a division to a third party will add value if the estimated sale price exceeds the present value of lost cash flows (including economies of scale lost as a result of the sell-off)

Management buy-out (MBO)

- Allows sale of a with the co operation of divisional management, and a lower risk of redundancies
- Less likely to attract the attention of the competition authorities than a sale to another company

Financing issues
- Equity and mezzanine finance element will be mainly provided by a venture capital/private equity firm
- Ambitious targets will be set for the MBO

Other types of MBO
- MBI
- BIMBO
- LBO

Demerger (spin-off)

- Spin-off of a corporate body into two or more separate and independent bodies, it does not raise finance
- The motives for a demerger are likely to be strategic
- Does not raise finance
- Aims to create a clearer management structure and to allow faster decision making
- Risks losing synergies between different parts of the group
  – It is also an expensive and time-consuming process
  – Assets and liabilities will have to be clearly segregated between the demerged units

Valuations

An asset beta for the unbundled division will be needed to calculate an appropriate cost of capital for valuing an unbundled division

Knowledge diagnostic

1. Types of unbundling

These include divestment, management buy-out and demerger.

2. Types of management buy-out

These also include leveraged buy-outs, management buy-ins, and buy-in management buy-outs.

3. Mezzanine finance

This is finance with the characteristics of debt and equity, and is commonly used by venture capitalists to finance MBOs.

4. Drawbacks of demergers

Cost, time and risk of losing synergies/economies of scale.

5. Valuing an unbundled entity

This is likely to require a cash-based valuation using a cost of capital based on the asset beta for the unbundled entity which has been regeared to reflect the gearing of the unbundled entity.

Further study guidance

Question practice

Now try the following from the Further question practice bank (available in the digital edition of the workbook):

Q27 AIR

Activity answers

Activity 1: Financing issues

(1) Forecast statements of profit or loss

	Year 1	Year 2
	$'000	$'000
Revenue	35,594	37,374
Operating costs	19,686	20,670
Direct operating profit	15,908	16,704
Central services from Lomax	(4,500)	(4,725)
VC loan interest at 18% on $15m	(2,700)	(2,700)
Bank loan at 8% (interest only)		
Year 1	(2,400)	
Year 2		(1,661)
Profit before tax	6,308	7,618
Tax at 20%	1,262	1,524
Profit after tax	5,046	6,094
Retained earnings	5,046	6,094

(2) Forecast levels of debt and equity

	Year 1	Year 2
	$'000	$'000
Reserves b/f	0	5,046
Reserves c/f	5,046	11,140
Share capital + closing reserves	12,546	18,640
Total debt at end of year (see working)	35,759	25,779
Gearing: debt/equity	285%	138%

Gearing at period end

Assuming no dividend is paid and ignoring the possible issue of new shares, the gearing at the end of two years is predicted to be 138%, which is significantly below the target of 200% needed to meet the condition on the bank's loan.

If conversion rights are then exercised, new share capital will be raised, reducing the gearing still further.

Cash flow

It is assumed that cash generated from operations is sufficient to repay the bank loan each year, which is by no means obvious from the figures provided.

Conclusion

As long as there is sufficient cash to finance the loan repayments, there will probably not be a problem in meeting the loan conditions.

Working

Using the profile of debt repayments provided we can calculate the debt outstanding at the end of each year.

	Year 1	*Year 2*
	$'000	$'000
Loan carried forward (see above)	20,759	10,779
VC loan	15,000	15,000
Total debt	**35,759**	**25,779**

Skills checkpoint 4

Commercial acumen

Chapter overview

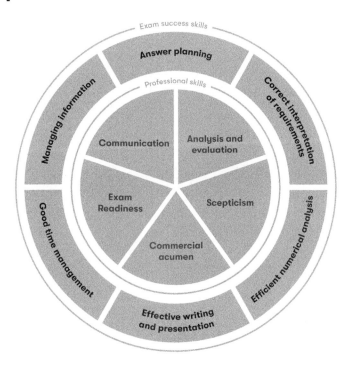

Introduction

Commercial acumen is one of the four professional skills that have been introduced to the AFM exam from 2022.

This skill will be examined in Section A of the exam, a compulsory 50 mark question, which tests all of the four professional skills for 10 marks in total.

This skill may also be examined in Section B, which consist of two compulsory scenario-based 25 mark questions each of which allocates 5 marks to professional skills. Each Section B question will contain a **minimum of two professional skills from Analysis and Evaluation, Scepticism and Commercial Acumen. Section B questions will state which of these professional skills are being tested.**

No Professional Skill will ever be worth more than five marks in a question.

As with the Technical marks **there will be slightly more marks available for candidates to score than the set amount.** For example, in a Section A question there are ten Professional Skills marks; however, those ten marks could be scored from a possible fourteen marks available. In a Section B question there are five Professional Skills marks; however, those five marks could be scored from a possible seven marks available.

AFM Professional Skill: Commercial acumen

Commercial acumen is about demonstrating an awareness that both your analysis and your recommendations are **practical and plausible** given the resources of a company and the situation it finds itself in.

Possible approaches to scoring marks for this professional include the following:

Demonstrating an awareness of organisational and external factors, which will affect the financial management decisions being considered

This can be demonstrated by making effective use of examples, probably from the scenario of a question (but occasionally using a practical real-world example) as part of your answer to an exam question.

For example, if a question says that a company is in a rapidly changing market (ie business risk is high) then this would often mean that it is more practical to use equity finance as opposed to debt.

This skill can also be demonstrated by making any relevant practical considerations.

For example, if a company that is reviewing its portfolio of shares holds shares in another company that is rumoured to be a take-over target then holding onto the shares may be sensible as share prices often rise during a take-over bidding process.

Recognising key issues in a given scenario and using judgement in proposing and recommending commercially viable solutions

This may involve recognising **key external constraints**.

For example, do funding constraints that are mentioned in a question mean that an investment decision may not be commercially viable.

Alternatively, it may involve **spotting commercial opportunities**, sometimes these may be **alternative opportunities** to those suggested in a question.

For example, in a question on takeovers it may be relevant to briefly mention other types of growth that may be suitable opportunities for a company to consider such as organic growth or a joint venture.

Possible pitfalls

- **Don't include irrelevant real-world examples**

Any example that you use will only gain credit if they are directly relevant to the issue being discussed. Practical examples are much more likely to come from the scenario of a question, and even here you are likely to focus on a small number of key examples.

- **Don't write at length about real-world examples**

Remember that there are likely to be no more than 2 or 3 marks for this skill, and that practical examples are much more likely to come from the scenario of a question.

Applying this professional skill

Like any of the professional skills, commercial acumen is not complicated and it involves doing what you should naturally be doing as you answer a question, ie being practical and sensible.

In some questions you may find it appropriate to signal that you are addressing this skill by using an appropriate sub-heading such as 'practical points' to signal where this skill is being addressed.

A simple approach here is to consider any constraints on decision-making that are signalled within a question, and to think about possible opportunities too.

Question practice

The solution to question 28 (Lamri), which is set as homework at the end of Chapter 16, gives an illustration of how this skill can be applied to score professional marks.

16

Planning and trading issues for multinationals

Learning objectives

On completion of this chapter, you should be able to:

	Syllabus reference no.
Advise on the theory and practice of free trade and the management of barriers to trade	A4(a)
Demonstrate an up-to-date understanding of the major trade agreements and common markets and, on the basis of contemporary circumstances, advise on their policy and strategic implications for a given business	A4(b)
Discuss how the actions of the World Trade Organisation, the International Monetary Fund, the World Bank and Central Banks can affect a multinational organisation.	A4(c)
Discuss the role of international financial institutions within the context of globalised economy, with particular attention to the Fed, Bank of England, ECB and Bank of Japan	A4(d)
Discuss the role of international financial markets with respect to the management of global debt, the financial development of the emerging economies and the maintenance of global financial stability	A4(e)
Discuss the significance to the organisation of the latest developments in world financial markets, such as the causes and impact of the recent financial crisis; growth and impact of dark pool trading systems; the removal of barriers to the free movement of capital; and the international regulations on money laundering.	A4(f)
Demonstrate an awareness of new developments in the macroeconomic environment, assessing their impact upon the organisation, and advising on the appropriate response to those developments both internally and externally	A4(g)
Advise on the development of a financial planning framework for a multinational organisation, taking into account:	A5(a)

- Compliance with national regulatory requirements (for example the London Stock Exchange admission requirements)
- The mobility of capital across borders and national limitations on remittances and transfer pricing
- The pattern of economic and other risk exposures in different national markets

	Syllabus reference no.
• Agency issues in the central co-ordination of overseas operations and the balancing of local financial autonomy with effective central control	
Determine a corporation's dividend capacity and its policy given:	A6(a)
• The corporation's short- and long-term reinvestment strategy	
• The impact of capital reconstruction programmes such as share repurchase agreements and new capital issues on free cash flow to equity	
• The availability and timing of central remittances	
• The corporate tax regime within the host jurisdiction.	
• The organisational policy on the transfer pricing of goods and services across international borders	
Advise, in the context of a specified investment programme, on an organisation's current and projected dividend capacity	A6(b)

Exam context

This chapter is drawn from Section A of the syllabus, but works well as a final chapter because it summarises a number of practical business issues faced by multinationals, many of which have already been introduced in earlier chapters.

This syllabus area contains a large number of learning objectives but actually has not featured heavily in exam questions, reflecting the largely **factual nature** of the subject matter. The Workbook identifies the **key facts** and **additional factual background** is provided via the Essential reading section, available in Appendix 2 of the digital edition of the Workbook.

Chapter overview

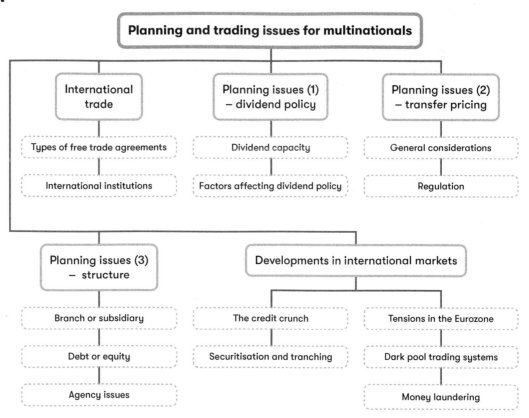

1 International trade

1.1 Types of free trade agreement

Multinational companies will encounter a variety of **different types** of international trade agreements.

These may provide protection to the company in the sense that competitors operating outside these areas may find it difficult to enter the market, or may create problems if the company is itself operating outside these areas and creates **barriers to trade** as they try to enter these markets.

1.1.1 Free trade area and customs unions

This exists when there is no restriction on the movement of **goods and services** between countries, but individual member countries impose their **own restrictions on non-members** (eg North American Free Trade Agreement [NAFTA]).

A **customs union** involves a free trade area between member countries and, in addition, **common external tariffs** applying to imports from non-member countries (eg Mercosur in South America).

1.1.2 Common and single markets

A **common market** encompasses the idea of a customs union but in addition there are moves towards creating free markets in each of the **factors of production** (eg labour, capital) and a move to **standardise market regulations** (eg safety rules).

Eventually a common market becomes a **single market with no restriction of movement** in each of the **factors of production** and **no regulatory differences** (ega citizen in the European Union (EU) has the freedom to work in any other country of the EU).

1.1.3 Economic Union

A common/single market may eventually evolve into **economic and monetary union** which will also **involve a common Central Bank, a common interest rate and a single currency.**

 Activity 1: Idea generation

Degli Co is a small manufacturing company based in a country that is applying for entry to the European Union (EU). Degli Co produces high-quality parts for aerospace companies, for domestic customers and also for companies that are based in the European Union.

Required

Discuss possible economic benefits to Degli Co of operating in a country that is within the EU.

Solution

Essential reading

See Chapter 16 Section 1 of the Essential reading for further discussion of general trading issues for multinationals.

The Essential reading is available as an Appendix of the digital edition of the Workbook.

1.2 International institutions

The activities of multinationals will be impacted by a number of different international institutions.

Types	Definition
World Trade Organisation (WTO)	**Supports the development of international trade,** the WTO provides a mechanism for **identifying and reducing trade barriers and resolving trade disputes.** The WTO will impose fines if members are in breach of their rules. Unless otherwise bound by free trade agreements, members trade under WTO rules, ie they can't selectively reduce tariffs for one country without offering this to all other WTO members (this is the **most-favoured nation principle).**
International Monetary Fund (IMF)	Supports the stability of the international monetary system by providing medium-term (3–5 year) loans **to countries with balance of payments problems,** such as problems in making debt repayments to international creditors, and provides advice on the **economic development** of countries. IMF loans come with stringent conditions. Countries must take **effective action to improve their balance of payments, eg reducing aggregate demand to** reduce imports and encourage firms to increase production for export markets. It has been suggested that the strict terms attached to IMF loans can lead to **economic stagnation** as countries struggle to repay these loans.
World Bank	**Lends** to creditworthy governments of developing nations to finance projects and **policies that will stimulate economic development and alleviate poverty.** The World Bank consists of two institutions: • The International Bank for Reconstruction and Development (IBRD) which focuses on middle-income and creditworthy poorer countries • The International Development Association (IDA) which focuses exclusively on the world's poorest countries Both provide finance for projects which are likely to have an impact on poverty. Loans are normally interest-free and have a maturity of up to 40 years. The World Bank directly **affects multinational companies** by **helping to finance infrastructure**

Types	Definition
	projects in developing economies. This creates a platform for other investment by multinationals (once reliable infrastructure is in place).
Central banks	Central banks normally have **control over interest rates** and **support the stability** of the financial system (eg by managing the risk of financial contagion).
	Financial contagion is where a crisis in one country spills to many other countries. One of the roles of central banks is to monitor the risk of financial contagion carefully and to increase their stimulus programmes where necessary.

Essential reading

See Chapter 16 Section 2 of the Essential reading for further discussion of individual central banks and international financial markets.

The Essential reading is available as an Appendix of the digital edition of the Workbook.

2 Planning issues (1) – dividend policy

2.1 Dividend capacity

Dividend capacity has been introduced in Chapters 1 and 8 as **'free cash flow to equity'** – it is a measure of **what is available for payment as dividend** after providing for capital expenditures to maintain existing assets and to create new assets for future growth.

Dividend capacity
Profits after interest, tax and preference dividends
less
debt repayment, investment in assets
plus
depreciation, any capital raised from new share issues or debt

In a multinational context, an additional complication is that dividend may be paid by foreign subsidiaries to the parent company, and in addition:

- Extra tax may be payable on the profits made by foreign subsidiary; and
- Withholding tax may be due on dividends paid by the foreign subsidiary.

Activity 2: Tax issues

DX Co, based in Country D, has estimated its dividend capacity from its domestic operations to be $14 million.

A subsidiary of DX Co, based in Country F, is forecast to make profits before tax of $3 million. It is proposed that the subsidiary should remit 75% of its post-tax profits as a dividend to DX Co.

The rate of corporation tax is 24% in Country D and 20% in Country F. A withholding tax of 10% is charged on any dividends remitted. The tax authorities in Country D base charge corporation tax on profits made by subsidiaries but give full credit for any foreign corporation tax already paid.

Required

Adjust the estimated dividend capacity of DX Co for the impact of the foreign subsidiary.

Solution

2.2 Factors affecting dividend policy

General factors affecting dividend policy have already been covered in Chapter 1. For a multinational, there are a few additional factors to consider.

Types	Definition
Financing	The financing needs of the parent company, eg dividend payments to external shareholders and capital expenditure in the home countries.
Agency issues	Dividend payments restrict the financial discretion of foreign managers and allow greater control over their behaviour (see Section 4).
Timing	A subsidiary may adjust its dividend payments in order to benefit from expected movements in exchange rates, collecting earlier (lead) payments from currencies vulnerable to depreciation and later (lag) from currencies expected to appreciate.
Tax	If tax liabilities are triggered by repatriation, these can be deferred by reinvesting earnings abroad. This is more of an issue for subsidiaries in low-tax countries, whose dividends trigger significant parent tax obligations.
Exchange controls	Controls involve suspending or banning the payment of dividends to foreign shareholders, such as parent companies in multinationals, who will then have the problem of **blocked funds** (see Section 3 Chapter 5).

3 Planning issues (2) – transfer pricing

The **dividend capacity** of a division of company may be influenced by the transfer pricing system that is being used. For example, if it is paying more for internally supplied goods and services, then a division's dividend capacity will be reduced.

3.1 General considerations

In deciding on their transfer pricing policies, multinationals take into account many financial factors:

Consideration	Achieved by
Exchange controls	Transfer pricing can be used to channel profits out of countries facing restrictions on their ability to repatriate dividends (exchange controls).
Financing	Transfer pricing may be used to boost the profits of a subsidiary, to make it easier for it to obtain funds in the host country.
Taxation	Transfer pricing may be used to channel profits out of high tax rate countries into lower ones.

3.2 Regulation

Transfer pricing is a normal and legitimate activity. **Transfer price manipulation**, on the other hand, exists when transfer prices are used to evade or avoid payment of taxes and tariffs.

The most common solution that tax authorities have adopted to reduce the probability of transfer price manipulation is to develop particular transfer pricing regulations based on the concept of the **arm's length standard**, which says that all MNC intra-firm activities should be priced as if they took place between unrelated parties acting at arm's length in competitive markets.

KEY
TERM

> **Arm's length standard:** This means that intra-firm trade of multinationals should be priced as if they took place between unrelated parties acting at arm's length in competitive markets.

Any attempts to distort the transfer price significantly run the risk of fines (from the governments affected by loss of tax revenue), and loss of business (directly from the governments affected by loss of tax revenue and indirectly due to the impact on reputation). Additionally, there may be agency affects arising from reducing the reported profit (and by implication performance) from divisional managers adversely affected by transfer pricing changes.

4 Planning issues (3) – structure

4.1 Branch or subsidiary

Firms that want to establish a definite presence in an overseas country may choose to establish a **branch** rather than a subsidiary. In many instances a multinational will establish a branch and utilise its initial losses against other profits, and then turn the branch into a subsidiary when it starts making profits.

A subsidiary is a separate legal entity and gives the impression of a long-term commitment. The parent company benefits from limited liability. The normal structure of many multinationals consists of a parent company (a holding company) with subsidiaries in several countries. The subsidiaries may be wholly owned or just partly owned.

4.2 Debt or equity

The **method of financing** a subsidiary will give some indication of the **nature and length of time** of the investment that the parent company is prepared to make.

A sizeable equity investment (or long-term loans from the parent company to the subsidiary) would indicate a long-term investment by the parent company.

Because subsidiaries may be operating with a guarantee from the parent company, higher gearing structures may be possible. As we have seen in Chapters 5 and 6, higher gearing can help to **reduce tax and to manage risk**.

In addition, local governments may directly or indirectly offer **subsidised debt finance**.

Types	Impact of overseas debt finance
Direct	Low cost loans may be offered to encourage multinational investment Other incentives may include exchange control guarantees, grants, tax holidays etc
Indirect	Local governments may reduce the interest rates to stimulate the local economy

So, it may be desirable for a subsidiary to operate with higher levels of debt, especially if it is operating in a high tax regime.

4.2.1 Thin capitalisation

However, many countries have rules that disallow interest deductions above a certain level when the entity is considered to be too highly geared. A company is said to be **thinly capitalised** when its capital is made up of a much greater proportion than usual of debt than equity.

Tax authorities may place a limit on the amount that a company can claim as a tax deduction on interest (for example as a percentage of EBIT), or may judge that a subsidiary contains artificially high gearing if its gearing level is higher than the group's gearing.

4.2.2 Local regulations

Where overseas equity is preferred, a listing on an overseas stock exchange may be considered. If so, it will be important to conform to local regulations.

For example, the London Stock Exchange requires at **least three** years of audited published accounts and for at least **25%** of the company's shares to be in public hands. A **prospectus** must be published containing a forecast of expected performance and future plans. The company will also have to be introduced by a **sponsoring firm** and to comply with the local **corporate governance requirements** (such as splitting the roles of Chairperson and CEO, and maintaining independent audit, remuneration and nomination committees).

A company must also show that it has enough working capital for at least the next 12 months.

4.3 Agency issues

Agency relationships exist between the **managers** at the **headquarters** of **multinational corporations (principals)** and the managers that run the **subsidiaries** of **multinational corporations (agents)**.

The **agency relationships** are created between the headquarters and subsidiaries of multinational corporations because the interests of the managers at the headquarters who are responsible for the performance of the whole organisation can be considerably different from the interests of the managers who run the subsidiaries.

The incongruence of interests between a multinational's headquarters and subsidiaries can arise not only due to concerns that can be seen in any parent-subsidiary relationship, but also due to the fact that the multinational's headquarters and subsidiaries operate in different cultures and have divergent backgrounds.

This **can be managed by**:

- The parent company ratifying key decisions taken by the subsidiary
- Managerial compensation packages tied in to the performance of the group
- High dividend payouts to reduce the funds available to local management
- High gearing increases the discipline on local management to manage cash flows effectively

PER alert

As part of the fulfilment of the performance objective 'evaluate investment and financing decisions' you are expected to be able to identify and apply different finance options to single and combined entities in domestic and multinational business markets. This section looks at the financing options available to multinationals which you can put to good use if you work in such an environment.

5 Developments in international markets

5.1 The credit crunch

A **credit crunch** is a crisis caused by banks being too nervous to lend money, even to each other.

Between 2007 and 2008 turmoil hit the global financial markets causing the failure of a number of high-profile financial institutions (eg Northern Rock in the UK, Lehman Brothers in the US). The crisis was caused by a number of factors:

- **Years of lax lending** by banks inflated a huge debt bubble: people borrowed cheap money and invested it in property. In the US, billions of dollars of 'Ninja' mortgages (no income, no job) were sold to people with weak credit ratings (sub-prime borrowers).

- Massive **trade surpluses** in some countries led to a flood of investment into countries with deficits (notably the US) which contributed to the asset price bubble that contributed to the **credit crunch**.

- The US banking sector packaged sub-prime home loans into mortgage-backed securities known as **collateralised debt obligations** (CDOs). These were sold on to investment banks as securities. The **credit risk rating** on these securities often reflected the selling bank's AA+ rating and not the real risk of default. When borrowers started to default on their loans, the value of these investments plummeted, leading to **huge losses by banks on a global scale**.

- In the UK, many banks had invested large sums of money in these assets and had to **write off billions of pounds in losses**. In addition some investment banks underwrote bond issues without fully understanding the risk – and were left holding the credit risk as the bonds defaulted. As banks' confidence was at an all-time low, they stopped lending to each other, causing a massive liquidity problem – a credit crunch. With bank lending so low, businesses were **unable to obtain funding for investments**, resulting in large reductions in output.

5.2 Securitisation and tranching

5.2.1 Securitisation

KEY
TERM

Securitisation: The process of converting illiquid assets into marketable securities.

Securitisation involves banks transfer lending such as mortgages to 'special purpose vehicles' (SPVs) which are then sold as collateralised debt obligations (CDOs). By securitising the loans, the bank removes the risk attached to its future cash receipts and converts the loan back into cash, which it can lend again.

5.2.2 Tranching

CDOs are a way of repackaging the risk of a large number of risky assets such as sub-prime mortgages. Unlike a bond issue, where the risk is spread thinly between all the bond holders, CDOs concentrate the risk into investment layers or 'tranches', so that some investors take proportionately more of the risk for a bigger return – and others take little or no risk for a much lower return.

Each tranche of CDOs is securitised and 'priced' on issue to give the appropriate yield to the investors. The 'investment grade' tranche will be the most highly priced, giving a low yield but with low risk attached; this is sometimes referred to as a senior tranche. Typical investors of **senior tranches** are insurance companies, pension funds and other risk-averse investors.

At the other end, the 'equity' tranche carries the bulk of the risk – it will be priced at a low level but has a high potential (but very risky) yield. These **junior tranches** (or subordinated debt) are **higher risk**, as they are not secured by specific assets. These tranches tend to be bought by hedge funds and other investors looking for higher risk–return profiles.

Tranching

A bank is proposing to sell $100 million of mortgage loans by means of a securitisation process. The mortgages have a ten-year term and pay a return of 8% per year. The bank will use 90% of the value of the mortgages as collateral.

- 60% of the collateral value will be sold as Tranche A: senior debt with a credit rating of A. This will pay interest of 7%.
- 30% of the collateral value will be sold as Tranche B: less senior debt with a credit rating of B. This will pay interest of 10%.
- 10% will be sold as subordinated debt with no credit rating.

The estimated cash flows would be:

Cash inflows

$8 million is expected to be repaid by the mortgage holders ($100m × 8%).

Cash outflows

Tranche A is the first to be paid and receive $100m × 0.90 × 0.6 × 0.07 = $3.78m

Tranche B is the next to be paid and receives $100m × 0.90 × 0.3 × 0.1 = $2.7m

The cash paid to the tranches with security (ie tranches A and B) is $6.48 million ($3.78m + $2.7m). The difference between cash received ($8 million) and cash paid to these tranches ($6.48 million) is $1.52 million.

This is paid to the holders of the subordinated debt who therefore receive a return of $1.52 million on an investment of $9 million ($100m × 0.90 × 0.1). This is a return of 1.52/9 = 16.9%.

If there are any mortgage defaults, cash inflows would fall and this would lead to lower returns for the holders of subordinated debt.

Only if cash inflows fell below $6.48 million will the holders of Tranche B be affected, and only if the income fell below $3.78 million would the holders of Tranche A be affected.

5.3 Tensions in the Eurozone

After the euro came into circulation in 2002, there was a rapid fall in interest rates (due to low interest rates in Germany, the dominant economy) which **led to a rapid increase in consumer spending**.

German economic policy continued to focus on export-led growth. The accumulation of surplus funds in Germany helped to finance excessive borrowing in Southern European economies. This, combined with low interest rates, led to **a sharp increase in the price of assets such as houses and shares** and thus reinforced a boom into a bubble.

Following the **credit crunch of 2007 to 2008**, asset prices in Southern Europe tumbled. In a number of European economies, it was **the bursting of the house price bubble**, not lax spending policies by the government, that led to a recession. Government borrowing ballooned **after** the 2008 global financial crisis because, for example, governments have had to fund bank bailouts.

Parts of Southern Europe have since faced severe recessions, because no-one wants to spend. Companies and mortgage borrowers were too busy repaying their debts to spend more, and governments were drastically cutting their spending back as well.

5.4 Dark pool trading systems

Since 2007, when legislation removed the monopoly status of European stock exchanges, there has been a rapid growth in trading systems for shares, especially off-exchange venues known as 'dark pools' where large orders are matched in private.

Dark pools allow large shareholdings to be disposed of without prices and order quantities being revealed until **after** trades are completed. Traditionally, when an investor wished to buy or sell securities on a stock market they would be **publicly identifiable once the order to buy or sell was made.**

One **impact of dark pools** has been to reduce transaction fees and to improve the prices that large institutional shareholders can obtain when they buy/sell shares.

However, because dark pools normally use information technology to keep the orders secret until after they've been executed, there is a **reduction in the availability of information and a threat to the efficiency of the stock markets.**

5.5 Money laundering

> **Money laundering:** Constitutes any financial transactions whose purpose is to conceal the identity of the parties to the transaction.

One effect of the free movement of capital has been the growth in **money laundering.**

Money laundering is used by organised crime and terrorist organisations but it is also used in order to avoid the payment of taxes or to distort accounting information.

Regulations differ across various countries but it is common for regulation to require **customer due diligence** ie to take steps to check that new customers are who they say they are. An easy way to do this is to ask for official identification. If customers are acting on behalf of a third party, it is important to identify who the third party is.

Staff should be suitably trained and a **specific member of staff** should be nominated as the person to whom any suspicious activities should be reported. Full documentation of anti-money laundering policies and procedures should be kept. Regulations may require that historic records including receipts, invoices and customer correspondence are kept.

 ### Essential reading

See Chapter 16 Section 3 of the Essential reading for further developments in world markets.

The Essential reading is available as an Appendix of the digital edition of the Workbook.

Chapter summary

Planning and trading issues for multinationals

International trade

Types of free trade agreements
- Free trade areas/customs unions
- Common/single market
- Economic Union

International institutions
- WTO, IMF
- World Bank (IBRD/IDA)
- Central banks

Planning issues (1) – dividend policy

Dividend capacity
- Affected by dividends from foreign subsidiaries
- Extra tax may be payable on the profits made by foreign subsidiary, and withholding tax may be due on dividends paid by the foreign subsidiary

Factors affecting dividend policy
- Financing
- Agency issues
- Timing
- Tax
- Exchange controls

Planning issues (2) – transfer pricing

General considerations
- Exchange controls
- Financing
- Taxation

Regulation
- Arm's length standard

Planning issues (3) – structure

Branch or subsidiary
- Branch: utilise initial losses against other profits
- Subsidiary: separate legal entity, gives impression of a long-term commitment, parent company benefits from limited liability

Debt or equity
- Debt: may be subsidised, thin capitalisation rules
- Equity: local exchange regulations need to be followed

Agency issues

Different interests of local management, managed by:
- Parent company ratifying key decisions
- Managerial compensation packages tied to the performance of the group
- High dividend payouts
- High gearing

Developments in international markets

The credit crunch

Triggered in 2007 by massive losses on CDOs

Securitisation and tranching
- Each tranche of CDOs is securitised and 'priced' on issue to give the appropriate yield to the investors
- Typical investors of **senior tranches** are insurance companies, pension funds and other risk-averse investors
- At the other end, the 'equity' tranche carries the bulk of the risk – these **junior tranches** tend to be bought by hedge funds and other investors looking for higher risk–return profiles

Tensions in the Eurozone

Continued downturn on some parts of the Eurozone after the credit crunch

Dark pool trading systems

Allow large shareholdings to be disposed of without prices and order quantities being revealed until **after** trades are completed

Money laundering

Regulation requires **customer due diligence** ie taking steps to check that your customers are who they say they are

Knowledge diagnostic

1. Free trade zones

Depending on the form these take can potentially benefit a multinational by offering frictionless trade and common regulatory standards.

2. International institutions

The IMF, the World Bank and the WTO all bring order and stability to the international financial system and provide benefit to multinationals as a result.

3. Dividend capacity

Dividends remitted by overseas subsidiaries will increase the dividend capacity of the parent company – but extra tax may be payable.

4. Transfer pricing

Methods need to be in line with requirements for an 'arm's length standard'.

5. Agency issues

Local subsidiary management may not act in the best interests of the 'group'.

6. Tranching

This is the pricing of CDOs in different 'investment layers'; each tranche of CDOs is securitised and 'priced' on issue to give the appropriate yield to the investors.

Further study guidance

Question practice

Now try the following from the Further question practice bank (available in the digital edition of the workbook):

Q28 *Lamri (a past 2010 ACCA exam question)*

Q29 *Strom (a past 2012 ACCA exam question)*

Further reading

There is a Technical Article available on ACCA's website, called 'Securitisation and tranching'. This article examines behavioural finance and is written by a member of the AFM examining team.

We recommend you read this article as part of your preparation for the AFM exam.

Activity answers

Activity 1: Idea generation

A single market area like the EU aims to remove barriers to trade and allow **freedom of movement** of production resources such as capital and labour within the EU. The EU also has a **common legal structure** across all member countries and tries to **limit any discriminatory practice** against companies operating in these countries.

The EU also erects **common external trade barriers** to trade against countries which are not member states.

Degli Co may benefit from operating within the EU because it may be protected from non-EU competition – companies outside the EU may find it **difficult to enter the EU** markets due to barriers to trade.

A common legal structure should ensure that manufacturing standards apply equally across all the member countries. This will **reduce compliance costs** for Degli, which may be an important issue for a small company with limited financial resources.

Having access to capital and labour within the EU may make it easier for the company to set up and attract resources (eg labour) from within the EU.

The company may also be able to access any grants which are available to companies based within the EU and will be able to bid for contracts with EU companies without any risk of discrimination.

Activity 2: Tax issues

	$m
Profits before tax of foreign subsidiary	3.00
Tax on profits paid in Country F 20%	0.60
Profits after tax	2.40
Dividend paid 75%	1.80
Withholding tax 10% on $1.80 million	(0.18)
Extra tax on profits 4% on $3.00 million profit (before tax)	(0.12)
Net cash received	1.50

This is the required adjustment, so the new dividend capacity is $14m + $1.5m = $15.5m

Skills checkpoint 5

Exam readiness

Chapter overview

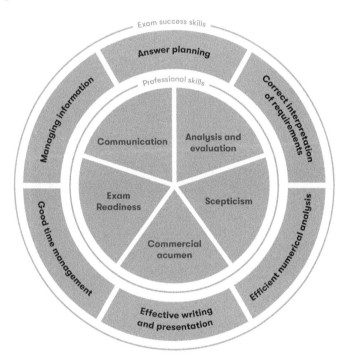

Introduction

Having covered the technical aspects of the syllabus and the four professional skills, you now need to make sure that you know how to use the computer-based exam software (CBE) so you are fully prepared for your AFM exam.

You should start to familiarise yourself with the CBE software as soon as possible using the ACCA's practice platform, where you will find a number of questions that are presented in the CBE software used in the real AFM exam.

We will explore how use the computer-based exam software (CBE) using section G of the AFM syllabus (consisting of four learning outcomes related to **employability and technology skills**) as a framework. We will also refer back to the **exam success skills** covered in the **introductory section of this workbook.**

G1 – Use computer technology to efficiently access and manipulate relevant information

CBE tools can be used to support the exam success skill of **managing information** (exam success skill 1).

Introduction and instructions

The first thing you will see when you load up a CBE is an introduction followed by a series of instructions on how to use the CBE software. The instructions in the ACCA practice platform also explain where it differs from the CBE software used in the live exam.

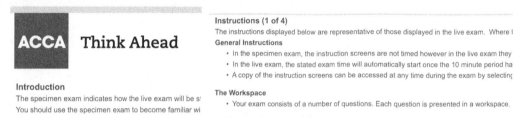

Workspace

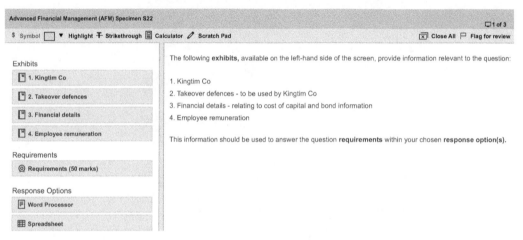

Once you have started the CBE and are in Question 1, you should note the various elements of the workspace:

- **Exhibits** – these contain more detailed information about the issues facing the company necessary to answering the question. The first exhibit will often contain important background information about the company; this could relate to any of the question requirements. Each of the remaining exhibits will normally **mainly relate to one of the requirements;** in this question exhibit 2 related to part a, exhibit 3 related to part b and exhibit 4 to part c. However, you will need to examine **all** of the exhibits before attempting **any of the question requirements** because an answer to that requirement may need to use small amounts of information from other exhibits.

- **Requirement(s)** – these will vary depending on the question but will specify what you are required to do and may direct you to use specific professional skills.

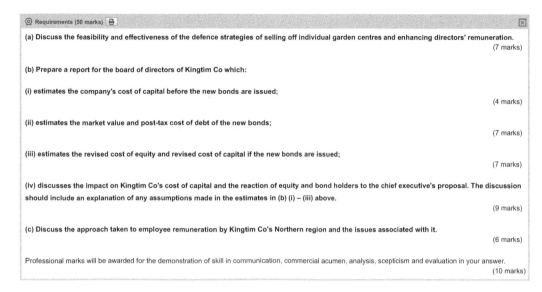

Requirements (50 marks)

(a) Discuss the feasibility and effectiveness of the defence strategies of selling off individual garden centres and enhancing directors' remuneration.

(7 marks)

(b) Prepare a report for the board of directors of Kingtim Co which:

(i) estimates the company's cost of capital before the new bonds are issued;

(4 marks)

(ii) estimates the market value and post-tax cost of debt of the new bonds;

(7 marks)

(iii) estimates the revised cost of equity and revised cost of capital if the new bonds are issued;

(7 marks)

(iv) discusses the impact on Kingtim Co's cost of capital and the reaction of equity and bond holders to the chief executive's proposal. The discussion should include an explanation of any assumptions made in the estimates in (b) (i) – (iii) above.

(9 marks)

(c) Discuss the approach taken to employee remuneration by Kingtim Co's Northern region and the issues associated with it.

(6 marks)

Professional marks will be awarded for the demonstration of skill in communication, commercial acumen, analysis, scepticism and evaluation in your answer.

(10 marks)

- **Response option(s)** – there will be a **word processor** option where you will type your answer and the option to use a **spreadsheet** as well.

You will probably have observed that with the exhibits, requirement and response options, the screen will start to get very cluttered. To help you manage all this information you can re-arrange how each of these windows looks on screen. They can all be moved around on the screen and can be re-sized (by clicking on the bottom right of an exhibit): you just need to get used to how they move and how you can arrange them.

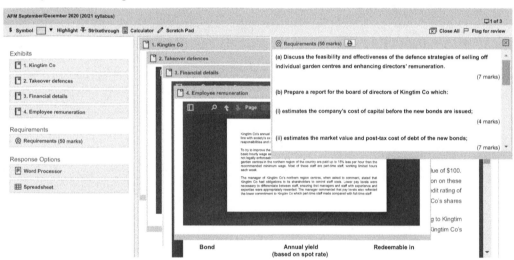

G2 – Work on relevant response options, using available functions and technology, as required by the workspace

CBE tools can be used to support the exam success skills of **answer planning** (exam success skill 3) and **efficient numerical analysis** (exam success skill 4).

Response options

All questions will have a **word processor** response option and a **spreadsheet** option as well. You can choose to use the option that works best for you but remember you can answer using **both options for a single requirement**.

For example, if the requirement to question 2 part (a) required some calculations and then an analysis of these calculations, the spreadsheet could contain the calculations, and the word processor could then discuss the calculations (referencing the spreadsheet calculations).

BPP LEARNING MEDIA

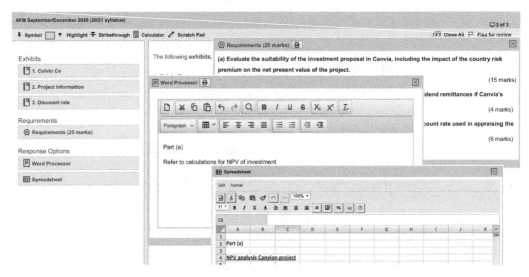

Within the workspace and response options, you will find a number of functions that will help you plan your answer, such as highlighting and formatting text, undo and redo and copy and paste.

As you will have noticed in the instructions at the start of the CBE, **there are many functions and formulae that can be used in the spreadsheet**, so you are advised to start using it as soon as possible to make sure you are able to use them.

You can then copy and paste numbers from the Exhibit into the spreadsheet to perform your analysis; however, you may need to reformat if copying from a table so be careful.

Other workspace functions

If you want to make notes while you are **planning** your answer you can use the **scratchpad** function embedded within the workspace. However, you should remember that the contents of the scratchpad won't be marked so it is better to set out the start of your answer clearly labelled as a plan and to do your planning there in the word processor so that it is visible to the examiner (and to you as you write your answer). In addition, if you run out of time you may score a small number of marks for the contents of your plan.

The workspace also contains a **calculator** function (you can use your own but it must not have the ability to enter and store data).

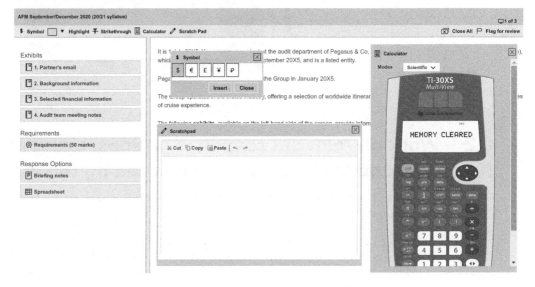

BPP
LEARNING
MEDIA

G3 – Navigate windows and computer screens to create and amend responses to exam requirements, using the appropriate tools

This supports the exam success skills of **managing information** (exam success skill 1), **correct interpretation of requirements** (skill 2) and **answer planning** (exam success skill 3), and **time management** (exam success skill 6).

Requirements

By now, you should be starting to feel more comfortable toggling between the various elements of the CBE – the exhibits, the requirement(s) and your response option(s). The requirements of the question can be copied into your answer plan (if you are showing this in the main response option) to make sure that your answer plan is linked to the question requirements. The mark allocation shown in the requirement can also be used to allocate the appropriate amount of time pre-question by multiplying the marks by the appropriate number of minutes per mark (see exam success skill 6 for details here). Note that there is no timer on the ACCA practice platform, but there is in the live exam.

The requirements of the question can also be copied into the start of your answer to ensure that as you write your answer you do not lose sight of the question's requirements.

One note of caution here, if you are writing a report (in question 1) the headings of the report should be based on the requirement, but the wording of the requirement should be adjusted so that it fits the style of a report (or communication marks will be lost).

For example, if the requirement is 'estimate the company's cost of capital before the new bonds are issued, 4 marks' then this could be simply adjusted to become a heading in a report saying 'estimate of the company's cost of capital before the new bond issue' (without showing the mark allocation).

Navigation tools

What about switching between questions? This can be done by accessing the **navigator** function on the bottom right-hand corner of the workspace:

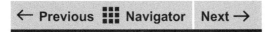

If you feel you need to move on but haven't finished what you wanted to say (perhaps you're stuck or you are concerned about time) the navigator gives you the option to **flag** it for review at a later stage to make sure that you haven't forgotten about it. There is also a **help** function which provides an overview of the instructions for both the workspace and the exam itself.

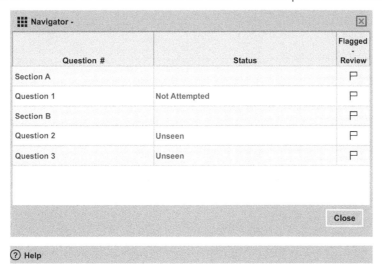

G4 – Present data and information effectively, using the appropriate tools

This supports the exam success skill of **effective writing and presentation** (exam success skill 5).

The formatting functionality in the word processor response option will help you to produce a more professional-looking answer, especially in Question 1 where the **professional skill of communication** is examined. However, remember to keep it simple! Tables, heading, bold text and underlining may all be useful where appropriate, but no marks are available for different font sizes or styles for headings.

Summary

Make sure that you practice questions in the ACCA CBE practice platform you have access to. This will help to familiarise you with the various elements of the CBE and how you can make use of them when answering questions.

Although there are syllabus outcomes on employability and technology skills, demonstration of these skills **won't specifically attract marks** in the same way that you are rewarded for technical and professional skills. However, familiarity with the technology that you are given in the CBE will help you to be **ready to perform effectively in the exam**.

Finally, as part of being **exam ready** please take the time to **review the guidance on scoring marks for professional skills** (worth 20 marks in the exam) given in the previous skills checkpoints 1-4 and also to **review the general guidance on exam success skills** given at the start of this workbook (especially **skill 4 covering efficient numerical analysis**).

Appendix 1: Mathematical tables and formulae

Formulae

Modigliani and Miller Proposition 2 (with tax)

$$k_e = k_e^i + (1-T)(k_e^i - k_d)\frac{V_d}{V_e}$$

The Capital Asset Pricing Model

$$E(r_i) = R_f + b_i(E(r_m) - R_f)$$

The asset beta formula

$$\beta_a = \left[\frac{V_e}{(V_e + V_d(1-T))}\beta_e\right] + \left[\frac{V_d(1-T)}{(V_e + V_d(1-T))}\beta_d\right]$$

The Growth Model

$$P_0 = \frac{D_0(1 + g)}{(r_e - g)}$$

Gordon's growth approximation

$$g = br_e$$

The weighted average cost of capital

$$WACC = \left[\frac{V_e}{V_e + V_d}\right]k_e + \left[\frac{V_d}{V_e + V_d}\right]k_d(1-T)$$

The Fisher formula

$(1 + i) = (1 + r) \times (1 + h)$

Purchasing power parity and interest rate parity

$$S_1 = S_0 \times \frac{(1 + h_c)}{(1 + h_b)}$$

$$F_0 = S_0 \times \frac{(1 + i_c)}{(1 + i_b)}$$

Modified internal rate of return

$$MIRR = \left[\frac{PV_R}{PV_I}\right]^{\frac{1}{n}}(1 + r_e) - 1$$

The Black-Scholes option pricing model

$$c = P_aN(d_1) - P_eN(d_2)e^{-rt}$$

Where:

$$d_1 = \frac{\ln(P_a/P_e) + (r + 0.5s^2)t}{s\sqrt{t}}$$

$$d_2 = d_1 - s\sqrt{t}$$

The Put Call Parity relationship

$$p = c - P_a + P_ee^{-rt}$$

Present value table

Present value of 1 ie $(1+r)^{-n}$

Where r=discount rate; n=number of periods until payment

Periods (n)	Discount rate (r)									
	1%	2%	3%	4%	5%	6%	7%	8%	9%	10%
1	0.990	0.980	0.971	0.962	0.952	0.943	0.935	0.926	0.917	0.909
2	0.980	0.961	0.943	0.925	0.907	0.890	0.873	0.857	0.842	0.826
3	0.971	0.942	0.915	0.889	0.864	0.840	0.816	0.794	0.772	0.751
4	0.961	0.924	0.888	0.855	0.823	0.792	0.763	0.735	0.708	0.683
5	0.951	0.906	0.863	0.822	0.784	0.747	0.713	0.681	0.650	0.621
6	0.942	0.888	0.837	0.790	0.746	0.705	0.666	0.630	0.596	0.564
7	0.933	0.871	0.813	0.760	0.711	0.665	0.623	0.583	0.547	0.513
8	0.923	0.853	0.789	0.731	0.677	0.627	0.582	0.540	0.502	0.467
9	0.914	0.837	0.766	0.703	0.645	0.592	0.544	0.500	0.460	0.424
10	0.905	0.820	0.744	0.676	0.614	0.558	0.508	0.463	0.422	0.386
11	0.896	0.804	0.722	0.650	0.585	0.527	0.475	0.429	0.388	0.350
12	0.887	0.788	0.701	0.625	0.557	0.497	0.444	0.397	0.356	0.319
13	0.879	0.773	0.681	0.601	0.530	0.469	0.415	0.368	0.326	0.290
14	0.870	0.758	0.681	0.577	0.505	0.442	0.388	0.340	0.299	0.263
15	0.861	0.743	0.642	0.555	0.481	0.417	0.362	0.315	0.275	0.239

(n)	11%	12%	13%	14%	15%	16%	17%	18%	19%	20%
1	0.901	0.893	0.885	0.877	0.870	0.862	0.855	0.847	0.840	0.833
2	0.812	0.797	0.783	0.769	0.756	0.743	0.731	0.718	0.706	0.694
3	0.731	0.712	0.693	0.675	0.658	0.641	0.624	0.609	0.593	0.579
4	0.659	0.636	0.613	0.592	0.572	0.552	0.534	0.516	0.499	0.482
5	0.593	0.567	0.543	0.519	0.497	0.476	0.456	0.437	0.419	0.402
6	0.535	0.507	0.480	0.456	0.432	0.410	0.390	0.370	0.352	0.335
7	0.482	0.452	0.425	0.400	0.376	0.354	0.333	0.314	0.296	0.279
8	0.434	0.404	0.376	0.351	0.327	0.305	0.285	0.266	0.249	0.233
9	0.391	0.361	0.333	0.308	0.284	0.263	0.243	0.225	0.209	0.194
10	0.352	0.322	0.295	0.270	0.247	0.227	0.208	0.191	0.176	0.162
11	0.317	0.287	0.261	0.237	0.215	0.195	0.178	0.162	0.148	0.135
12	0.286	0.257	0.231	0.208	0.187	0.168	0.152	0.137	0.124	0.112
13	0.258	0.229	0.204	0.182	0.163	0.145	0.130	0.116	0.104	0.093
14	0.232	0.205	0.181	0.160	0.141	0.125	0.111	0.099	0.088	0.078
15	0.209	0.183	0.160	0.140	0.123	0.108	0.095	0.084	0.079	0.065

Annuity table

Present value of an annuity of 1 ie $\dfrac{1-(1+r)^{-n}}{r}$

Where r=discount rate; n=number of periods

Periods (n)	1%	2%	3%	4%	5%	6%	7%	8%	9%	10%
1	0.990	0.980	0.971	0.962	0.952	0.943	0.935	0.926	0.917	0.909
2	1.970	1.942	1.913	1.886	1.859	1.833	1.808	1.783	1.759	1.736
3	2.941	2.884	2.829	2.775	2.723	2.673	2.624	2.577	2.531	2.487
4	3.902	3.808	3.717	3.630	3.546	3.465	3.387	3.312	3.240	3.170
5	4.853	4.713	4.580	4.452	4.329	4.212	4.100	3.993	3.890	3.791
6	5.795	5.601	5.417	5.242	5.076	4.917	4.767	4.623	4.486	4.355
7	6.728	6.472	6.230	6.002	5.786	5.582	5.389	5.206	5.033	4.868
8	7.652	7.325	7.020	6.733	6.463	6.210	5.971	5.747	5.535	5.335
9	8.566	8.162	7.786	7.435	7.108	6.802	6.515	6.247	5.995	5.759
10	9.471	8.983	8.530	8.111	7.722	7.360	7.024	6.710	6.418	6.145
11	10.368	9.787	9.253	8.760	8.306	7.887	7.499	7.139	6.805	6.495
12	11.255	10.575	9.954	9.385	8.863	8.384	7.943	7.536	7.161	6.814
13	12.134	11.348	10.635	9.986	9.394	8.853	8.358	7.904	7.487	7.103
14	13.004	12.106	11.296	10.563	9.899	9.295	8.745	8.244	7.786	7.367
15	13.865	12.849	11.938	11.118	10.380	9.712	9.108	8.559	8.061	7.606

(n)	11%	12%	13%	14%	15%	16%	17%	18%	19%	20%
1	0.901	0.893	0.885	0.877	0.870	0.862	0.855	0.847	0.840	0.833
2	1.713	1.690	1.668	1.647	1.626	1.605	1.585	1.566	1.547	1.528
3	2.444	2.402	2.361	2.322	2.283	2.246	2.210	2.174	2.140	2.106
4	3.102	3.037	2.974	2.914	2.855	2.798	2.743	2.690	2.639	2.589
5	3.696	3.605	3.517	3.433	3.352	3.274	3.199	3.127	3.058	2.991
6	4.231	4.111	3.998	3.889	3.784	3.685	3.589	3.498	3.410	3.326
7	4.712	4.564	4.423	4.288	4.160	4.039	3.922	3.812	3.706	3.605
8	5.146	4.968	4.799	4.639	4.487	4.344	4.207	4.078	3.954	3.837
9	5.537	5.328	5.132	4.946	4.772	4.607	4.451	4.303	4.163	4.031
10	5.889	5.650	5.426	5.216	5.019	4.833	4.659	4.494	4.339	4.192
11	6.207	5.938	5.687	5.453	5.234	5.029	4.836	4.656	4.486	4.327
12	6.492	6.194	5.918	5.660	5.421	5.197	4.988	4.793	4.611	4.439
13	6.750	6.424	6.122	5.842	5.583	5.342	5.118	4.910	4.715	4.533
14	6.982	6.628	6.302	6.002	5.724	5.468	5.229	5.008	4.802	4.611
15	7.191	6.811	6.462	6.142	5.847	5.575	5.324	5.092	4.876	4.675

Standard normal distribution table

$Z = \frac{(x-\mu)}{\sigma}$	0.00	0.01	0.02	0.03	0.04	0.05	0.06	0.07	0.08	0.09
0.0	.0000	.0040	.0080	.0120	.0159	.0199	.0239	.0279	.0319	.0359
0.1	.0398	.0438	.0478	.0517	.0557	.0596	.0636	.0675	.0714	.0753
0.2	.0793	.0832	.0871	.0910	.0948	.0987	.1026	.1064	.1103	.1141
0.3	.1179	.1217	.1255	.1293	.1331	.1368	.1406	.1443	.1480	.1517
0.4	.1554	.1591	.1628	.1664	.1700	.1736	.1772	.1808	.1844	.1879
0.5	.1915	.1950	.1985	.2019	.2054	.2088	.2123	.2157	.2190	.2224
0.6	.2257	.2291	.2324	.2357	.2389	.2422	.2454	.2486	.2518	.2549
0.7	.2580	.2611	.2642	.2673	.2704	.2734	.2764	.2794	.2823	.2852
0.8	.2881	.2910	.2939	.2967	.2995	.3023	.3051	.3078	.3106	.3133
0.9	.3159	.3186	.3212	.3238	.3264	.3289	.3315	.3340	.3365	.3389
1.0	.3413	.3438	.3461	.3485	.3508	.3531	.3554	.3577	.3599	.3621
1.1	.3643	.3665	.3686	.3708	.3729	.3749	.3770	.3790	.3810	.3830
1.2	.3849	.3869	.3888	.3907	.3925	.3944	.3962	.3980	.3997	.4015
1.3	.4032	.4049	.4066	.4082	.4099	.4115	.4131	.4147	.4162	.4177
1.4	.4192	.4207	.4222	.4236	.4251	.4265	.4279	.4292	.4306	.4319
1.5	.4332	.4345	.4357	.4370	.4382	.4394	.4406	.4418	.4430	.4441
1.6	.4452	.4463	.4474	.4485	.4495	.4505	.4515	.4525	.4535	.4545
1.7	.4554	.4564	.4573	.4582	.4591	.4599	.4608	.4616	.4625	.4633
1.8	.4641	.4649	.4656	.4664	.4671	.4678	.4686	.4693	.4699	.4706
1.9	.4713	.4719	.4726	.4732	.4738	.4744	.4750	.4756	.4762	.4767
2.0	.4772	.4778	.4783	.4788	.4793	.4798	.4803	.4808	.4812	.4817
2.1	.4821	.4826	.4830	.4834	.4838	.4842	.4846	.4850	.4854	.4857
2.2	.4861	.4865	.4868	.4871	.4875	.4878	.4881	.4884	.4887	.4890
2.3	.4893	.4896	.4898	.4901	.4904	.4906	.4909	.4911	.4913	.4916
2.4	.4918	.4920	.4922	.4925	.4927	.4929	.4931	.4932	.4934	.4936
2.5	.4938	.4940	.4941	.4943	.4945	.4946	.4948	.4949	.4951	.4952
2.6	.4953	.4955	.4956	.4957	.4959	.4960	.4961	.4962	.4963	.4964
2.7	.4965	.4966	.4967	.4968	.4969	.4970	.4971	.4972	.4973	.4974
2.8	.4974	.4975	.4976	.4977	.4977	.4978	.4979	.4980	.4980	.4981
2.9	.4981	.4982	.4983	.4983	.4984	.4984	.4985	.4985	.4986	.4986
3.0	.4987	.4987	.4987	.4988	.4988	.4989	.4989	.4989	.4990	.4990

This table can be used to calculate N(d1), the cumulative normal distribution functions needed for the Black–Scholes model of option pricing. If d1 > 0, add 0.5 to the relevant number above. If d1 < 0, subtract the relevant number above from 0.5.

Index

Bibliography

ACCA. (2018) 'ICOs: real deal or token pressure. Exploring Initial Coin Offerings', ACCA [Online] Available at: https://www.accaglobal.com/pk/en/professional-insights/technology/ICOs-real-deal-or-token-gesture.html [Accessed 13 October 2021]

BBC. (11 February 2014) Myanma Air signs nearly $1bn leasing deal. *BBC* [Online] Available from: http://www.bbc.co.uk/news/business-26131019 [Accessed 13 October 2021].

BBC. (25 March 2015) Kraft shares soar on Heinz merger. *BBC* [Online] Available from: http://www.bbc.co.uk/news/business-32050266 [Accessed 13 October 2021].

BBC. (12 October 2015) Dell agrees $67bn EMC takeover. *BBC* [Online] Available from: http://www.bbc.co.uk/news/business-34505553 [Accessed 13 October 2021].

Chester, J. (2018) 'Can your start-up run an ICO?', Forbes [Online] Available at: https://www.forbes.com/sites/jonathanchester/2018/02/28/can-my-startup-run-an-initial-coin-offering/?sh=39d36fc15a30 [Accessed 13 October 2021]

Davies, R. (15 December 2015) Starbucks pays UK corporation tax of £8.1m. *Guardian* [Online]. Available from: http://www.tradeleo.com/news/starbucks-pays-uk-corporation-tax-of-lb8-1m-350.html [Accessed 13 October 2021]

Economist. The Big Mac Index. *Economist* [Online] Available from:

https://www.economist.com/big-mac-index [Accessed 13 October 2021].

Lielacher, A. (2017) 'Understanding token types', Bitcoin Market Journal [Online] Available at: https://www.bitcoinmarketjournal.com/ico-token/ [Accessed 13 Octobe 2021].

New York University Stern School of Business. (January 2016) Price and Value to Book Ratio by Sector (US) Stern NYU [Online] Available from: http://pages.stern.nyu.edu/~adamodar/New_Home_Page/datafile/pbvdata.html [Accessed 13 October 2021].

Ryan, B. (2007) *Corporate Finance and Valuation.* London, Cengage Learning.

Standard & Poor's. (30 April 2015) Default, Transition, and Recovery: 2014 Annual Global Corporate Default Study And Rating Transitions [Online] Available from http://aeri.es/irconference/docs/agenda/1710%20Carlos%20Garrido%20Rating.pdf [Accessed 13 October 2021].

Watson, D. and Head, A. (2013) *Corporate Finance Principles and Practice.* 6th edition. Pearson Education Limited.

Tell us what you think

Got comments or feedback on this book? Let us know.
Use your QR code reader:

Or, visit:
https://bppgroup.fra1.qualtrics.com/jfe/form/SV_9TrxTtw8jSvO7Pv